UNDERSTANDING REALITY

UNDER-STANDING REALITY

A Taoist Alchemical Classic

by Chang Po-tuan

With a Concise Commentary
by Liu I-ming

Translated from the Chinese
by Thomas Cleary

University of Hawaii Press • Honolulu

Printed in the United States of America
98 99 00 01 02 03   9 8 7 6 5

Library of Congress Cataloging-in-Publication Data

Chang, Po-tuan, 10th/11th cent.
  Understanding reality.

  Translation of: Wu chen p'ien.
  Bibliography: p.
  1. Taoism—Doctrines—Early works to 1800.
2. Alchemy—Religious aspects—Taoism—Early works
to 1800. I. Liu, I-ming, 18th cent. II. Cleary,
Thomas F., 1949-   . III. Title.
BL1923.C51613   1987   299'.5142   87-25539
ISBN 0-8248-1103-8
ISBN 0-8248-1139-9 (pbk.)

CONTENTS

ACKNOWLEDGMENTS

Thanks are due to a number of people for their invaluable assistance in this project: to Wang Po-hsueh, for unparalleled inspiration in Taoist studies; to Wong Leok Yee and Liu Shih-i, for their help in the study and interpretation of Taoist teachings on spirit and energy; and to Sha-ch'uan Ho-tzu, the most remarkably ordinary person I have ever met, for unique demonstrations of the art of integrating being and nonbeing.

T.C.

FOREWORD

Taoism, in many forms, has long had an important role in the development of Chinese civilization, particularly in the fields of natural science, medical arts, and psychology. An extremely complex phenomenon, Taoism has used many media of expression and influenced many realms of thought and action through its long history. Among its modes of projection and spheres of influence may be counted philosophy, politics, religion, folklore and mythology, satire and other forms of humor, visual art and design, poetry, music and song, drama and fiction, herbal and psychosomatic medicine, physical education, martial arts, military strategy, and alchemy, both material and spiritual.

In view of this remarkable profusion of forms, any attempt to establish historical links joining every one of the forms of activity that have been labeled Taoist meets with formidable problems. Perhaps the single most widely accepted Taoist text is the famous *Tao Te Ching,* but since the meanings of this often cryptic work cannot be definitely established by ordinary literary methods, and interpretations vary enormously at certain points, the notion of affiliation through association with the teachings of the *Tao Te Ching* is of dubious value. Moreover, Taoist literature has noted for over two thousand years the existence of degenerations and aberrations under the rubric of the Tao; thus an assumed link between different forms of Taoism may well be one that has in fact lapsed, or one that was from the beginning fabricated by false analogy.

Nevertheless, if one were to hypothesize an inner link among quite different forms of Taoism (without presuming to encompass everything called Taoistic in this hypothesis), a key to the rationale behind the enormous variety of frameworks through which Taoist teachings and practices have been presented might be found in the opening lines of the *Tao Te Ching* itself: "A path that can be verbalized is not a permanent path; terminology that can be designated is not a constant terminology." The first part of this opening statement might also be read, "A path which can be taken as a path is not a permanent path," and understood to refer to the distinction between means and end. From this point of view, it might be said that like Buddhism, a parallel teaching which emphasizes ongoing reformation of doctrine and praxis to meet contemporary needs, Taoism has appeared in many guises throughout the ages, corresponding to changing conditions in its host society.

While it is beyond the scope of the present study to enter very far into the maze of Taoist history, it is of some interest to glance at a few outstanding manifestations of Taoism while pursuing this theme of adaptation to the times. For example, one of the oldest texts of Taoism, presented in the form of a divination manual, was composed in a time when divination was formally considered a branch of government. Later, in an era when all serious thinkers wrote in the subject of political and social science, another classic appears in a form that can be read as a treatise on political and social theory. During a period marked by the accelerated rise of hegemonism and tyranny, yet another text appears libertarian, even libertine and anarchic. Under similar conditions, with the rise of militarism, a classic manual of military strategy advocates a policy of minimal expenditures of lives, energy, and material. Satire and fantastic poetry appear during a time of social upheaval and decay of an old order along with its world view; grass roots political organization emerges under the same conditions. Religious texts come to the fore during the growth of Chinese Buddhist churches, and collections of sayings of Taoist adepts parallel similar developments in Ch'an Buddhist literature. Martial arts are refined in an era marked by the overthrow of an alien dynasty as well as by repeated popular uprisings. Colloquial drama and fiction transmitting Taoist ideas appear during a time of growth of vernacular literature. Most recently, secularized Taoistic teachings are published as therapeutic arts after an anti-religious communist revolution.

This is, of course, a very simplistic picture of Taoism, somewhat in the spirit of Taoist imagery itself, designed to evoke a certain point of view and not to define historical fact. The historical origins of Taoism, like nearly everything else about it, are extremely obscure, veiled in allegory and myth; it may be that much of the material relating to the question of origins consists of, or is interlarded with, initiatory lore, the understanding and application of which would vary according to circumstances. Sometimes Taoism is called the Huang-Lao teaching, after two important figureheads of the teaching alleged to have lived thousands of years ago; but even these people are presented in tradition as transmitters rather than originators of Taoistic teachings. Certain cultural prototypes often associated with Taoism are said to have gained their knowledge through systematic observation, contemplation, and experiment; other teachings are attributed to spiritual revelations. A Taoist encyclopedia says that "Taoism" antedating all formulations is found in a recondite realm of mind where the customary divisions of thought do not exist.

In short, it may well be that the origins or derivations of Taoism cannot be positively ascertained by conventional methods; this situation is due not only to the variety and nature of the data in Taoistic literature, but also to the paucity of associated data which would pin the origins of Taoism to specific times, people, or places. What seems to be a common theme is the idea that Taoism transcends history—vertically, so to speak, in the sense that it claims contact with another dimension of experience beyond the terrestrial, and horizontally in that it claims to reach back before history. Taoist tradition generally associates its early articulation on the terrestrial plane with the very beginnings of proto-Chinese civilization, but also claims ongoing or periodically renewed contact with a higher source. It is not, of course, at all necessary to give literal credence to any of the fantastic tales of Taoist history in order to appreciate them as representations of the common contention that the structure of the universe as perceived by the conventionally socialized mind, within its framework of time and space, is not absolute, and that there exists within humanity the potential for extradimensional perception.

In a sense, it might be possible to interpret the presence of so many marvels and wonders in Taoist lore as an indication of interest in human possibilities. It has often been observed, moreover, that much the same descriptions of extraordinary powers alleged to be available through esoteric knowledge are to be found all over the world. What is perhaps more significant than such possibilities is their effect on the world, and some esoteric traditions stress the issue of the use and function of supernormal knowledge and power more than the mere fact of their possibility. Within Taoism, the question of the actual individual and collective benefit or harm deriving from the exercise of knowledge and power led some practitioners to subordinate everything in their path to the quest for permanent stabilization of consciousness.

Among these practitioners were the Taoists of the schools which came to be known by the name of Complete Reality. Complete Reality Taoism, which arose as a distinct movement between the eleventh and thirteenth centuries, was concerned with the totality of experience and with furthering human progress in the realms of both conventional and ultimate truth. This concern manifested itself accordingly in both social and mystical practices, as the followers of Complete Reality strove to encompass what they considered to be the essence of Buddhism and Confucianism as well as Taoism.

The impact of Complete Reality Taoism was very powerful, and in some areas it superseded the aged and failing schools of Ch'an Buddhism, which had for centuries exerted enormous influence on Chinese civilization. To be sure, Complete Reality Taoism had much in common with Ch'an Buddhism, notably including concentrated meditation exercises and the practice of introducing fresh views of traditional teachings. Among the literary formats used in the projection of Complete Reality Taoism was the vocabulary and imagery of alchemy, one of the most ancient and widespread realms of interest in China, now adopted by these new Taoists as an allegory for a process of inner transformation and sublimation. The present text, *Understanding Reality*, is one of the classics of this spiritual alchemy, and is still considered a basic document of Taoist mental science.

UNDERSTANDING REALITY

INTRODUCTION

Understanding Reality (Chinese *Wu Chen P'ien*) is one of the basic classics of Taoist spiritual alchemy as practiced in the Complete Reality (Ch'uan-chen) school of Taoism. Writing in the year 1841, the Taoist Chu Chung-t'ang described its status within the tradition in these terms: "Wei Po-yang of the Eastern Han dynasty (23–220 C.E.) first revealed the celestial mechanism and expounded its esoteric truths, composing the *Ts'an T'ung Ch'i*. . . . In the Sung dynasty (960–1279) Chang Tzu-yang composed the *Wu Chen P'ien*. Both texts are perennial guides to the study of the Tao." [1]

Chang Po-tuan, styled Tzu-yang, lived from approximately 983 to 1082. He is considered the founder of the so-called southern school of Complete Reality Taoism. As he lived before the widespread public recognition and institutionalization of Complete Reality Taoism that took place under the successors and descendants of Wang Che (1113–1171), founder of the northern school, little is known about his life. Indeed, apart from his retrospective recognition as the first patriarch of the southern school of Complete Reality Taoism, Chang is mainly known simply as the author of *Understanding Reality,* considered a basic text by practitioners of both northern and southern schools.

Chang Po-tuan originally studied Confucianism but eventually turned to esoteric studies after repeated failure to pass civil service examinations. He also read widely in secular subjects, including law, mathematics, medicine, military science, astronomy, and geography. According to one source, he experienced an awakening while studying Buddhist literature, but as his attainment of "the Tao of unification with the fundamental" was still incomplete, he continued to travel in search of enlightenment. [2]

Chang's search ended when he met the Taoist master Liu Ts'ao in western China in the year 1069. Liu is supposed to have learned the secrets of Taoism from Chung-li Ch'uan and Lu Tung-pin, who are also said to have later been the teachers of Wang Che in the middle of the twelfth century.[3] In any case, Chang is believed to have learned the esoteric lore of alchemy from Liu Ts'ao and to have subsequently completed the process successfully. Finally he became a teacher in his own right, though there is no trace of his ever having founded any sort of organization;[4] near the end of his life he composed *Understanding Reality* and entrusted it to a patron, requesting him to circulate it: "All I have learned in my life is herein," he is reported to have said on this occasion. "Circulate it, and someday there will be those who arrive at the way through this book."[5]

According to Chang's own preface to his *Understanding Reality,* he composed this text because he thought alchemical literature and its exegesis in his time obscure and confused. He also wished to emphasize the confluence of Buddhism, Confucianism, and Taoism, even adding an appendix devoted to Buddhist subjects.

The present translation of *Understanding Reality* is based on, and includes, the commentary of Liu I-ming, a Ch'ing dynasty Taoist who like Chang Po-tuan was deeply versed in Buddhism and Confucianism as well as Taoism, and expressly dedicated his works to removing obscurities surrounding technical terminology in alchemical literature. Liu felt that alchemical terminology, originally a protective device, had become a field for imagination, resulting in all sorts of aberrated cults; his commentaries on Taoist classics are thus marked by great simplicity, directness, and unequivocal repudiation of practices he regarded as ineffective or harmful.

As with Chang Po-tuan, there is no evidence of Liu I-ming's membership in any formal organization, and the details of his life are rather obscure. According to his own writings, which date from the end of the eighteenth century through the first quarter of the nineteenth century, he left home at the age of eighteen in search of truth, and followed teachings which he eventually rejected as degenerate after meeting a teacher who instilled in him a sense of the essential importance of balance. Thirteen years later he met another teacher whose guidance enabled him to resolve all his doubts. For twenty years he practiced concealment in the world while working on himself, and in places as widely separated as Ninghsia and Fukien, he assumed the various guises of traveling merchant, Confucian scholar, manual laborer, and recluse. Sometimes he appeared as a mystic, sometimes he worked as a teacher, or else engaged in construction and repair of public facilities such as roads and bridges. Eventually he rebuilt an abandoned Taoist cloister and lived there for another twenty years. During this period he seems to have attracted a circle of disciples and composed commentaries on classics such as the *I*

Ching, the *Ts'an T'ung Ch'i*, and *Understanding Reality*, along with a considerable number of original poems and essays.[6]

The comparative study of Chinese alchemical lore is an immense task, full of inconsistencies. A modern Taoist says, "Chinese alchemical texts are not unified into a system; without extensive study and thorough investigation, it is hard to understand them. Why is it that no one with profound learning in Taoism has come forth to organize them?"[7] That there is a certain irony underlying this question becomes apparent when one reflects again on the opening statement of the *Tao Te Ching*. In any case, by way of introduction to the present work, I will simply focus on the main points of the teaching of *Understanding Reality* as Liu explains it,[8] and append a glossary-index to deal with special terms not touched upon in the introduction. The basic concepts which seem to stand out for emphasis here are yin and yang, the five elements, and essence and life; in addition, the use of *I Ching* signs and the question of praxis will be briefly considered.

Yin and yang

The concept of yin and yang forms one of the basic and pervasive themes of Taoist thought, used to describe all manner of oppositions and complementarities in the physical and metaphysical worlds. In the teachings of Complete Reality Taoism as we find them in the present work, yin and yang have a number of associations which represent various qualities and procedures involved in Taoist methods of human development.

Generally speaking, three aspects or phases of Taoist practice are expressed in terms of yin and yang. These are referred to as fostering yang while repelling yin, blending yin and yang, and transcending yin and yang. In interpreting these phases, the associations of yin and yang differ according to the specific process being described.

In Taoism one of the basic equivalents of yin and yang is the pair of terms "heaven and earth." At one level of interpretation, heaven refers to a world-transcending higher consciousness, beyond the bounds of ordinary thought and emotion; earth refers to the experience of the everyday world. The complete or "real" human being is considered a balanced combination of these two levels of experience; this is expressed in the Taoist slogan "being beyond the world while living in the world." Thus to maintain contact with the higher, vaster dimension of "celestial" consciousness while at the same time living effectively in the "earthly" domain is one meaning of blending or uniting yin and yang.

4 *Introduction*

However, since the effort to achieve a harmonious union of these two "poles" of human potential is usually undertaken after temporal conditioning has already become ingrained, so that the "mundane" prevails over the "celestial," there is the work of "repelling yin" and "fostering yang." The aim of this practice is to bring about a balance in which celestial consciousness guides earthly consciousness. In religious terms, this is described in Liu I-ming's commentary as "unconsciously following the laws of God." In secular terms, it is sometimes described as the body obeying the mind, or desire conforming to reason.

A practical procedure for repelling yin and fostering yang often presented in Taoist texts basically consists of standing aloof from the dominant mundane aspect of the mind—that is, acquired habits of thought and feeling—in order to increase awareness of the recessive celestial mind, which is considered the original, primordial mind.

Complete Reality Taoism finds an indication of this practice in the famous lines of the ancient classic *Tao Te Ching*: "Effect emptiness to the extreme, guard stillness carefully; as myriad things act in concert, I thereby watch the return" (XVI). According to the Complete Reality interpretation, emptiness and stillness refer to quieting the mental talk which sustains the acquired world view and habitual involvement therein. "As things act in concert, I thereby watch the return" is taken to mean that during this practice one leaves things to themselves, not becoming involved with external objects but instead, by means of emptiness and stillness, "watching" for the "return" of yang, the original mind which has been obscured by acquired mental habits and entanglement in things of the world. So according to the Complete Reality school's understanding of this practice, stillness is not an end but a means, and the practice of emptiness and stillness is supposed to have a definite climax and outcome.

The process of repelling yin is often called the "yin convergence," and Complete Reality texts speak of operating the yin convergence as well as repelling the yin convergence. Thus it has two meanings: excluding mundane conditioning to the extent that it will not interfere with or imprison higher potential; yet including mundane conditioning to the extent that it is necessary or useful for life in the world.

A convenient illustration of the balance of exclusion and inclusion may be found in the habit of language. Language is a form of conditioning which is both potentially useful and potentially debilitating. The usefulness of language is a matter of common experience and so needs no further comment. If one is so conditioned by language, on the other hand, that one's whole experience is molded by fixed labels and categories, compelled by the associations and structures afforded by a particular language, or by language in general, then this habit has become restrictive, like a prison of the mind. Modern psychologists recognize that automatic associations or reactions to labels, be they emotive or intellectual, effectively block absorption of information, to say nothing of understanding; this is a basic point of Taoist learning theory.

The same point is made in the opening lines of the *Tao Te Ching*—"A path that can be verbalized is not a permanent path, terminology that can be designated is not constant terminology." This might be paraphrased by saying that there is always more than what can be encompassed by any formulation, whether that formulation be a word, a language, a system of thought, or a whole culture. This does not deny the relative validity or usefulness of any such tools; rather it affirms the existence of greater potential, the possibility of progress and freedom.

Therefore Complete Reality Taoist teaching does not say that mundanity or conditioning is evil, only that it should be a servant rather than a master. From this standpoint, mundane conditioning is not bad per se, it is the source of what is bad—the suffocation of the organic living potential of the individual and community. One advantage of being able to stand aside from the mundane and recover the awareness of the unconditioned primordial mind is that it allows a more objective assessment of the value or otherwise of particular habits or patterns of behavior; and it allows leeway within which to modify behavior.

What the Complete Reality Taoist strives for is to attain autonomy, the freedom to be or not to be, to do or not do, according to the needs of the situation at hand. In this sense the adept is said to transcend yin and yang, reaching an undefinable state in which one "does nothing, yet does anything." This is alluded to in the present text in expressions such as "neither being nor nonbeing, neither material nor void." The accomplished Taoist in this sense is neither a worldling nor an otherworldly anchorite, but uses both involvement and withdrawal as necessary means to an ultimate balance and completeness.

Another pair of important terms analogous to heaven and earth is "the mind of Tao and the human mind." According to the *Chung Ho Chi*, the mind of Tao is the "shining mind," while the human mind is the "wandering mind." What the Taoist tries to do, in these terms, is to still the wandering and sustain the shining, effecting thereby a stabilization of lucid awareness.

This practice is also suggested by another famous line of the *Tao Te*

Ching, "Empty the mind, fill the belly" (III), which is interpreted to mean clearing the human mind of its ramblings and preoccupations, and filling the center of the being—representing the focus of life—with the direct awareness of reality.

The mind of Tao and the human mind are also associated with "real knowledge" and "conscious knowledge." Real knowledge is held to be nondiscursive, immediate knowing, originally inherent in the human being and not the product of learning. Conscious knowledge is the everyday awareness of ordinary life, formed by training and experience. The Taoist aim is to open consciousness and thereby allow greater access to reality, bypassing mental habit, stabilizing conscious knowing by real knowledge so that it is not subject to distorting influences. This is also expressed in terms of making real knowledge conscious and conscious knowledge real.

Real knowledge and conscious knowledge are in turn associated with "sense and essence." Essence is the essence or fundamental nature of consciousness itself; sense is its function. In the conditioned state, essence is frozen into personality and temperament, while sense wanders into feelings. The effort here is to join sense and essence; this may be described as developing a sense of the real essence of mind, and sensing reality directly from the essence of consciousness rather than through the acquired psychological configurations of temperament. This is said to involve keeping consciousness open and fluid while clearing sense of subjective feelings; this means transcendence of restrictive mental fixations through the greater perspective afforded by the mind of Tao.

Yin and yang are also commonly defined as flexibility and firmness, and these terms are then applied to other yin/yang associations. For example, the essence of conscious knowledge in the human mind is said to be flexible, because it has no definite form originally; the sense of real knowledge in the mind of Tao is said to be firm, because it is objective and unequivocal. The joining of these two means that the flexible consciousness, instead of conforming to the arbitrary influences of history and environment, is stabilized by the firmness of real knowledge. Without conscious knowing, it is said, there is no point of access to real knowing; without real knowing, on the other hand, there is no stable objectivity of consciousness.

The qualities of flexibility and firmness, or softness and hardness, have numerous other points of reference besides their application to the essence of conscious knowledge and the sense of real knowledge. In his *Shen Shih Pa Fa*, Liu I-ming describes firmness as strength, sturdiness, decisiveness, keenness, incorruptibility, and indomitability; he also associates it with detachment, independence, serenity, will, consistency, dedication, and objectivity. As for flexibility, Liu defines this in terms of self-control, humility, consideration of others, simplicity, sincerity, and modesty; he also refers to flexibility as tolerance, courtesy, self-examination, freedom from compulsive habit, contentment, and absence of random thought and imagination. All of these qualities and practices may thus be suggested by the simple terms yin and yang; in respect of these associations, it is the blending of yin and yang that is the aim, and these forms of yin and yang are sometimes given the special name of true yin and true yang.

Speaking in general terms about the need to balance flexibility and firmness, Liu I-ming in his *Wu Tao Lu* says that if one is always "hard," one will be impetuous, aggressive, and impatient; on the other hand, if one is always "soft," one will vacillate and be ineffective. Balance, he concludes, calls for firmness of will with flexibility in action, neither rushing ahead nor lagging behind. The correct balance of yin and yang, in terms of these qualities and applications of firmness and flexibility, is considered important both for social life as well as for spiritual life.

In the context of spiritual practice, yin and yang also correspond to stillness and movement, both of which are used in Complete Reality Taoist training. Stillness may mean actual physical stillness, commonly used as an aid to achieving inner stillness; it is also used to mean the stilling of certain undesirable qualities such as vindictiveness and greed, and it is used to refer to a state of inward tranquility in the midst of action.

Movement has a number of meanings in Complete Reality Taoist praxis; it may mean travel, physical exercise, psychosomatic exercise, or ordinary activity in the world. Charitable activities in particular are often given special emphasis as being an important part of the overall process of human development, encompassing inner benefit to oneself within outward benefit to others.

A somewhat more subtle meaning of stillness and movement is essence and function of awareness. This association appears in the context of a specific exercise described as silencing the mind to revert from function to essence, until quiescence reaches a climax followed by spontaneous activation of the conscious potential formerly stifled by mental routine. One of the finer points of Taoist practice here is to discern the exact quality of the movement following stillness, to determine whether it is in fact movement of the primordial mind of Tao, or whether it is mixed with the acquired human mentality.

As in Ch'an Buddhism, Complete Reality Taoist teaching asserts that stillness produced by concentration alone is not necessarily sufficient to break through the boundaries of psychological conditioning, and may only hold it in temporary abeyance. Altered states thus produced are called "phantom elixir," because they vanish in time. According to the Taoist theory of blending and transcending yin and yang, in the final analysis there is supposed to be no fixed duality between stillness and movement; in Liu I-ming's commentary on *Understanding Reality*, this balanced integration is referred to by means of an expression from the *I Ching*, "Tranquil and unperturbed, yet sensitive and effective," and by a common Taoist phrase, "Always calm yet always responsive, always responsive yet always calm." This is considered to be a basic aspect of the uniting of heaven and earth within humanity, a primary aim of Taoist practice.

The five elements

The concept of the "five elements," like that of yin and yang, is one of the basic descriptive frameworks found in the Complete Reality school of Taoism. So well established was the notion of five elements composing the universe in ancient Chinese thinking that it became routine to classify things in terms of fives—five notes in music, five viscera in physiology, five constants and five virtues in sociology, five senses and five emotions in psychology. It was no doubt convenient for Taoists as well to use this time-honored scheme to structure some of their teachings.

In the Complete Reality school's projection of Taoism, one of the most common constructs for referring to the unification or reconstitution of the human being is called "assembling the five elements." The five elements are represented by the physical elements of fire, water, metal, wood, and earth; these in turn stand for conscious knowledge, real knowledge, sense, essence, and intent. Thus, substituting these equivalents, the assembling of the five elements represents the same blending of yin and yang that has been discussed above: the essence of conscious knowledge and sense of real knowledge are united, with this unification being accomplished through the medium of intent, or will, the concentrated attention used to bridge the acquired gap between the conscious and the unconscious.

Another construct based on the five elements is the contrast between "going along" and "reversal." The form of this construct derives from the ancient idea that the five elements in one order overcome one another, while in another order give rise to one another: Taoist "reversal" inverts both orders. To interpret this scheme, it is necessary to introduce

the idea of the conditioned versus the primordial five elements. In Taoist
terminology, the conditioned five elements are antagonistic or harmful to
one another whereas the primordial five elements cooperate with and foster one another; the conditioned five elements are fragmented whereas
the primordial five elements are unified.

The classic order of production of the five elements is wood-fire-earth-
metal-water-wood-, and so on. In the conditioned state, "wood" stands
for temperament, "fire" for volatility, "earth" for arbitrary intentions,
"metal" for feelings, "water" for desire. In these terms, temperament
produces volatility, volatility produces arbitrary intentions, intentions
produce feelings, feelings produce desires, desires produce temperament.
This represents a circle of conditioning, somewhat reminiscent of the
Buddhist idea of the twelvefold circle of conditioning.

In the primordial state, wood stands for essence, fire for open consciousness, earth for true intent, metal for true sense, and water for real
knowledge. Hence, reversing the order of wood-fire-earth-metal-water-
wood-, essence produces real knowledge, real knowledge produces true
sense, true sense produces true intent, true intent produces open consciousness, open consciousness produces essence.

The classic order of the mutual overcoming of the five elements is wood-
earth-water-fire-metal-wood-. The conditioned equivalents produce the
circle of temperament overcoming will so that the latter degenerates into
arbitrary intentions; arbitrary intentions overcome real knowledge so that it
degenerates into desire; desires overcome consciousness so that it becomes
volatile and unstable; volatility overcomes sense so that it fragments into
feelings; feelings overcome essence so that it is molded into temperament.
This is another way of describing the circle of conditioning.

Reversing the mutual-overcoming cycle, essence overcomes feelings so
they return to true sense; true sense overcomes volatility so that it returns
to clear consciousness; clear consciousness overcomes desire so that it
returns to real knowledge; real knowledge overcomes willfulness so that it
returns to true intent; true intent overcomes temperament so that it
returns to essence.

In dealing with Taoist teachings, it is useful to remember that virtually
every didactic device employed in Taoism, even within a particular school
of Taoism, can be defined in different ways, with the result that there is no
one standard scheme that is universally applied. The importance of this
provision in dealing with Taoist literature may be guessed from the fact that
it derives from the opening statement of the *Tao Te Ching*. One and the
same author may even use different explanations at different times.

This variety of interpretative methods is certainly much in evidence when it comes to a pervasive framework such as the five elements. In his *Shuo P'o Hsiang Yen*, for example, Liu I-ming gives another treatment of the reversal of the five elements that could profitably be applied to the present text. According to this interpretation, fire produces wood in the sense that the essence of a human being is refined in the "furnace" of creation—that is, through experience—to become stabilized; water produces metal in the sense of true sense passing through desire to become undefiled. The reversal of earth then means the reversal of intention and orientation—using the world for self-refinement rather than for self-indulgence.

Another important set of associations of the five elements is the so-called five bases. In the present text, the five bases, or fundamental elements of a human being, are referred to as basic essence, basic sense, basic vitality, basic spirit, and basic energy. The first two, essence and sense, have already been discussed as the essence of consciousness and the sense of real knowledge; the remaining three form the so-called three jewels or three treasures, an important trinity in Complete Reality Taoist thought.

Vitality, energy, and spirit might be defined as the fundamental productive, kinetic, and conscious forces of life. In Taoism they are said to be originally one, yet spoken of as threefold because of their temporal specialization into the energies of sexuality, metabolism, and thought. There are practices which involve the temporal conditioned forms of the three treasures—sexual exercises, breathing exercises, and controlled imagination; but these are said (by numerous authors, including Chang Po-tuan, author of *Understanding Reality*) to be limited in that they do not produce permanent results. In addition, there are said to be mental and physical dangers associated with such practices. Many texts therefore make a point of dismissing them or relegating them to a secondary place.

The metaphysical practice based on the three treasures is generally seen as a progressive refinement: refining vitality into energy, refining energy into spirit, refining spirit into space, and finally breaking through space to merge with the reality of the Tao. This is sometimes described as a progressive detachment and shifting from awareness of the body to awareness of breath, from awareness of breath to awareness of mind, from awareness of mind to awareness of space, from awareness of space to awareness of the Tao, or objective reality.

In certain systems generally classified as belonging to a "lesser vehicle" of Taoism, the vitality, energy, and spirit are associated with specific physical locations. The vitality is associated with the genital or umbilical region, the energy with the area of the solar plexus, and the spirit with the head. These areas are then successively made the focus of concentration, according to the stage of practice; some practitioners, however, concentrate only on one point. In either case, it is commonly noted that this type of practice has the advantage of ease, but also has the disadvantages of being incapable of producing final realization and also having undesirable and potentially dangerous side effects. Such are the dangers of this sort of practice, in fact, that some teachers (such as Liu I-ming) appear to reject it entirely. Modern Taoist literature abounds with warnings in this connection, particularly in reference to concentration on points in the head.

In a different dimension of interpretation, the "upward" progression of vitality-energy-spirit-space-Tao may be used to illustrate an important contention of Complete Reality Taoism. The degeneration of humankind from its original "celestial" state, it is held, is characterized by a "downward" regression of thought into aggression and greed—mundane manifestations of spirit, energy, and vitality. Complete Reality praxis attempts to reverse this regression, channeling vitality and energy "upward" to boost consciousness. This boosting is enhanced by clarification and purification of consciousness so as to make it "spacelike" and therefore receptive to objective reality. Complete Reality Taoist literature using Buddhist terminology also equates vitality, energy, and spirit with the realms of desire, form, and formlessness, similarly indicating a progressive refinement.

In the present text, Liu I-ming's commentary on *Understanding Reality,* the "five bases" represent the energies of the five elements in the primordial, unconditioned state; in the temporal conditioned state, they degenerate into five "things" which are referred to as the wandering higher soul, the ghostlike lower soul, the earthly vitality, the discriminating mind, and the errant intent.

This concept of higher and lower souls derives from an ancient Chinese idea of multiple souls which separate from the individual at death; one group rises up, while one group sinks down. Traditionally, both higher and lower souls are multiple, but in Complete Reality Taoist usage this factor is ordinarily irrelevant, and it is convenient to use the singular form when translating this particular text. The higher and lower souls tend to be ill defined, or undefined, but in some literature, including the present text, the association of the higher soul with imagination and the lower soul with emotion may suggest itself to the modern reader. This interpretation accords, at any rate, with the association made here of the conditioned form of the essence or nature of consciousness with the higher soul, and of conditioned sense or feeling with the lower soul. Those familiar with Western psychoanalytic terminology might also be tempted to see the ego or superego and id in the higher and lower souls.

The earthly vitality, here called the conditioned form of the basic vitality, generally refers to sexuality. In Complete Reality Taoism, sexuality has no moral associations, and its operation and employment are treated as a practical issue. The basic premise in this regard is that sexual activity can either boost or deplete energy; the fundamental aim of Complete Reality praxis seems to be to control and consciously direct sexuality—neither celibacy nor indulgence, according to Chang Po-tuan, author of *Understanding Reality,* will take one to the goal. In Chang's southern school of Complete Reality Taoism, sexual intercourse (both physical and mental) was used to cultivate energy, bliss, and health, especially in the case of practitioners of advanced age. As with breathing exercises and psychosomatic concentration practices, sexual techniques are considered hazardous if improperly performed. Taoist literature abounds with warnings about the misuse of sexuality, both technically and generally; as with other aspects of life in the world, the matter is presented as a question of whether one is controlled by one's energies or in control of them.

The discriminating mind refers to conceptualization. This is regarded as a characteristic of the human mind, conditioned by personal and collective history; it is useful for everyday affairs but ultimately limited and limiting. One feature of the discriminating mind is that it cognizes multiplicity; without the balancing factor of direct perception of organic unity, it is prone to fragmentary awareness and bias. Furthermore, as the patterns according to which the discriminating mind organizes and rationalizes its activities are associated with and influenced by social and cultural identity, they tend to become intimately bound up with emotion, which then increases the tendency to narrowness and prejudice.

As is the case when speaking of the human mentality in general, Complete Reality Taoist teachings often appear extremely negative in their attitudes toward the discriminating mind; it is explained that this is because such teachings are addressed to those in whom the discriminating mind has through long use developed into a jealous tyrant which seeks to exclude or discount knowledge not within its range. It is interesting to note in this connection that attainment of enlightenment in Complete Reality Taoism is said to be easier for women and children than for adult males; one reason for this could be that women and children in post-tribal society have traditionally had less of a stake in, and hence less compulsive need to uphold and defend, the conceptual rationale of a given system. According to Liu I-ming, for example, flexibility is the beginning of the practice of the Tao; and as this quality is conventionally demanded of women and children to a greater extent than it is of men, it might be said that women and children have a head start in Taoist practice in this respect.

The errant intent is considered a degeneration or deviation of the "true intent." True intent is autonomous will or concentration, associated with truthfulness, sincerity, and reliability, which acts as the focal point of Taoist practice, and of life as a whole, in what is called a "real" or "free" human being. Errant intent, on the other hand, is more willfulness than will, and it is influenced by external pressures and subjective desires. In contrast to the sober, deliberate focus of "true intent," the activity of "errant intent" is unstable and fickle.

The five bases and five things are further said to contain, respectively, five virtues and five thieves. The five virtues represent qualities which are held to simultaneously promote social health and personal development. The five thieves are emotions and cravings, called thieves or bandits because their indulgence robs the individual of energy, reason, and inner autonomy. This drainage is held to be the cause of physical and mental decline. Thus the aim of Complete Reality Taoism is to govern the five things by the five bases, and subordinate the five thieves to the five virtues.

The ancient idea of the five virtues seems to have taken final shape in the work of the second century B.C. Confucian scholar Tung Chung-shu, who is said to have introduced the old scheme of the five elements into Confucianism. Prior to this, the great Confucian thinker Mencius (372–289 B.C.) had spoken of four virtues: benevolence, justice, courtesy, and knowledge. He considered benevolence an outgrowth of sympathy, justice an outgrowth of shame at doing evil, courtesy an outgrowth of deference, and knowledge or wisdom an outgrowth of judgment or a sense of right and wrong. Mencius considered the bases of these virtues to be inherent in all people.

The names of the five virtues are variously translated in English, illustrating different aspects or implications of the qualities they represent. Benevolence is associated with humanity, kindness, and compassion. Justice is associated with righteousness and duty. Courtesy is associated with decorum and social grace. Knowledge or wisdom is associated with investigation of things and understanding of principles. In general, these virtues are not rigidly defined, being applied in different ways by different interpreters according to context. In Taoist texts, mention is also made of relevant attitudes and actions such as loving people, promoting social welfare, deferring to others, and pursuing theoretical and practical studies.

The fifth virtue, truthfulness, is perhaps the quality most precisely defined in Complete Reality Taoism. The word can be translated as faith or trust, but in this school of Taoist practice it is specifically associated with sincerity and truth, and regarded as the central quality which gives all the other virtues authenticity. It thus is seen as constituting the core of the individual.

Essence and life

The inner and outer integration of the human being is called the science of essence and life *(hsing-ming hsueh),* and this term is commonly used to indicate the general subject matter of Complete Reality Taoist study. This expression is particularly significant in that it illustrates the contention of the Complete Reality school that both mundane and transcendental development are important for the realization of human completeness.

In Confucian tradition, where the term seems to originate, *hsing-ming* generally means human nature and destiny; in Complete Reality Taoist usage, it means essence and life, defined as mind and body, or spirit and energy. These are said to be one in the primordial state, then divided by temporal conditioning; in this sense the science of essence and life is aimed at restoration of the primal organic unity of mind and body, spirit and energy.

As in the expression "essence and sense," in this case essence also means the basic nature of consciousness, so it may be called mind or spirit. The special study of the science of essence deals with realization of this basic nature. In terms of Plato's metaphor of the cave, the study of essence is commonly practiced by turning the attention from the shadows on the wall to the source of the light itself. Done not by discursive thought but by a direct inner sense, this is what is known in Ch'an Buddhism as "seeing essence" *(chien-hsing),* and Complete Reality Taoist texts often use the Ch'an expression "turning the attention around to look inward" to describe a basic practice used in both schools for this purpose.

The science of life, dealing with the energy of being, includes physical exercise, massage, psychosomatic exercise, energy conservation, and conduct in general. While some manifestations of the study may thus be primarily physical, nevertheless even physical exercises are generally accompanied by certain mental postures or attitudes. The special emphasis of this part of Taoist study is health and well-being. The practices involved in the science of life may be complex, and it is generally in this area that most differences among individual teachers and sects within Complete Reality Taoism are found.

Among the various types of physical exercise, the two systems best known in the Complete Reality tradition are the *pa tuan chin,* "eight step brocade," and the *t'ai chi ch'uan,* "absolute boxing." The former is

said to have been transmitted by Chung-li, ancestor of Complete Reality
Taoism; the invention of the latter is attributed to the extraordinary Ming
dynasty adept Chang San-feng, whose work is often cited in Complete
Reality literature. Eight step brocade is quite simple while absolute boxing is fairly intricate; both systems have numerous variations, and both
are still in popular use.

There are also various systems of massage, generally included under the
rubric of *tao-yin,* "induction," which may combine stretching and bend-
ing with massage. Induction practices are noted for their effects on circu-
lation, and are recommended for maintaining health. Like eight step brocade and absolute boxing, induction practices seem to have taken on a
life of their own in the course of time, and may be presented simply as
exercises for health, without necessarily including the total context of
Complete Reality theory and practice.

The main psychosomatic exercise seen in Complete Reality Taoism is
what is known as the "waterwheel" *(ho-ch'e).* This involves generation of
inner heat by concentration or sexual arousal, then circulating this heat
through the psychic channels called the active and passive *(tu* and *jen)*
channels, up the spine, through the head, and down the center line of
the front of the torso. An abbreviated version of this exercise, using the
active channel up the spine to the brain, is called "returning the vitality
to repair the brain" *(huan ching pu nao).* This is often, though not necessarily, practiced in conjunction with sexual intercourse; in the male, ejaculation is suppressed, either by muscular contraction or external pressure,
creating an extremely intense and prolonged orgasm, the heat of which is
then conducted by concentration up the spine into the brain, where it
"burns" away mundane thoughts and feelings by bliss.

Some Taoists do not use the waterwheel or brain-repairing exercises,
instead emphasizing the practice of energy conservation as a means of
preserving health and extending life. Energy conservation involves mini-
mizing the use of the mind and senses: this includes both exercises of
extreme withdrawal and quiescence as well as general reduction of unnec-
essary expenditures of energy. It is a rather common Taoist contention
that excitation of thought and emotion drains people of energy, and
thus hastens deterioration of the organism. Disconnection of emotion,
thought, and even sense from objects is a three-level restorative exercise
believed to aid in recovery of depleted energy and thus in maintenance of
physical health. As previously mentioned, in Complete Reality Taoism
withdrawal and quietude are not general life patterns or goals of Taoist
practice, but specific techniques to be applied only at appropriate times.

The general practice of avoiding frivolous waste of energy involves not only relinquishment of compulsive mental and physical activity in pursuit of stimulation, but also the harmonization of the individual with the social milieu. In this sense, social ethics, insofar as they promote interpersonal harmony, are considered an integral part of the "science of life," helpful in reducing both psychic and physical wear and tear on all concerned. In his introduction to *Understanding Reality,* Chang Po-tuan mentions the overt teachings of Confucius as being mainly concerned with "life," citing the five virtues and "four no's"—no willfulness, no fixation, no insistence, no egotism. These attitudes are thus considered beneficial both in the context of life in the ordinary world and in the context of higher psychological development, by fostering the accumulation of the energy needed to sustain enhanced consciousness.

In sum, the pursuit of the "science of essence and life" calls for the inner and outer integration of the total human being. This means the inward unification of the psychological and physical energies and their faculties of expression, combined with outward unification of the individual with the environment. Both inner and outer harmonizations are viewed as essential in forming a channel through which proceeds a continuous flow of energy between "heaven and earth."

The use of *I Ching* signs

In common with other Taoist alchemical literature, *Understanding Reality* uses certain signs from the ancient classic *I Ching* in presenting its teachings. The most common of these are the four signs called *heaven, earth, fire,* and *water.*

The signs *heaven* ☰ and *earth* ☷ are the "parent signs" representing pure yang and pure yin, respectively. These two signs thus may be used to indicate qualities or modes of being or praxis, such as movement and stillness, associated with yin and yang. As in the case of the terms yin and yang, the associations of the signs and their components differ according to the context of usage.

The sign *fire* ☲ is generally used to refer to awareness, particularly the consciousness in the human mind. *Fire* is treated as a modification of heaven, indicating that awareness is originally "celestial." The yin -- component in the middle of *fire* ☲ is understood in two ways, according to the specific sense of yin applied. In one sense, yin stands for flexibility, adaptability, and receptivity; in this sense, in the middle of *fire* ☲ it represents the quality of openness or flexibility that is originally a characteristic of consciousness. Hence *fire* can be "open consciousness." In another sense, yin stands for mundanity, conditioning, susceptibility; in this case *fire* ☲ symbolizes fundamentally celestial awareness having been invaded by mundane influences, producing the human mentality, which is centered on and susceptible to the things of the world.

In contrast to the conscious knowledge of the human mind represented by *fire* ☲, the sign *water* ☵ is used to refer to the real knowledge of the mind of Tao. The yang — component in the middle stands for the originally integrated real knowledge that has become buried by mundane conditioning, here represented by the two yin -- components surrounding it. Thus a basic operation of Taoist alchemy is described as taking the solid yang — out of *water* ☵ and using it to replace the broken yin -- inside *fire* ☲ so as to produce whole *heaven* ☰. This means, in other words, to retrieve real knowledge from the overlay of artificial conditioning, and use that to replace the mundanity infecting conscious knowledge, thereby restoring the basic completeness of the primordial celestial mind. Associated nuances of this operation are explained in the commentary to the text.

Another way in which this combination is expressed is in terms of "inversion of *fire* and *water.*" In the ordinary worldly human being, it is said, fire is above water: just as fire rises, consciousness is volatile and given to imagination and wandering thought; and just as water flows downward, real knowledge tends to become submerged in the unconscious, to sink away into oblivion. Thus when fire is above and water below, consciousness and real knowledge go their separate ways and do not combine. Therefore Taoist alchemy speaks of inverting fire and water so that they interact—water "cools" fire, in the sense that real knowledge stabilizes consciousness and removes volatility, while fire "warms" water, in the sense of consciousness bringing real knowledge into action in life.

The eight basic signs of the *I Ching* are also used to represent fundamental elements involved in human development; hence the alchemical expression "the crucible of the eight trigrams." In this scheme, *heaven* ☰ is firmness, *earth* ☷ is flexibility, *fire* ☲ is awareness, *water* ☵ is danger, *thunder* ☳ is action, *mountain* ☶ is stillness, *lake* ☱ is joy, and *wind* ☴ is obedience.

As we have already seen, however, the usage of the signs in Taoist texts may vary just like that of any other symbol or expression. One of the signs often used more or less in isolation from others is *thunder* ☳, representing one yang appearing under two yins, symbolizing the appearance of the primordial mind after profound quiescence: ☷ turning to ☳ stands for the resurgence of the celestial after the climax of the stilling of the mundane; here the "action" of thunder means activation of the innate potential of the original mind. In another context, however, *thunder* ☳ represents essence, paired with *lake* ☱ representing sense: *thunder* as "action" here refers to the excitable nature of temperament, which is the conditioned form of essence; and *lake* as "joy" refers to emotional feelings, the conditional form of sense.

A number of six-line signs of the *I Ching* are also used in alchemical texts to represent phases of practice. Among the most commonly encountered are *difficulty* ䷂ and *darkness* ䷃, as in the standard expression "difficulty in the morning, darkness at night." This maxim is generally used to allude to the so-called "martial" and "cultural" phases of the alchemical work, involving active struggle and passive nurturance. These complementary aspects of practice are also known as doing and nondoing, striving and nonstriving.

Also mentioned in *Understanding Reality* are the pairs *obstruction* and *tranquility, settled* and *unsettled. Obstruction* ䷋ represents failure of yin and yang to interact and combine, thus obstructing human progress; *tranquility* ䷊ stands for the interaction of yin and yang, which is the basis of growth. Similarly, *settled* ䷾ symbolizes the interaction of *fire* and *water,* conscious knowledge and real knowledge, thus producing balance; while *unsettled* ䷿ indicates the isolation of *fire* and *water* from one another, resulting in bias.

Finally, *Understanding Reality* also alludes to what are known as the six yang signs and six yin signs. The six yang signs are *return* ䷗, *overseeing* ䷒, *tranquility* ䷊, *great power* ䷡, *parting* ䷪, and *heaven* ䷀. Conversely, the six yin signs are *meeting* ䷫, *withdrawal* ䷠, *obstruction* ䷋, *observing* ䷓, *stripping away* ䷖, and *earth* ䷁. These signs are not used in this case according to their individual values as outlined in the *I Ching,* but simply as representations of the gradual growth of yang followed by merging with yin: hence they symbolize the "yang fire" and "yin convergence," the two predominant operations of the alchemical process.

Praxis

One of the interesting features of *Understanding Reality* is that it does not give details of any concrete form of practice through which the alchemical transformation is to be accomplished. This can be easily appreciated on the principle that practices can have their intended effect only when performed according to proper measure, which depends on individual needs and timing. What the text does indicate is what is to be achieved through the alchemical work; the specific method, tailored to the individual case, is to be learned in person from an adept.

It is sometimes said that there are three thousand six hundred practices in Taoism; some writers repudiate all formal practices as "sidetracks," hinting at the metaphysical nature of the Tao and confirming the contention that truth is formless. In his preface to *Understanding Reality*, Chang Po-tuan mentions some common exercises such as star-gazing, visualization, breathing exercises, massage, incantation, celibacy, fasting, fixation of attention, and sexual yoga, and says that the effects of such practices are all impermanent, at best leading to physical health and well-being.

Generally speaking, the most pervasive practical concern in Complete Reality Taoism appears to be the purification and deautomization of the mind so as to make it sensitive to reality; and it is well known that practitioners commonly practiced quiet sitting as an aid in accomplishing this. Nonetheless, Liu I-ming, who generally presents an interpretation of *Understanding Reality* characteristic of the "pure serenity" approach of the northern school of Complete Reality Taoism, which emphasized quiet sitting, still makes a point of repudiating even this as a magic key to enlightenment. There are indisputable indications that Liu did himself practice abstract trance in quiet sitting, but he did not preach it as a mechanical cure-all; rather, he emphasized more the use of everything in life as a means of self-refinement, with abstract trance a means of finding the "medicines" of unconditioned spirit and energy, which subsequently have to be refined in the "furnace" of everyday life. There is no indication that he, or Chang Po-tuan for that matter, ever set up any sort of fixed program for students to follow.

Perhaps the most provocative issue in Complete Reality practice is the difference in the approaches of the so-called northern and southern schools. As noted in the beginning of this introduction, both schools are believed to derive from the teachings of Chung-li Ch'uan and Lu Tung-pin, and to have the same goal; nevertheless there are methodological differences. One modern Taoist puts it this way: "Whatever the school, all practitioners gather the unique unconditioned energy; the way of getting it and the provenance are not the same, but the accomplishment is one."[9]

The main difference in the methods of the northern and southern schools apparently lies in the use or otherwise of sexual yoga and the waterwheel exercise. This is suggested by the epithets given to the schools based on their practices: the northern school is commonly called the sect of "pure serenity," referring to silent meditation, while the southern school is often called the sect of "grafting" or "twin cultivation of yin and yang," in reference to the use of sexual exercises.

One modern Taoist gives an interesting explanation of the reason for this difference: "The northern school emphasizes purity and stillness, as transmitted by Ch'iu Ch'ang-ch'un (a disciple of Wang Che); the southern school emphasizes grafting, as transmitted by Chang Po-tuan. Ch'ang-ch'un's lineage involved people who practiced the Tao in youth or middle age, none of whom were over sixty years old. Chang Po-tuan's lineage mostly included elderly people over eighty, whose temporal vitality and energy were insufficient and had to be replenished by grafting; therefore it is also called the method of mutual supplementation of yin and yang. However, after replenishment, they also had to practice in the same way as the school of pure serenity." [10]

As usual, however, the situation does not seem to have been quite as clear-cut as generalizations make it appear. Although differences in method and emphasis apparently came to be exaggerated by some groups as a basis for sectarianism, nevertheless those Taoists who continued to emphasize the unity of the goal insist that the documents of the northern and southern schools can be interpreted coherently in each other's terms. For example, a modern Taoist says, "The books of the southern school may be interpreted perfectly well in terms of the practice of pure serenity." [11] Another says, "The southern and northern schools are extremely difficult to differentiate. Chang Po-tuan's *Understanding Reality* is, to be sure, a specialist book of the southern school, but it can also be viewed as an alchemical classic of the northern school. What one sees in it depends on the person." [12]

A further complication arises when we consider the southern school to be marked by the use of "grafting," sexual yoga for energy boosting, since Chang Po-tuan himself deemphasizes sexual practices in his own preface to *Understanding Reality,* and so does Tao-kuang, third patriarch of the southern school, in his commentary on this text. These apparent denials may, of course, be protective camouflage, not only to guard against outside interference by scandalized Confucian authorities, but also to guard against abuse of such practices by ignorant imitators, because sexual yoga is held to be potentially hazardous, as a modern Taoist explains: "The interaction of yin and yang (here meaning female and male) is inconceivable; if the practice of the southern school is not done properly, it can easily cause illness." [13]

According to other modern Taoists who speak of the differences and similarities of the two schools, the grafting practice of the southern school must be combined, as previously noted, with the pure serenity practice of the northern school: "If one wants to practice the yin-yang twin cultivation of the southern school, unless one has sufficient grounding in the practice of pure serenity one will be unable to be unminding in face of objects; many have failed in the eleventh hour because of this."[14] "In the practice of the southern school, even if one can obtain elixir from one's partner, one must then resume the practice of pure serenity, embrace the fundamental, preserve unity, return to emptiness and go back to nothingness; only thus can one achieve final settlement. Otherwise, hopes of attaining reality will in the end vanish."[15]

In sum, the aim of Complete Reality Taoism is to be a "real human being" rather than a willy-nilly product of socio-cultural accident, to be fully awake, autonomous, capable of exercising free will and of perceiving reality directly without artificial constructs. It is not necessary to believe in the possibility of attaining this goal to draw the lesson from religious history that arbitrary adoption of formal practices because of tradition or attraction can simply automatize people in another way, just "adding chains to fetters," in the Ch'an phrase. The value of texts like *Understanding Reality* is not in providing an A to Z manual of Taoist enlightenment, but in providing a theoretical basis for understanding the elements of a praxis in the context of a comprehensive framework, in relation to specific possibilities. This removes the charisma from externals and focuses attention on effect, so that a system can be assessed in terms of what it does rather than what it looks like.

Notes

1. *Ting P'i Shang-yang-tzu Yuan Chu Ts'an T'ung Ch'i* (Hsin Wen Feng Publishing Co., Taiwan, 1978), p. 4.

2. See *Hsuan Men Pi Tu* (Tzu Yu Publishing Co., Taiwan, 1965), and *Li Tai Shen Hsien Shih* (Hsin Wen Feng Publishing Co., Taiwan, 1978).

3. There are obvious chronological problems involved in trying to trace Complete Reality Taoism back beyond Chang Po-tuan and Wang Che. Liu Ts'ao is said to have lived in the tenth century, a hundred years before Chang Po-tuan met him. Lu Tung-pin, to whom a vast body of apocrypha is attributed, is said to have lived in the eighth century. Chung-li is generally said to have been a man of the T'ang dynasty, but his teacher was supposedly born in the middle of the second century C.E. Taoists, of course, have long claimed that a sort of hibernation or suspended animation can be achieved by practice; interestingly enough, amid con-

temporary fears for the planet, scientists in the West have recently begun to seriously examine the question of whether human hibernation is possible, quite apart from any interest in Taoism. If the works of Chang Po-tuan and Wang Che are studied on the basis of the Ch'an Buddhist maxim, "Refer everything to yourself," historical concerns subside to the relatively superficial plane of terminology and organizational patterns.

4. In general, the formation of large organizations in Taoist history relates more to economic and political conditions than to intrinsic qualities of Taoism. Taoist circles such as that represented by Chuang Tzu were apparently esoteric in the sense that they had no readily identifiable social presence. Stories of the encounters of Chung-li Ch'uan, Lu Tung-pin, and Liu Ts'ao are centered on individual, personal recognition and interaction. Indications of the situation in the times of Chang Po-tuan and Wang Che seem to point to individuals or small groups of associates; the organizational boom of Complete Reality Taoism took place after Wang's time and was connected with social factors such as alienation of the gentry from politics under foreign rule, disturbed conditions in northern China due to military action, and the recognition and entitlement of Wang's successor Ch'iu Ch'ang-ch'un by the Mongol hegemon Jenghiz Khan.

5. *Li Tai Shen Hsien Shih*, scroll 4.

6. Other classics commented on by Liu include the *Yin Fu Ching*, attributed to Huang Ti; *Huang Ting Ching*, attributed to Tung Hua; *Ch'iao Yao Ke*, attributed to Lu Tung-pin; *Wu Ken Shu*, by Chang San-feng; and *Chin Tan Ssu Pai Tzu*, by Chang Po-tuan. For Liu's explanation of the *I Ching*, see my *The Taoist I Ching* (Shambhala, Boston, 1986); for his explanation of *Chin Tan Ssu Pai Tzu*, see my *The Inner Teachings of Taoism* (Shambhala, Boston, 1986).

7. Li Lo-ch'iu, *Fang Tao Yu Lu* (Chen Shan Mei Publishing Co., Taiwan, 1965), p. 2.

8. Again, in the spirit of the *Tao Te Ching*, it must be remembered that no claims of unique validity can be made for this or any other interpretation. For broader studies in alchemical lore, see Joseph Needham's *Science and Civilization in China*, 5 vols. (Cambridge University Press). For some indication of the variety of interpretative frameworks applied to alchemical terms, see *Chung Ho Chi* in volume 17 of *Tao Tsang Chi Yao* (Hsin Wen Feng Publishing Co., Taiwan, 1976). For Liu I-ming's critical examination of metaphysical and physical interpretations of Taoist symbolism, see my *The Inner Teachings of Taoism*.

9. Li Lo-ch'iu, *Fang Tao Yu Lu*, p. 321.

10. Ibid., p. 251.

11. Ibid., p. 330.

12. Ibid., p. 349.

13. Ibid., p. 119.

14. Ibid., p. 332.

15. Ibid., pp. 327–328.

UNDERSTANDING REALITY
A Direct Explanation

I

Sixteen verses,
representing "eight ounces" of yin
and "eight ounces" of yang,
forming "one pound" of elixir

1

IF YOU DO NOT SEEK THE GREAT WAY TO LEAVE THE PATH OF
DELUSION, EVEN IF YOU ARE INTELLIGENT AND TALENTED
YOU ARE NOT GREAT. A HUNDRED YEARS IS LIKE A SPARK, A
LIFETIME IS LIKE A BUBBLE. IF YOU ONLY CRAVE MATERIAL
GAIN AND PROMINENCE, WITHOUT CONSIDERING THE DE-
TERIORATION OF YOUR BODY, I ASK YOU, EVEN IF YOU AC-
CUMULATE A MOUNTAIN OF GOLD CAN YOU BUY OFF IMPER-
MANENCE?

The realm of dust is the world of sound and form, the land of name
and gain where misery is taken for pleasure, where the artificial is taken to
be real. Diminishing the vitality, wearing out the energy, destroying
essence and life, in it there is death only. Those who realize this and can
go beyond it are the people of attainment; those who are unaware of it
and fall into it are people astray. Therefore since ancient times the
immortals and real people who achieved the Tao took care of their family
and social duties when they were young, thereby fulfilling human ethics;
when they reached the age of forty they practiced the Tao of not stirring
the mind, whereby they preserved their essence and life. After all, a hundred years is only a brief interval; a lifetime of glory and disgrace is a
blink of an eye. If you do not know how to return to the fundamental and
go back to the origin, to return to the root and go back to life, when the
limit of your time here comes, even if you have a pile of gold you'll leave
empty-handed. Our author says, "Even if you accumulate a mountain of
gold, can you buy off impermanence?" Truly this is a golden bell, a drum
of truth, to wake everyone up.

2

THOUGH HUMAN LIFE HAS A LIMIT OF A HUNDRED YEARS,
THE LENGTH OF LIFE, AND WHETHER IT WILL BE DIFFICULT
OR SMOOTH, CANNOT BE KNOWN BEFOREHAND. YESTERDAY
RIDING A HORSE THROUGH TOWN, TODAY A SLEEPING
CORPSE IN A COFFIN: FAMILY AND WEALTH CAST OFF, THEY
ARE NOT YOUR OWN POSSESSIONS; WITH EVIL DEEDS COM-
ING ON, YOU CANNOT FOOL YOURSELF. IF YOU COME UPON

THE GREAT ELIXIR WITHOUT EVEN LOOKING FOR IT, HAVING
COME UPON IT, YOU ARE A FOOL IF YOU DO NOT REFINE IT.

Worldly people compete and struggle for fame and profit, not resting
day or night. They assume their lives will never end, and they will be able
to go on forever enjoying happiness. How can they realize that no one can
know beforehand how long they will live, whether their lives will be difficult or easy, or whether their lives will be filled with gain or loss. Do not
say people rarely live to be a hundred years old—even if they do, they still
cannot escape the grave. We frequently see people who do not take life or
death seriously; but after all there are countless numbers of people who
die horrible and violent deaths even as they walk along the road, as they
talk and laugh. While your eyes are open, your family and goods are
yours, but when your eyes close forever everything is one void. You do not
take anything at all along with you when you go; only the demons of your
misdeeds come back to you for a thousand years. It is better to see
through worldly affairs as soon as possible, and hasten to call on enlightened teachers, whereby to seek the great elixir. If your potential and circumstances are meet, and you do find the great elixir, this is very fortunate, a great basis; set right about refining it with the best of your power,
and you can leave death and enter life, thereby comprehending impermanence. If you do not willingly and straightforwardly cultivate it, you
are ruining yourself and throwing yourself away; such fools are on a par
with those who cannot see through worldly things—after all they will die;
then what is the value of knowledge?

3

IF YOU ARE GOING TO STUDY IMMORTALITY, YOU SHOULD
STUDY CELESTIAL IMMORTALITY; ONLY THE GOLD ELIXIR IS
WORTHWHILE. WHEN THE TWO THINGS JOIN, SENSE AND
ESSENCE MERGE; WHEN THE FIVE ELEMENTS ARE COMPLETE,
THE TIGER AND DRAGON INTERTWINE. STARTING WITH
HEAVEN-EARTH AND EARTH-EARTH AS GO-BETWEENS, FI-
NALLY THEY HAVE HUSBAND AND WIFE CONJOIN HAPPILY.
JUST WAIT FOR THE ACHIEVEMENT TO BE COMPLETED TO PAY
COURT TO THE NORTH PALACE GATE; IN THE LIGHT OF NINE-
FOLD MIST YOU RIDE A FLYING PHOENIX.

The first two sections told people to see through things of the world and hasten to seek the great elixir whereby to shed birth and death. The way to shed birth and death is the way of learning immortality. But there are numerous classes of immortals. Those who comprehend essence and project the yin soul are ghost immortals. Those who understand life and keep their bodies in the world are earthly immortals. Those who understand both essence and life, who have bodies outside their bodies, who are both physically and mentally sublimated and who join the Tao and merge with reality, are celestial immortals. Though the spirit of ghosts is the yin soul and can exit and enter at will, still since the abode is not permanent they still have the affliction of abandoning one body and entering another. Though earthly immortals keep their bodies in the world, still they cannot free the spiritual body and still have the burden of the illusory body relying on things. Of these two, one falls into having death, one falls into having birth—both are equally unable to completely shed birth and death. Only celestial immortals shed the illusory body and achieve the spiritual body; they go beyond creation, and have no birth or death. Able to shed birth and death, their life span is equal to heaven, never decaying.

If students want to shed birth and death, they should learn celestial immortality; if they want to learn celestial immortality, they cannot do so but by the great science of gold elixir. Gold is something incorruptible; elixir is a symbol for blending without hindrance. Incorruptible, freely blending, the undifferentiated one energy is like the measureless empty sphere of heaven, enclosing everything, invulnerable to anything. Therefore after the way is accomplished, one is called a celestial immortal; because of being forever incorruptible, this is also called a gold immortal; because of appearing and disappearing unfathomably, this is also called a spirit immortal. In reality, gold immortals and spirit immortals are all celestial immortals. If you want to learn celestial immortality, there is no method of doing so save the science of the gold elixir.

This gold elixir is the innate knowledge and innate capacity received by humans from heaven—it is completely good, with nothing bad in it; the completely perfect spiritual faculty, it is formed of a coagulation of primordial positive energy. Therein are included yin and yang, therein are stored the five elements: that is, there is the energy but not the substance —it cannot be compared to the conditioned corporeal polluted matter of an individual body. If it is passed through yin convergence and yang fire and refined to perfection, it becomes eternally incorruptible—this is called the great restored elixir of gold liquid through sevenfold reversion and ninefold restoration.

Gold elixir is another name for the unfragmented original essence; there is no gold elixir besides the original essence. This elixir is inherent in everyone, not more in sages or less in ordinary people. It is the seed of immortals and enlightened ones, the root of saints and sages. It is only that as long as it has not been put through fire and refined, when the positive culminates it must turn to negative, when waxing culminates it must wane, and it falls into the temporal: intellectual knowledge develops and private desires get mixed in; temperament emerges and the natural good dims, innate knowledge and innate capacity both lose their innocence, and there is no more body of pristine purity.

Therefore ancient sages set up the method of reversion and restoration of gold elixir, just to have people return home and recognize their ancestor, to revert to what is fundamentally inherent. Why is it called reversion and restoration? Reversion means the self comes back after it has gone; restoration means the self is regained after it has been lost.

When the spiritual root of the fundamental essence is obscured, it is because yin and yang are not in harmony and the five elements harm each other. If yin and yang are united and the five elements are assembled, the former completeness is regained.

As for the "two things" mentioned in the text, one is hard, one soft, one firm, one submissive, one real knowledge, one conscious knowledge, one true sense, one conscious essence. Real knowledge is included in the mind of Tao, and controls hardness and firmness; it emerges as true sense. Conscious knowledge hides in the human mind, and controls softness and submission; it is receptive as conscious essence. When real knowledge and conscious knowledge separate, one is firm when one shouldn't be firm, and submits to what one shouldn't submit to: hardness and softness lose their proper measure, and true sense and conscious essence turn into false feeling and false nature. When real knowledge and conscious knowledge are conjoined one is firm where one should be firm and submits to what one should submit to; hardness and softness are properly timed, and false feeling and false nature turn into true sense and true essence. Is it not clear when the author here says, "When the two things join, sense and essence merge"?

As for the "five elements," they are the five energies of metal, wood, water, fire, and earth. In the primordial state, these five energies constitute the five bases—basic essence, basic sense, basic vitality, basic spirit, and basic energy. In the conditioned state, they constitute five things—the wandering higher soul, the ghostlike lower soul, the earthly vitality, the discriminating mind, and the errant intent. The five bases contain the five virtues of benevolence, justice, courtesy, knowledge, and truthfulness; the five things contain the five thieves, which are joy, anger, sadness, happiness, and lust. When the five elements are complete, the primordial and the temporal are conjoined, and the five bases control the five things. The "dragon" is yang; it commands the life-impulse. It belongs to the sphere of "wood" in the eastern direction. In humans, it is the essence. The "tiger" is yin; it commands the death-impulse. It belongs to the sphere of metal, in the western direction. In humans it is sense. When the five elements are not in harmony, their natures become isolated; the five bases turn into the five things, and the five virtues change into the five thieves; the dragon remains in the east and the tiger in the west, essence is disturbed and sense is awry, thus becoming temperament and errant feeling, so that the energy of death saps the energy of life.

When the five elements are complete and whole, they all return to one nature; the five things turn into the five bases, the five thieves change into the five virtues. The dragon coils, the tiger sits, essence is stabilized and feelings are forgotten, thus constituting true sense and real essence; so the energy of death becomes the energy of life.

The path of spiritual alchemy is no more than harmonizing hard and soft, causing firmness and submissiveness to balance each other and essence and sense to unite with each other. When essence and sense unite, yin and yang join and the five elements are complete; this is the primordial noumenon of heaven. It is wholly good, with no evil, the basic phenomena of innate knowledge and capacity—hence the gold elixir is restored.

But after the primordial original basis is lost and scattered, essence goes east while feeling goes west, and hard and soft do not interact. If there is no harmonizing substance to convey communication, they will be cut off from each other and not know each other at all. The harmonizing substances are the two earths, the heaven-earth and the earth-earth.

The heaven-earth is in charge of movement, and is in the domain of yang; the earth-earth is in charge of stillness, and is in the province of yin. That which is quiescent and unmoving is earth-earth; that which is sensitive and effective is heaven-earth. Among the five virtues, the two earths are real truthfulness. When real truthfulness is in the center, essence is stable; when the function of true stability is externalized, sense is harmonious. When essence is stable and sense harmonious, essence and sense return to the root, like husband and wife in blissful embrace. Benevolence, justice, courtesy, and knowledge return to one truthfulness; essence and sense, vitality and spirit, join in one energy. Heaven, earth, and humanity meet, the five energies go back to the basis, return to the origin and revert to the fundamental, and the gold elixir congeals. One name for this is the spiritual embryo.

Then go on to advanced cultivation, entering from doing into nondoing, nurturing it warmly for ten months, making it solid and complete, firmly sealed. Take out the excess of firm sense, augment the insufficiency of submissive essence. Using the natural true fire, beginning in the morning, flowing on unceasingly at night, burn away the conditioned mundane energy. Producing substance from no substance, going from subtle to apparent, when the energy is full and the spirit complete, with a peal of thunder you shed the shell, and have a body outside the body. Then the accomplishment is achieved, and you go to the celestial court, the "North Palace," riding on a phoenix, flying aloft in broad daylight, becoming a pure celestial immortal. Wouldn't that be pleasant? The original true essence is called the gold elixir; with the physical elements as the furnace, it is forged into a ball. Those who realize this ascend to the ranks of sages right away; those who do not know it are sunk for myriad eons. How can those with will not work on this?

4

THIS METHOD IS THE SUBLIME AND REAL OF THE REAL. IT ALL DEPENDS ON ONESELF ALONE, APART FROM OTHERS. ONE KNOWS INVERSION ONESELF, STARTING FROM FIRE AND WATER. WHO DISCERNS FLOATING AND SINKING, ESTABLISHES HOST AND GUEST? IN THE GOLD CRUCIBLE, IF YOU WANT TO KEEP THE MERCURY WITHIN CINNABAR, IN THE JADE POND FIRST SEND DOWN THE SILVER WITHIN WATER. THE SPIRITUAL WORK OPERATING THE FIRING DOES NOT TAKE A WHOLE DAY BEFORE IT BRINGS OUT THE ORB OF THE SUN IN THE DEEP POOL.

The foregoing section said that cultivating the gold elixir requires that essence and sense be joined into one, and the five elements all be complete; only then can it be accomplished. However, while the medicinal substances are easy to know, the firing process is most difficult.

The firing process is the process of the method of cultivation and refinement. Master Lu said that those of superior virtue make their bodies complete by means of the Tao, this being because their pure yang is not yet broken, while those of lesser virtue extend their lives by means of techniques, because water and fire have already formed. In general, those of lesser virtue need artificial methods.

Method means technique: without method, without technique, one cannot return to the basis and revert to the origin; when the life-foundation is unstable, the great Tao is difficult to achieve. Therefore the author says here, "This method is the sublime and real of the real. It all depends on oneself alone, apart from others." The method called the real and sublime is an utterly real and utterly sublime method. As the method leads to the real, one can appropriate yin and yang and take over creation, turning enlivening and killing around, reverse the working of energy. As the method leads to the sublime, even spirits and ghosts cannot fathom it, divination cannot read it. In the primordial state, nature does not differ from it; in the temporal state, it obeys the times of nature. So it is the way to become a sage; it is impenetrable by the minor methods of all auxiliary techniques.

Wherein lies the marvel of the real method of refinement? The marvel is in inversion alone. Inversion means inversion of yin and yang and reversal of creation. As for fire and water, *fire* ☲ is male outside and female inside; the female inside is true yin, which in people is conscious knowledge concealed within the human mind. When the human mind stirs, conscious knowledge flies, like the rising of flames of fire. *Water* ☵ is dark outside and light inside; the light inside is true yang, which in people is real knowledge, inherent in the mind of Tao. When the mind of Tao is obscured, real knowledge is obscured, like water flowing downward.

By inverting these, we produce the mind of Tao and stabilize the human mind. When the mind of Tao emerges, real knowledge is strong and firm, and the pure and whole water rises. When the human mind is stabilized, conscious knowledge is flexible and adaptive, and the rising, drying fire descends. When water rises and fire descends, they equalize each other.

Conscious knowledge is essence; essence is in the province of wood: the essence of wood is soft, and it easily floats up. Real knowledge is sense; sense is in the province of metal: the sense of metal is hard, and it easily sinks down. Conscious knowledge floating up and acting in affairs is the "host"; there is artificiality within the real. Real knowledge sinking and not being manifest is the "guest"; the artificial overcomes its reality. This is the usual course. To "establish host and guest" is to make the sense of real knowledge the host, causing that which sinks to float up, and to make the essence of conscious knowledge the guest, causing that which floats up to sink down. With host and guest inverted, metal and wood join.

When fire and water mix, and metal and wood join, the mind of Tao is strong, and the human mind submits to it. Real knowledge and conscious knowledge are joined into one, essence and sense commingle. How could the gold elixir then not crystallize?

However, this real, sublime method is not material and not void; it is done unbeknownst to others, where only one can know oneself. That is why the text says, "One knows oneself," and it also says "Who discerns?" People do not discern it—you know it yourself. That snatching of potential is invisible and unknowable to anyone.

In this path, there is before and after, there is intensity and relaxation; if you do not know the subtle function of before and after, intensity and relaxation, even if you can recognize the medicinal substances inversion will be impossible to effect and host and guest will not be determined. Therefore the text follows right up with "In the gold crucible, if you want to keep the mercury within cinnabar, in the jade pond first send down the silver within water." Here, "gold" is something hard, "jade" is something soft; the "crucible" is something for refining the elixir, the "pond" is something for nourishing the fire. The gold crucible and jade pond symbolize the path of cultivation of reality; hardness and softness is its body.

The human mind belongs to *fire* ☲ , which is based on the body of *heaven* ☰ . This is the gold crucible, containing the fire of *earth* in the second place (– –) as conscious knowledge; this is that in which the softness and adaptability of *earth* ☷ is balanced in the center—that is, the original innate capacity. The human mind is originally empty and clear, its immaterial spirit unclouded: because it is mixed with conditioned discriminating consciousness, awareness is used to produce illusion; perceiving objects, it arouses dust, raising waves along with the wind, without a moment's rest, like the mercury within cinnabar, which flies when it meets fire and is most difficult to keep. This is what the *Ts'an T'ung Ch'i* refers to when it says, "The bead flowing in the sun always tries to leave the person."

The mind of Tao belongs to *water* ☵ , which is based on the body of *earth* ☷ . This is the jade pond, containing the water of celestial unity (—) as real knowledge; this is that in which the hardness and firmness of *heaven* ☰ is balanced in the center—that is, the original innate knowledge. Because of falling into the temporal state, working with conditioned energy, the true energy recedes, yang falls into yin, the real is covered by the artificial, one sinks in the ocean of desire, and innate knowledge is obscured, like silver in water, virtually nonexistent, barely existent. Silver is metal; silver in water is the metal concealed in water. This metal primordially is the innate knowledge of the original essence; in the temporal state it is the real knowledge of the mind of Tao. By that real knowledge one reaches strength and health, so it is represented metaphorically as true lead. By that real knowledge one becomes immortal and attains the Tao, so it is represented metaphorically as true seed.

Sages since antiquity have all comprehended essence and life by gathering these same medicines. Though the conscious knowledge of the human mind is easily moved, if you get the real knowledge of the mind of Tao to control it, the consciousness will return to reality and will not fly off. Instability is due to the unsettledness of the consciousness of the human mind, which in turn is due to lack of the mind of Tao. If you want to retain the conscious knowledge of the human mind, you must first set down this real knowledge of the mind of Tao. Where there is the true seed of real knowledge, there is inner autonomy which is unmoved by contaminated energies; then the conscious knowledge of the human mind naturally stabilizes and does not fragment.

The mind of Tao is used to control the human mind, the human mind is made to follow the mind of Tao; real knowledge governs conscious knowledge, conscious knowledge nurtures real knowledge. Hard and soft balance each other, firm and submissive become as one, essence and sense conjoin; within a short time they crystallize into a single round, luminous jewel, its spiritual light shining brightly, invulnerable to any aberrant energies. Therefore the treatise says, "The spiritual work operating the firing does not take a whole day before it brings out the orb of the sun in the deep pool." The spiritual work is the silent operation of the light of the spirit being careful when alone; the fire is the harmonious energy of real knowledge and conscious knowledge, hard and soft, merging into one. Operating the firing means being careful and wary about the unperceived, operating this real knowledge and conscious knowledge so the hard and soft unite, not letting any garbage stay in the mind. This fire of spiritual work is like setting up a pole and seeing its shadow, shouting into a valley conveying one's voice; if you do it straightforwardly without reservations, it won't take all day before you can restore the positive from within the negative, like the sun emerging in a deep pond, negative energy receding of itself.

The essential point in this section is the words "if you want to keep" and "first send down." Therein is the meaning of "first developing control over the person, duty not extending to a guest"—if you get the meaning of this, then inverting yin and yang and uniting the four forms is as easy as turning your hand over. This is the form of the method of the outer elixir. "Outer elixir" is another name for the restored elixir. Because it is gone and comes back, is lost and restored, it is called the outer elixir and also called the restored elixir. After the elixir has been restored, it then is the inner elixir; this is the distinction between the inner and outer elixir.

5

THE TIGER LEAPS, THE DRAGON SOARS, THE WIND AND WAVES ARE ROUGH; IN THE CORRECT POSITION IN THE CENTER IS PRODUCED THE MYSTERIOUS JEWEL. FRUIT GROWS ON THE BRANCHES, RIPE AT THE END OF THE SEASON; HOW CAN THE CHILD IN THE BELLY BE ANY DIFFERENT? THE SOURCE OF NORTH AND SOUTH OVERTURNS THE TRIGRAM SIGNS; THE FIRING PROCESS OF MORNING AND EVENING JOINS THE PIVOT OF HEAVEN. YOU SHOULD KNOW THE GREAT HERMIT IS CONCEALED IN THE CITY; WHAT IS THE NECESSITY OF KEEPING TO TRANQUIL SOLITUDE DEEP IN THE MOUNTAINS?

The preceding section spoke of the matter of restored elixir; this one speaks of the way of the great elixir. The way of the great elixir is the work of one time. This one time joins the qualities of heaven and earth, joins the light of sun and moon, joins the order of the four seasons. It is hard to find and easy to mistake. If there is any carelessness, the energy of primordial true unity is lost. The primordial truly unified energy is the restored elixir; it is formed by the combination of hard and soft energies based on the restored elixir, so it is called the truly unified energy. It is not that there is a truly unified energy apart from the restored elixir.

When the restored elixir is obtained, the mind of Tao is firm and strong, and the human mind is soft and docile; real knowledge and conscious knowledge merge into one, round and bright. This is the innate knowledge and innate ability, tranquil and unperturbed, sensitive and effective, the property of the original self. This property is called the true lead because of its essential firmness; it is also called the male tiger because of the robustness of its energy. The true lead, or male tiger, is one single flowing energy, all good, with no evil; it is simply preservation of the natural reality of the innate knowledge and capacity. Once you have managed to recover this natural reality, you need to return this natural reality to where the five elements do not reach, before your parents gave birth to you; only then can it be an everlasting incorruptible natural reality.

So when natural reality has been recovered, nurture it, guarding it carefully and storing it securely. Become utterly empty, quiet, and sincerely intent; when filled with positive energy, from ultimate stillness you again go into motion, and the spiritual sprouts emerge.

At this time, the positive light emerges from its lair, like the robustness of the tiger, its momentum unstoppable: quickly meet it with the point of fire of clear consciousness in the true essence. The fire of clear consciousness is called the female dragon. "The tiger leaps, the dragon soars" is a representation of the gathering of yin and yang. As for "wind and waves are rough," when the tiger emerges from its cave wind rises, and when the dragon emerges from its pool waves arise. This means the contact of yin and yang: dragon and tiger mate, essence and sense merge, joining into one, entering the center.

The primordial energy comes from nothingness and congeals into a bead of jewel: "The spiritual embryo assumes form." The spiritual embryo is the "valley spirit," the valley spirit is the spirit of mystery and femaleness merging into one. The mystery of yang is the tiger, sense; the femaleness of yin is the dragon, essence. When essence and sense join, the spiritual embryo forms; when the mysterious female stands, the valley spirit is born. When you get to this state, doing is ended and nondoing appears; it is no longer necessary to strive—leave it to nature. It is like fruit growing on the branches—eventually they will ripen; the child in the belly will one day be born.

But though the consolidation of the spiritual embryo calls for nondoing, there is still the work of preventing danger and being wary of peril, which one must know.

As for "The source of north and south overturns the trigram signs," south is fire, and north is water: with the spiritual embryo consolidated, a harmonious energy permeates; water and fire return to the source, naturally heating and boiling together. Let it proceed naturally; one must successfully avoid both inattentiveness and forcing the issue.

As for "the firing process morning and evening joins the pivot of heaven," morning is the beginning of a day, when the yang energy works; evening is the beginning of a night, when the yin energy works: the pivot of heaven is the incipience of energy, yin and yang. When yang is appropriate, use yang; when yin is appropriate, use yin: the waxing and waning of the firing accords with the potentials of morning and evening. This is the accomplishment of work by day and cautious by night.

Do not be inattentive, yet do not force; working by day and cautious at night, nurture it warmly for ten months, exchange the temporal trigrams, free the primordial spiritual body. Your life depends on yourself, not on heaven. This is the Tao. It is cultivated among humanity, done in the marketplace. The great function of great potential, the realistic work of true action, is not the study of vacant, inactive quiescence; that is why it says, "You should know the great hermit is concealed in the city; what is the necessity of keeping to tranquil solitude deep in the mountains?"

6

EVERYONE ORIGINALLY HAS THE HERB OF LONG LIFE: IT'S JUST THAT THEY DON'T UNDERSTAND IT, AND THROW IT AWAY IN VAIN. WHEN THE SWEET DEW DESCENDS, HEAVEN AND EARTH JOIN; WHERE THE YELLOW SPROUTS GROW, WATER AND FIRE MIX. A FROG IN A WELL WOULD SAY THERE IS NO DRAGON'S DEN; HOW COULD A QUAIL IN A CAGE KNOW THERE IS A PHOENIX NEST? WHEN THE ELIXIR IS FULLY DEVELOPED, NATURALLY GOLD FILLS THE ROOM; WHAT IS THE NEED TO LOOK FOR HERBS AND PRACTICE BURNING REEDS?

The preceding three sections explain the restored elixir, the great elixir, the medicinal substances, and the firing process. However, it may happen that students may get the false idea that the gold elixir is made by burning and forging ordinary substances; therefore this section follows up quickly with a warning about this.

The gold elixir is the fundamental essence of innate knowledge and innate capacity inherent in people. This essence is intrinsically complete in everyone; it is not more in sages or less in ordinary people. It is not obtained from another, it is inherent in oneself. If you accord with it, you ascend directly into the realm of sages; essence is stabilized, life is solidified, never to disintegrate. This fundamental essence of innate knowledge and innate capacity is the great elixir of long life.

Those who are deluded do not investigate the true principles of sages, do not consider the basis of essence and life; they abandon what is near and seek afar, reject the true and accept the false. Thus they waste their lives, growing old without fulfillment, foolishly throwing themselves away. Is this not to be pitied and lamented?

The firm quality of innate knowledge inherent in people is received from heaven—this is "heaven." The original adaptable quality of innate capacity is received from earth—this is "earth." The original spirit of open awareness without obscurity is the spiritual essence, which is a product of the energy of earth—this is "fire." The original pure, unadulterated vitality is true sense, which is a product of the energy of heaven—this is "water." If people can be both firm and adaptable at once, then the heaven and earth within themselves join. This is like sweet dew descending and washing the heart; vexations are shed all at once. If people can avoid dissipating their vitality and spirit, then the water and fire in themselves will mix, and the original energy will be restored.

The descent of sweet dew is purity of heart; the growth of the yellow sprouts is tranquility of mind. The unique spiritual true essence of innate knowledge and innate capacity hangs in space, silent, unstirring; sensing, it accomplishes effects. Ever responsive, it is ever tranquil: creation cannot move it, things cannot cramp it. One's destiny depends on oneself, not on heaven; the path of long life is herein.

How can a frog in a well know of the existence of this dragon cave? How can a quail in a cage know of the existence of this phoenix nest? Those who hear tell of medicinal substances and firing and imagine it refers to some chemical process do all kinds of strange things—they still do not know that when the cultivation of the great elixir is complete, gold and jade fill the room, preserving life, making the body sound, riches beyond compare. How can any material things be worthy of attachment?

7

IF YOU WANT TO KNOW THE LOCATION OF THE RIVER SOURCE WHICH PRODUCES THE HERB, IT IS JUST IN THE SOUTHWEST, ITS ORIGINAL HOMELAND. WHEN LEAD MEETS

THE ARISING OF THE YOUNGER WATER, YOU SHOULD
GATHER QUICKLY; WHEN METAL COMES TO THE PASSING OF
THE MIDDLE OF THE LUNAR MONTH, IT WON'T DO TO
TASTE. SEND IT BACK TO THE EARTHEN POT AND SEAL IT
TIGHTLY; NEXT PUT IN FLOWING PEARL, TO COMBINE WITH
IT. FOR THE WEIGHT OF THE MEDICINE TO BE ONE POUND
REQUIRES TWO TIMES EIGHT; ADJUST THE FIRING PROCESS
HARMONIOUSLY, RELYING ON YIN AND YANG.

The preceding section says everyone has the herb or medicine of
immortality, but it still doesn't say where and when this herb grows;
therefore this section reveals the facts about the growth of the herb, to
enable students to work on it according to the time, and be careful with
the firing process.

The southwest is the direction of *earth* ☷; it is the realm where the
new moon returns, where yin at its extreme gives birth to yang. In people, this is the time of beginning movement when stillness has reached its
extreme. This movement from the extreme of stillness is precisely when
the great medicine appears. However, this movement is not the stirring of
emotions at external influences, and it is not the stirring of thoughts in
the mind. It is the movement of the innate knowledge of the natural
mind, the movement of the real knowledge of the mind of Tao.

This innate knowledge of the natural mind and real knowledge of the
mind of Tao are represented as medicinal substances because they are able
to transcend the ordinary and enter into the spiritual, to rise from death
and return to life. Because at the time of extreme stillness, when all
entanglements have ceased, the innate knowledge of the natural mind
and the real knowledge of the mind of Tao have a point of brilliance
which reveals a glimpse of them, this is represented as the place where the
medicine or "herb" is produced. Because the innate knowledge of the
natural mind and real knowledge of the mind of Tao are white within
black, coming from within empty nothingness, movement born from
stillness, like a river having its source in a spring, this is represented as the
river source where the herb is produced.

This herb, in the primordial state, is the innate knowledge of the natural mind; in the temporal state, it is the real knowledge of the mind of
Tao. The mind of Tao is a reflection of the natural mind, real knowledge
is a reflection of innate knowledge. Because the natural mind falls into
the temporal state, it cannot abide forever; sometimes it appears, and is

called by another name, the mind of Tao. Because innate knowledge sinks into the sea of desire, its radiant energy is obscured; on the occasions when it is not obscured, it is called by another name, real knowledge. After you have reached the point of reversion and restoration, the mind of Tao is as before the natural mind, and real knowledge is as before innate knowledge.

Sometimes appearing and sometimes not being obscured is the homeland of the mind of Tao and its real knowledge. That is to say, in this place of sometimes appearing and sometimes not being obscured there is a point of primordial, real, unified living potential subsisting there. If you use this point of living potential and cultivate it in opposition to the usual course of conditioning and deterioration, it shouldn't be hard to return to the natural mind and its innate knowledge by way of the mind of Tao and its real knowledge.

But for the return not to be difficult, it is necessary to know clearly where the source of the river is, movement coming from the extreme of stillness. Lao Tzu said, "Effect emptiness to the extreme, guard stillness carefully; as myriad things act in concert, I thereby watch the return." The *I Ching* says, "Repeating the path, coming back in seven days." Both of these point to this river source where the mind of Tao and its real knowledge arise.

Once you know the river source where the medicine is produced, you need to understand the timing for practical application. The subtle application of cultivation of the elixir is just a matter of taking the uniform taste of the mind of Tao as the matrix of the elixir. Because the mind of Tao is firm and strong, containing within it the sense of real knowledge, it is represented as true lead. Within lead there is silver; it is black outside, white inside: within the mind of Tao there is real knowledge, which is dark outside and light inside. So the immortals and real people have all likened the mind of Tao and real knowledge to elixir and lead; they were unwilling to speak explicitly, being cautious lest the wrong people misappropriate it.

When the real knowledge of the mind of Tao is covered and buried by emotion and desire and has sunken deeply, it cannot get itself out; once you know the river source, you can gradually collect it and restore it. The method of restoration is to be sought while in the midst of emotion and desire. Real knowledge is the product of heaven, pure clear yang "water," which is the "elder water." Emotional desire is the product of earth, polluted yin "water," which is the "younger water." The elder water is hidden within the younger water; but for the arising of younger water, the elder water would not appear, and the true lead would not be manifest. "When lead meets the arising of the younger water" is the mixing of the two energies, yin and yang, when the younger water has just arisen but is not yet used, the elder water has not yet dispersed and real knowledge is not yet obscured: you must gather it quickly and return it to the "crucible," which is like a womb in suspension—then emotional desire will not be activated and will disappear of itself.

As for "When metal comes to the passing of the middle of the lunar month," once you have gotten real knowledge to come back, you use this point of true sense of real knowledge, increase and expand it, progressing to the correct balance of firm strength, the pure unadulterated vitality. This is light refining white metal out of lead, its color fully bright and clear. When you reach this stage, innate knowledge and innate capacity are clear and unobscured, able to deal with things, whether indirectly or directly, acting or not acting, at will, going along freely, everywhere being the Tao. This is like the bright moon in the sky, lighting up the world to view, penetrating the darkness. One can then cease to employ effort involving increase and decrease, give up doing and enter nondoing.

If you do not know the firing process, before fulfillment of the preparations is complete fullness will wane, light will return to darkness, like after the middle of the lunar month, when yin arises within yang. Real knowledge will be damaged, the true will go into obscurity and the false will come. What will be there is the pollution of temporal conditioning —it is not worth tasting. Therefore, when real knowledge has returned to completeness, you must quickly send it into the "earth pot" in the center and seal it up tightly, not letting even a little of it leak out. Then you take the flowing pearl of open awareness in the fundamental essence and mix it in, using yin to balance yang, using emptiness to nourish substantiality. Guarding against danger, wary of perils, aim for attaining unity of firmness and flexibility, balance of yin and yang, with twice eight ("eight ounces each"), no excess or lack, progressing until the slag is removed and the gold is pure, after there is not so much as a speck of temperament any more.

However, if you want a full measure of the two eights, it all depends on adjusting the firing process harmoniously, understanding maturity and immaturity, knowing to be content with sufficiency, distinguishing what bodes well and what bodes ill, discerning when to hurry and when to relax. When it is time to advance yang, then advance yang; when it is time to operate yin, then operate yin. Then great and small are unharmed, both countries are sound. The primordial real whole energy will naturally come forth from nothingness, will crystallize and not disperse, and the spiritual embryo will take on form.

Adjusting the firing is properly harmonized by firmness and flexibility not becoming stationary. When "the weight of the medicine is one pound," firmness and flexibility both wind up in correct balance, the two eights balance each other; there is yang in yin, there is yin in yang—yin and yang merge, firmness and flexibility sublimate. Tranquil, unstirring, yet sensitive and effective; sensitive and effective, yet tranquil and unstirring—it is something eternally imperishable.

The moon waxing to fullness is a secret passed on by word of mouth; the subtlety of the time reaching midnight is transmitted by mind. The medicinal substances are hard to know, and the firing process is not easy to understand. Students should hasten to find a genuine teacher.

This section includes within it the medicinal substances, the firing process, the subtle application of the restored elixir; it is the most critical of the sixteen sections in the first part, and should be studied carefully, without passing over a single word lightly. If you actually have some understanding, go to a genuine teacher for affirmation; you know myriad things by way of a single statement.

8

REFINING THE THREE YELLOWS AND FOUR SPIRITS, IF YOU LOOK FOR HERBS, IT IS NOT REAL ANYMORE. YIN AND YANG, FINDING THEIR COUNTERPARTS, RETURN TO INTERCOURSE; WHEN THE TWO EIGHTS MATCH, THEY NATURALLY JOIN CLOSELY. THE SUN IN THE POOL IS SCARLET, SHADES VANISH; THE MOON ON THE MOUNTAIN WHITE, THE HERB SPROUTS ARE NEW. IF PEOPLE OF THE TIME WANT TO KNOW THE TRUE LEAD AND MERCURY, IT IS NOT ORDINARY CINNABAR AND QUICKSILVER.

The preceding section says that the gold elixir can only be produced by the combination of two medicines, true lead and true mercury; however, people might get the wrong idea that the gold elixir is a material substance made by refinement with fire, so this section follows up quickly with the saying, "Refining the three yellows and four spirits, if you seek herbs, it is not real anymore." The three yellows are sulfur and sulfur compounds; the four spirits are cinnabar, quicksilver, lead, and saltpeter. The three yellows and four spirits are not of a kind with us, so how can they extend our lives? How can they enable us to understand our essence? If they do not function to extend life and understand essence, they are useless, not the real path.

The *Triple Analogue* says, "It is easy to work with what is of the same kind, hard to work with what is not of the same kind." People are born as receivers of the twin energies of yin and yang of heaven and earth, so they have the yin and yang energies in their bodies. As for the qualities of yin and yang, yang is firm and yin is yielding; the quality of firmness governs life, the quality of yielding governs essence. This firmness of yang and yielding of yin is the wellspring of essence and life.

As for the "counterparts" mentioned in this section, yang has yin as its counterpart, yin has yang as its counterpart; so firmness and yielding respond to each other, like a husband and wife suddenly meeting after a long separation, never failing to have intercourse.

As for "two eights," yang within yin is true yang, sound strength in correct balance; yin within yang is true yin, flexible adaptability in correct balance: firmness and flexibility both return to correct balance, yin and yang match each other, without partiality. Naturally they join intimately and merge into one energy, solidifying so that it does not dissolve.

When yin and yang have their counterparts in each other and balance each other, the primordial is restored within the temporal. The mind of Tao is firm, strong and sound, the human mind is yielding, flexible and adaptable. Real knowledge and conscious knowledge combine, and the original spiritual root of innate knowledge and innate capacity appear from within nothingness, like the scarlet sun at the bottom of a pool rising up, shades naturally disappearing, like the crescent moon over the mountain hanging on high, the medicinal sprouts fresh and new. This is because the sane energy arises and aberrant energy naturally recedes, the real returns and the false dissolves.

The scarlet of the sun in the pond and the white of the moon over the mountain both depict the emergence of true yang and the reappearance of the natural mind. Then knowledge and capacity are both innocent— this is called the gold elixir. This gold elixir is the true yin and true yang inherent in oneself, formed by the combination of the firm and the flexible. This is the true treasure which completes and perfects essence and life—it is not made by firing cinnabar and quicksilver.

9

THE SUBSTANCE OF THE YIN-VITALITY WITHIN YANG IS NOT FIRM; IF YOU ONLY CULTIVATE ONE THING, IT WILL RESULT IN INCREASING WEAKNESS. BELABORING THE BODY AND CONCERN WITH REFLECTIONS IS NOT THE PATH; SWALLOW-ING AIR AND INGESTING FOG IS CRAZY. EVERYONE IDLY SEEKS THE CONQUERING OF LEAD AND MERCURY; WHEN WILL THEY GET TO SEE THE DRAGON AND TIGER COME DOWN? I URGE YOU TO FIND OUT THE PLACE WHERE YOUR BODY WAS BORN; GOING BACK TO THE BASIS, RETURNING TO THE ORIGIN, THIS IS THE PRODUCTION OF THE MEDI-CINE.

The preceding section says that the medicinal substances of the gold elixir are not external chemicals or herbs, that those who cultivate the Tao must do it in their own bodies. What they still don't know is that after the primordial true yang has slipped away, what people have in their bodies is only the yin vitality within yang. The yin vitality is not only sex-ual fluid; all bodily fluids and also air are yin vitality. Their substance is not firm; they are there as long as the body subsists, they disappear when the body dies. Their existence or nonexistence depends on the phantas-mic body: if you cultivate this one thing, the yin vitality within yang, and want to preserve the body thereby, you will feel increasingly weak, and will ultimately not succeed. Those in the world who belabor their bodies, concerned with reflections, swallow air and ingest fog, and do all sorts of other such practices, either cultivate yin vitality or replenish the yin vital-ity, are off the right track; the more they work, the further off they will become. How can they conquer the true lead and true mercury and return them to one energy, how can they chase the true dragon and true tiger and join them into one?

The path of the gold elixir is the path of giving life to the body; the path of giving life to the body is the path of uniting yin and yang. When yin and yang unite, there is living potential therein. The way of giving life to humans uses the ordinary father and mother to give birth to the phantasmic body; the way of giving life to immortals uses the spiritual father and mother to give birth to the real body. The spiritual father is the sound strong real knowledge; the spiritual mother is the flexible adapt-able conscious knowledge. Giving birth to humans and giving birth to immortals both are in the realm of yin and yang, but there is a distinction between the spiritual and the mundane, between going in reverse and going along with the usual course. If people thoroughly investigate the principle of giving birth to the body, and achieve great understanding and great penetration, and know clearly how the father and mother can meet, how they can mate, how conception takes place, how gestation takes place, how the development of the fetus takes place, how birth is accomplished, how nursing is done, how action is accomplished, and how growth and maturation are accomplished, then the whole process of practice of the Tao will be clear, and one can go straight ahead, return to the origin, arise from death and restore life, preserve life and make the body complete, becoming master of the great medicine. After all, the great way of cultivating reality is just this principle of giving birth to the body; there is nothing else to it. How can those who take the side doors, cultivating only one thing, yin alone or yang alone, sticking to emptiness or clinging to forms, know this exists?

10

TAKE A GOOD HOLD ON THE TRUE LEAD, AND SEEK ATTEN-TIVELY; DO NOT LET YOURSELF PASS THE TIME TAKING IT EASY. JUST USE THE EARTHLY SOUL TO CAPTURE THE RED MERCURY; NATURALLY THERE WILL BE THE HEAVENLY SOUL TO GOVERN THE WATER METAL. IT COULD BE SAID THAT WHEN THE PATH IS LOFTY THE DRAGON AND TIGER SUBMIT; ONE MIGHT SAY THAT WHEN THE VIRTUE IS GREAT GHOSTS AND SPRITES ARE RESPECTFUL. ONCE YOU KNOW LIFE IS ETERNAL, EQUAL TO HEAVEN AND EARTH, VEXATIONS HAVE NO WAY TO RISE IN THE MIND ANYMORE.

The preceding section teaches people to find out where the body is born and return to the origin. But to go back to the root and return to the origin requires knowledge of the uniform flavored great medicine of true lead. When you know the true lead, you know the one, and myriad tasks are finished—everything else is easy.

The true lead is nothing else but the aforementioned real knowledge of the mind of Tao. Real knowledge is also called the true seed. If you do not know the true seed, there is no basis for practicing the Tao, and whatever you do will be a waste of effort. That is why it says, "Take a good hold on the true lead and seek attentively."

The words "Seek attentively" contain the directed work of investigating principles, examining things to bring about knowledge. If students want to practice the great Tao, nothing is better than to first investigate true principles. The approach to practice follows naturally. If you do not investigate and penetrate, you beg in vain for the celestial jewel—this has no reality or truth to it, and is only wasting time.

The "earthly soul" and the "water metal" are yang within yin, both symbols of real knowledge. The "heavenly soul" and "red mercury" are yin within yang, both symbols of conscious knowledge. "Just use the earthly soul to capture the red mercury" means to control conscious knowledge by real knowledge. "Naturally there will be the heavenly soul to govern the water metal" means to nurture real knowledge by conscious knowledge.

Real knowledge is "firm," in the province of yang, and is the "husband." Conscious knowledge is "flexible," in the province of yin, and is the "wife." The husband governs the wife, the wife obeys the husband; the wife obeys the husband, the husband loves the wife. When husband and wife have each other, the living potential always exists. Real knowledge and conscious knowledge unite, firmness and flexibility return to the center, changing into innate knowledge and innate capacity, tranquil and unstirring, yet sensitive and effective. The spiritual embryo then takes on form; when you reach this stage, the path is lofty and dragon and tiger submit; the virtue is great and ghosts and sprites are respectful. Then life is eternal, equal to heaven and earth; how can vexations arise in the mind anymore?

11

THE YELLOW SPROUTS AND WHITE CLOUDS ARE NOT HARD TO SEEK; THOSE WHO ARRIVE MUST RELY ON DEPTH OF VIRTUOUS PRACTICE. THE FOUR FORMS AND FIVE ELEMENTS ALL DEPEND ON EARTH; THE THREE BASES AND EIGHT TRIGRAMS ARE NOT APART FROM ELDER WATER. REFINED INTO SPIRITUAL SUBSTANCE, THEY ARE INSCRUTABLE TO MEN; HAVING DISSOLVED ALL THAT IS NEGATIVE AND HARMFUL, ONE IS INVULNERABLE TO GHOSTS. I WISH TO LEAVE THE

SECRET AMONG HUMANKIND, BUT I HAVE NOT YET MET A
SINGLE PERCEPTIVE PERSON.

The preceding section says that when the path is lofty and virtue great,
the dragon and tiger, ghosts and sprites, all become docile and obedient;
that is, where there is the Tao there must be virtue, and where there is virtue there must be the Tao. The ultimate Tao is not complicated, the fire
and medicine are not remote; the white clouds are right before your eyes,
the yellow sprouts grow in your own home. If you are straightforward,
you can obtain them at will; that's why it says they are "not hard to seek."
However, this path is to transcend the ordinary and enter sagehood, to
rise from death and return to life, something rare in the world. Even
though it is not hard to seek, it can only be known by those of great virtue
and great practice. Therefore it says, "Those who arrive must rely on
depth of virtuous practice." In effect, it is for the superior person of virtuous practice that it is not hard to seek.

The "four forms" are the four energies of metal, wood, water, and fire;
add earth, and they make the five elements. The "three bases" are the
basis of heaven, the basis of earth, and the basis of humankind. Also the
upper basis, middle basis, and lower basis constitute three bases too. The
"eight trigrams" are the yin and yang of the four forms and five elements: *heaven* ☰ is yang metal, *lake* ☱ is yin metal; *water* ☵ is yang
water, *mountain* ☶ is yin water; *thunder* ☳ is yang wood, *wind* ☴ is
yin wood; *fire* ☲ is yang fire, *earth* ☷ is yin fire. Although the eight trigrams are distributed among the yin and yang of the four forms, *earth* ☷
and *mountain* ☶ also contain the two earths, heaven-earth and earth-
earth. *Earth* ☷ is yin earth, *mountain* ☶ is yang earth. The energies of
the five elements are also therein.

In humankind, the five elements are the five bases—essence, sense,
vitality, spirit, and energy; in action, they are the five virtues—benevolence, justice, courtesy, wisdom, and truthfulness. In humans, the three
bases are the basic vitality, the basic energy, and the basic spirit. In
humans, the eight trigrams are the firm and flexible essences of the five
bases and five virtues. The four forms, three bases, and eight trigrams are
all transformations of the five elements, and do not exist separately.
When it says, "the four forms and five elements all depend on earth," it
means that benevolence, justice, courtesy, and wisdom develop based on
truthfulness. When it says "the three bases and eight trigrams are not
apart from elder water," it means essence, sense, spirit, and energy are
not apart from vital unity.

The "yellow sprouts" are the living potential of earth; truthfulness is in the center. The "white clouds" are the light clarity of water, vitality arriving at unity. When benevolence, justice, courtesy, and wisdom return to truthfulness, and preserve the mean, the yellow sprouts gradually grow. When essence, sense, spirit, and energy return to one, being vitality, being unified, the white clouds fly in the sky, unity of vitality keeps in the center.

Cultivate and refine this, growing in strength the longer you persevere, and the mind of Tao will always be active while the human mind will always be tranquil. Real knowledge and conscious knowledge unite, and a round and bright pearl hangs in space. Ever responsive yet ever tranquil, untrammeled by form or emptiness, you appear and disappear according to the times, unopposed by nature in the primordial state, serving the seasons of nature in the temporal state.

Unopposed even by nature, how much less by people, or by ghosts or sprites; people cannot know you, ghosts cannot attack you. This is not idle talk. This path is most simple and easy; it is quintessential, uncomplicated. Those who know it rise at once to the rank of sages, without awaiting twelve years of training. However, there are few people in the world who practice virtue, there are no real true people. Most consider the Tao far away when in fact it is near at hand. The author says, "I want to leave the secret among humankind, but I haven't met a single perceptive person yet." Is it not a pity?

12

YIN AND YANG ARE ALSO EQUAL IN PLANTS AND TREES; IF ONE IS LACKING THEY DO NOT FLOWER. WHEN THE GREEN LEAVES FIRST UNFOLD, YANG IS ACTING FIRST; WITH THE SUBSEQUENT BLOOMING OF SCARLET FLOWERS, YIN FOLLOWS ALONG. THE ORDINARY COURSE IS IN DAILY ACTION; THE TRUE SOURCE REVERSES THIS, BUT WHO IS THERE WHO KNOWS? I INFORM THOSE OF YOU WHO STUDY THE TAO: IF YOU DO NOT KNOW YIN AND YANG, DO NOT ACT AT RANDOM.

The preceding section said virtue must be cultivated; this one says the Tao must be understood. The *I Ching* says, "One yin and one yang is called the Tao." It also says, "Heaven and earth incubate, myriad things develop; male and female join their vitality, myriad beings evolve." The path of the gold elixir operates entirely through the strength of yang and the adaptivity of yin: when yin and yang unite, they produce the elixir and prolong life; when yin and yang are at odds, they turn away from each other, causing loss of life. Take a look at things like plants and trees: "When the green leaves first unfold, yang is acting first; with the subsequent blooming of scarlet flowers, yin follows along." Yin and yang are not apart from each other; extending the analogy, we find the ordinary course of all sentient beings does not take place outside of yin and yang.

But while the ordinary course follows along, the path of immortals goes in reverse. Following along means going along with yin and yang in the ordinary course; reversing means reverse operation of yin and yang. People of the world only know the way to go along, and do not know the way of reverse operation. Therefore they pursue artificial objects and stray from the true source; when yang culminates, they shift to yin, and when yin culminates they die.

For students, the first move is to get to know both yin and yang. When you know yin and yang, you know the true source. The true source is the door of the "mysterious female." The birth of yin is herein, the birth of yang is herein too; following is herein, and reversing is herein too. When you know the eternal and return to the root, you ascend at once to the realm of the sages.

However, there is not only one kind of yin and yang. There is primordial yin and yang, and there is conditioned yin and yang. There is yin and yang within life, and there is yin and yang within essence. There is real yin and yang, and there is artificial yin and yang. There is external yin and yang, and there is internal yin and yang. It is necessary to study all these kinds of yin and yang and understand them clearly before starting the alchemical work. If you do not know the real yin and real yang, and act at random, you will turn away from the real and enter the artificial, forgetting your own essence and life.

13

IF YOU DO NOT KNOW THE INVERSION WITHIN THE MYSTERY, HOW CAN YOU KNOW TO PLANT A LOTUS IN FIRE? LEADING THE WHITE TIGER, GO BACK HOME AND NURTURE

IT; YOU WILL PRODUCE A BRIGHT PEARL ROUND AS THE
MOON. STAY RELAXED BESIDE THE ALCHEMICAL FURNACE
AND WATCH THE FIRING PROCESS; JUST SETTLE YOUR SPIRIT
AND BREATH, AND LEAVE IT UP TO NATURE. WHEN ALL
MUNDANITY HAS BEEN STRIPPED AWAY, THE ELIXIR IS COM-
PLETE; LEAPING OUT OF THE CAGE OF THE ORDINARY, LIFE
IS MYRIAD YEARS.

The preceding section tells people to recognize yin and yang; this section tells people to find out about the work. The work is the method of
inverting yin and yang. If you don't know the method of inversion of yin
and yang, how can you know the subtlety of planting a lotus in fire?

What is inverted? The white tiger is associated with metal, which is the
sound strong energy in the middle of the palace of *heaven* ☰. This is
called the mind of Tao; in action it is the sense of real knowledge. Because
of mixture with temporal conditioning, doing things with the human
mentality, the mind of Tao is not manifest, true sense is obscured, and
deluded feelings arise. This is like the white tiger leaving one's own home
and going out, running to another house and injuring people. Inversion
means while in the midst of deluded feelings to restore true sense, and
combine it with true essence. This is like leading the white tiger from
another's house back to your own home and taking care of it.

Once true sense is restored, true essence becomes manifest; essence and
sense cleave to one another, and the primordial true one energy comes
from nothingness and forms a pearl like the full moon, its light shining
bright throughout the world, as if in the palm of one's hand. This is what
the *Ts'an T'ung Ch'i* means when it says, "When metal first comes back
to essence, it can be called restored elixir." Once the restored elixir is crystallized, innate knowledge and innate capacity are nonstriving when still,
spontaneous when in action, equanimous and serene on the path of balance.

The medicine is the fire, the fire is the medicine; the work of gathering
is effortless. Just settle the spirit and breath, letting them be natural.
Using the energy of the harmony of yin and yang in the furnace of creation, the true fire burns away the mundanity of conditioning, producing
pure celestial energy. This is called the completion of the elixir; ingesting
this, you become liberated and transformed, leap out of the cage of the
ordinary, and live as long as heaven, never to die.

14

THREE, FIVE, ONE: IT IS ALL THREE WORDS; THOSE WHO UN-
DERSTAND ARE RARE IN ALL TIMES. THREE IN THE EAST,
TWO IN THE SOUTH, TOGETHER MAKES FIVE; ONE IN THE
NORTH AND FOUR IN THE WEST ARE THE SAME. EARTH IN
ITS OWN ABODE HAS THE PRODUCTION NUMBER FIVE.
WHEN THE THREE MEET, THEY FORM AN INFANT. THE IN-
FANT IS ONE, CONTAINING TRUE ENERGY; IN TEN MONTHS
THE FETUS IS COMPLETE, AND ENTERS THE SPIRITUAL FOUN-
DATION.

The preceding section talks about the principle of reversing yin and
yang; this section talks about the work of assembling the five elements. In
the beginning of human life, the natures of the inherent five elements
are originally one energy which is undifferentiated. Their natures become
individuated because of mixture with conditioning: metal and wood are
unjoined, water and fire are unmixed, true earth is buried, false earth
grows wildly, essence goes awry and life is shaken, positive energy runs
out and negative energy becomes total, so it is impossible not to die.

The author here brings up the three words "three," "five," and "one"
to teach people to assemble the five elements and return them to one
house, restoring innate knowledge and innate capacity, the whole natural
self. However, the three words "three," "five," and "one" have confused
untold numbers of intrepid people, past and present. Those who have
understood are few enough to count.

This "three" and "five" are the production numbers of the five elements according to the River Diagram. To the east is the third element,
wood; south is two, fire: fire produces wood, so fire and wood are one,
together making one five. To the west is the fourth element, metal; north
is the first, water: water produces metal, so water and metal are one,
together making one five. Earth in the center constitutes one five by
itself.

If practitioners of the Tao can understand these three fives, and cultivate them in reverse, combining the four forms and aggregating the five
elements, then essence, sense, vitality, energy, and spirit congeal; benevolence, justice, courtesy, wisdom, and truthfulness are the same energy.
This is called "the three meet." In Confucianism, this is called the Great
Ultimate, or the principle of heaven, or ultimate good, or perfect sincer-

ity. In Taoism this is called the infant, or the primordial one energy, or the spiritual embryo, or the restored elixir. In Buddhism this is called complete awakening, or true emptiness, or the reality body, or the sacred relic, or the wish-fulfilling gem. There are various such names, all referring to the naturally good original essence. The path restores the innate knowledge and innate capacity of the original essence, going back to the fundamental, returning to the root: incubating and nurturing it for ten months, the energy is replete, the spirit is whole; one escapes from the ocean of misery, has a body outside the body, and enters the unborn and unperishing spiritual foundation.

15

IF YOU DO NOT KNOW THE TRUE SOURCE, REAL LEAD, WHATEVER YOU DO WILL BE IN VAIN: CELIBACY WILL IDLY CAUSE YIN AND YANG TO BE SEPARATED, FASTING WILL FU-TILELY MAKE YOUR STOMACH EMPTY; PLANTS AND WOOD, GOLD AND SILVER, ARE ALL TRASH, CLOUDS AND MIST, SUN AND MOON, ARE VACUOUS; EVEN BREATHING EXERCISES AND MEDITATION HAVE NO RESEMBLANCE TO THE MATTER OF THE GOLD ELIXIR.

The preceding section said you only enter the spiritual foundation when you have gathered the five elements and returned them to one energy. But to aggregate the five elements requires knowledge of the primordial truly unified energy; only then can you begin. The one yang in *water* ☵ is the centrally balanced sound strong energy of *heaven* ☰, the real knowledge of the mind of Tao, represented as real lead. This is a product of celestial unity, and contains the primordial truly unified energy, which is the generative energy that produces beings. Attainment of sagehood is therein, attainment of buddhahood and immortality is therein; it is the root of sages, the seed of immortals and Buddhas, the true source of the gold elixir. This is what is referred to by the saying, "If you know that one, myriad tasks are done." If you do not know the real true lead, you have no source, no basis of cultivating the gold elixir. Then whatever practices you do—celibacy, fasting, burning plants and wood to refine gold and silver, drinking in clouds and mist, sun and moonlight, breathing exercises, meditation and visualization—either sticking to emptiness or clinging to forms, is all a waste of effort and has no connection with the matter of the gold elixir.

16

THE WORDS OF THE MYRIAD BOOKS ON IMMORTALITY ARE ALL THE SAME—THE GOLD ELIXIR ALONE IS THE ROOT SOURCE. THE SUBSTANCE IS PRODUCED ON THE GROUND OF THE POSITION OF *EARTH*, PLANTED IN THE CHAMBER OF INTERCOURSE IN THE HOUSE OF *HEAVEN*. DO NOT THINK IT STRANGE THAT THE CELESTIAL WORKING HAS BEEN LEAKED —IT IS BECAUSE STUDENTS ARE CONFUSED AND IGNORANT.

Because the foregoing fifteen sections have at times spoken of going along, at times of going in reverse, sometimes explain separately, sometimes explain together, sometimes indicate the medicines, sometimes indicate the firing process, distinguish true and false and set forth right and wrong, with subtle gradations, scattered without as yet being put into order, this section sums up the intent of the preceding fifteen sections, indicating to people the path of utter simplicity and ease, lest they get confused by the complexity of the matter and find it difficult to progress.

Since ancient times the immortals and real people, the alchemical texts and Taoist books, have used a thousand similes, a hundred metaphors, setting up symbols and terms, exerting their powers of description to bring to light the marrow of the Tao. Although their terminology is different, the principles are the same—all of them explain the root source of the gold elixir. This is not like the situation in later eras when the more books there were the more people got confused, each clinging to his own views, pursuing them into side tracks. They did not know the root source of the gold elixir is only a matter of taking from *water* ☵ to fill in *fire* ☲, returning *earth* ☷ to *heaven* ☰.

"The substance is produced on the ground of *earth*" is the one yang in the center of *water* ☵. "The chamber of intercourse in the house of *heaven*" is the one yin in the center of *fire* ☲. *Water* ☵ is based on the body of *earth* ☷, therefore it is called the position of *earth*. *Fire* ☲ is based on the body of *heaven* ☰, so it is called the house of *heaven*. By *heaven* it is easy to know, by *earth* it is easy to do. *Heaven* is firm and strong, *earth* is flexible and obedient. Because of this firm strength, it is easy to know, without getting into difficulty; because of this flexible obedience, it is simple to do, without forcing. In people, easy knowing and simple doing are the original nature of the innate knowledge and capacity.

In the beginning of human life, strength and obedience are as one, firmness and flexibility are merged. Without being consciously cognizant of it, they follow the laws of God; round, luminous, clean, naked, there is only the single fundamental nature of innate knowledge and innate capacity, without any pollution. Reaching the age of sixteen, the celestial culminates, giving rise to the mundane; people become conditioned and do things with mundane energy. Reason and desire get mixed up, strength and obedience do not balance each other, firmness and flexibility lose their proper measure.

At this point the celestial is overcome by the mundane, and natural reality is obscured. This is like *heaven* mixing with *earth;* the yang in the middle of *heaven* ☰ enters the palace of *earth* ☷, so that the trigram of *earth* is filled in and becomes *water* ☵. The mundane taking the position of the celestial, intellectual knowledge gradually developing, is like *earth* mixing with *heaven:* the yin in the middle of *earth* goes into the palace of *heaven,* so the trigram of *heaven* is emptied and becomes *fire* ☲.

When natural reality is obscured, the mind of Tao is concealed and is faint. When intellectual knowledge develops, the human mentality grows and is insecure. Being faint means being virtually nonexistent, barely surviving; the celestial does not predominate over the mundane. Being insecure means producing feelings in regard to objects; the mundane predominates over the celestial.

However, though the mind of Tao is faint and the human mentality is perilous, the mind of Tao is still not entirely obliterated, and the human mentality is still not entirely prevalent. The mind of Tao is not entirely obliterated in that sometimes it may produce clarity in the midst of obscurity; this is called real knowledge. Nevertheless, it is inconsistent, now here, now gone. The human mind is not entirely predominant in that it can adapt to situations; this is called conscious knowledge. However, it uses consciousness to produce illusions.

The practice of alchemy is to restore the celestial in the midst of the mundane, to extract the real knowledge of the mind of Tao, to transmute the conscious knowledge of the human mind so that conscious knowledge returns to reality: then real knowledge is consummately conscious, the mind of Tao is sound and strong, the human mind is flexible and submissive, yin and yang commingle, hard and soft correspond, strength and obedience are balanced. When reality and consciousness do not separate, we return to the innate knowledge and innate capacity of before, the state of the creative foundation. This is called taking from *water* to fill in *fire*, and also called planting *heaven* by *earth*.

Actually, "the substance is produced on the ground of the position of *earth*, planted in the chamber of intercourse in *heaven*" means taking from *water* ☵ and filling in *fire* ☲. Taking from *water* means the yang fallen in the center of *water* comes out, and *water* ☵ becomes *earth* ☷; filling in *fire* means the yin mixed in the center of *fire* changes, and *fire* ☲ becomes *heaven* ☰.

When the bodies of *heaven* and *earth* are formed, the mysterious female is established, and the valley spirit exists; the gold elixir crystallizes, and essence and life come into our hands, not constrained by conditioning.

This is the celestial mechanism transmitted once in ten thousand eons. The immortals and real people of antiquity were unwilling to make it explicit, but our author is so kind and compassionate that in sixteen poems he reveals what the ancients did not reveal. At the end he points directly to the root source of the gold elixir; the celestial mechanism has been revealed too much. If people understand the subtle meaning herein, they will ascend directly to the realm of sages.

II

Sixty-four verses
modeled on the number of signs
in the *I Ching*

1

On the crucible and furnace (2 verses)

FIRST TAKE *HEAVEN* AND *EARTH* FOR THE CRUCIBLE, NEXT TAKE THE MEDICINES OF RAVEN AND RABBIT AND COOK THEM. ONCE YOU HAVE CHASED THE TWO THINGS BACK INTO THE YELLOW PATH, HOW COULD THE GOLD ELIXIR NOT BE PRODUCED?

Heaven is strong, taking its symbol from the sky; *earth* is submissive, taking its symbol from the ground. In humans, these are the natures of firmness and flexibility. In the sun there is a raven, which is the yin within yang; among the trigrams, this is *fire* ☲. *Fire* ☲ is yang outside and yin inside; the one yin inside is true yin, which in humans is the conscious knowledge latent in the human mind. In the moon is a rabbit, which is yang within yin; among the trigrams, this is *water* ☵. *Water* is yin outside and yang inside; the one yang inside is true yang, which in humans is the real knowledge inherent in the mind of Tao.

"First take *heaven* and *earth* for the crucible" means you use firmness and flexibility for the substance of production of the elixir. "Next take the medicines of raven and rabbit and cook them" means you use real knowledge and conscious knowledge for the function of the production of the elixir. Cooking and refining real knowledge, nothing in it is not real; so firmness winds up in correct balance. Cooking and refining conscious knowledge, there is no obscurity in it; so flexibility winds up in correct balance. When firmness and flexibility have both returned to correct balance, the mind of Tao is strong and the human mind submits to it; real knowledge and conscious knowledge, though two, are unified. This is likened to chasing raven and rabbit back into the yellow path; the "yellow path" is the middle way, which is the path traveled by the sun.

The sun traverses the middle path, the moon traverses nine paths. There are two each of blue, red, white, and black paths, which are apart from the yellow path: inside and outside, together they make eight paths. When sun and moon meet, sun and moon travel in concert; adding this, altogether there are nine paths. When sun and moon converge is referred to as the two things returning to the yellow path.

When people are first born, they only have the single essence of real consciousness with innate knowledge and innate capacity; they do not have either the human mentality or the mind of Tao. It is only after mixing with the conditioned state that there is a division between the human mind and the mind of Tao, a distinction between real knowledge and conscious knowledge. The mind of Tao is that which is unconfused in all situations: not being confused is real knowledge.

The human mind is only capable of conscious knowledge, not of real knowledge; its nature is weak, so it is called yin. Since the mind of Tao has real knowledge, it is also capable of conscious knowledge; its energy is strong, so it is called yang. Even sages have the human mind, and even ordinary people have the mind of Tao. Sages have the human mind in that they cannot annihilate perception; ordinary people have the mind of Tao in that they have moments of lucidity. The reason sages are different from ordinary people is simply that in them reality and consciousness are unified, they have knowledge and perception, and they are capable of permanent lucidity. The reason ordinary people are different from sages is that for them reality and consciousness are separated, and though they have knowledge and perception they are incapable of permanent lucidity.

The human mind has discriminatory awareness in it, which uses consciousness to create illusions: seeing objects, it gives rise to feelings, reverberating with whatever influences it. So consciousness takes refuge in the false, and the human mind is insecure. With the human mind insecure, perverse energies are rampant and sane energy weakens; the mind of Tao does not come to the fore, and becomes faint.

Practice of Tao refines the firmness of the real knowledge of the mind of Tao, restoring it to proper balance, and refines the flexibility of the conscious knowledge of the human mind, restoring it to proper balance. This is the joining of firmness and flexibility, the matching of strength and submission: precisely unified, one maintains true balance; innate knowledge and innate capacity are merged in the celestial design, and unified energy flows. How could the gold elixir not be produced?

The gold elixir is produced by the solidification of two energies, strong and yielding; true knowledge and conscious knowledge return to proper balance, and heaven and humanity merge, a precious pearl hangs in space, illumining everywhere. The gold elixir forms, at first subtle, becoming manifest, at first raw, becoming ripe. How could anyone not be emancipated?

2

SETTING UP THE FURNACE AND CRUCIBLE IS PATTERNED ON
HEAVEN AND *EARTH;* REFINING THE SUNLIGHT AND MOON-
LIGHT STABILIZES THE YANG AND YIN SOULS. CONGEALING
AND DISSOLVING, THE INCUBATING WARMTH PRODUCES
TRANSMUTATION; PRESUMPTUOUSLY DO I IDLY DISCUSS THE
MYSTERIOUS AND MARVELOUS.

The furnace is that whereby the fire is operated, the crucible is that
whereby the medicines are refined. The science of the gold elixir patterns
the furnace on the flexible submissiveness of *earth,* gradually progressing
in an orderly way: it models the crucible on the firm strength of *heaven*
cooking fiercely and forging quickly. Capable of being firm, capable of
being flexible, capable of being strong, capable of being submissive, with
a firm will, getting stronger as time goes on, the crucible and furnace
steady, not shaking, not moving, one can thereby cull the medicine and
operate the fire.

The conscious knowledge of the human mind is yang outside, yin
inside; it is like sunlight, which radiates outward. The real knowledge of
the mind of Tao is like moonlight, stored within. The external yang of
conscious knowledge belongs to the yang soul; the external yin of real
knowledge belongs to the yin soul. The sunlight yang soul of conscious
knowledge is what is called the spirit which is spirit; the moonlight yin
soul of real knowledge is called the spirit which is not spirit.

"Spirit which is spirit" means there is artificiality within the real;
"spirit which is not spirit" refers to containing reality within the artificial. "Refining sunlight and moonlight" means melting away the artificiality within reality of the conscious knowledge of the human mind, and
refining out the reality within artificiality of the mind of Tao. When false
consciousness is removed, real consciousness is steady; then the yang soul
doesn't fly off, but is stabilized. When real knowledge is revealed, false
knowledge vanishes; then the yin soul doesn't dissolve, but is stabilized.

Once the yang soul and yin soul are stabilized, then real knowledge
and conscious knowledge, sense and essence, merge into each other and
solidify into one energy, warm and gentle, transmuting by collecting and
dispersing, tranquil and unstirring yet sensitive and effective. Every step
is the celestial mechanism; the spiritual subtlety herein cannot be
described in words.

3

On the crescent moon furnace (2 verses)

STOP WASTING EFFORT AT AN ALCHEMICAL OVEN; TO REFINE
THE ELIXIR YOU MUST SEEK THE CRESCENT MOON FURNACE.
IT HAS OF ITSELF THE NATURAL TRUE FIRING—YOU DO NOT
NEED PURPLE COAL OR BELLOWS.

The crescent moon refers to the moon of the third day of the lunar
month, appearing as a hook of light in the direction of *earth* (southwest).
That light curves upward, that is why it is called the crescent moon. What
this crescent moon symbolizes in humans is a point of yang light shining
through in the middle of extreme quiet. Among the trigrams, it is *thunder* ☳. This is what is referred to by the lines, "On the third day *thunder*
appears in the west; on the curving river bank the moonlight gleams."
This point of yang light is nothing but the light of the mind of Tao. In
alchemy, what is hard to get is the mind of Tao; once the mind of Tao
appears, the principles of nature are clearly evident, and strong energy
gradually becomes active; then the whole world is spiritual medicine,
which you may take freely—everywhere is the Tao. The medicine is the
fire, the fire is the medicine; there is of itself the furnace of natural evolution, the fire of truth—what is the need for an alchemical oven, working
with coal and bellows?

4

IN THE CRESCENT MOON FURNACE, JADE FLOWERS GROW; IN
THE CINNABAR CRUCIBLE, QUICKSILVER IS LEVEL. ONLY
AFTER HARMONIZATION BY MEANS OF GREAT STRENGTH
CAN YOU PLANT THE YELLOW SPROUT, WHICH GRADUALLY
DEVELOPS.

The crescent moon furnace is, as mentioned before, the mind of Tao.
As for the jade flowers, jade means something warm and soft, in the
province of yin, while flowers mean something luminous, in the province
of yang; so the jade flowers are yang within yin, representing the real
knowledge in the mind of Tao.

The cinnabar crucible is the human mind. Quicksilver is something fluid and unfixed. This is in the province of yin, and is the yin within yang, representing the conscious knowledge of the human mind. When the mind of Tao is always manifest and real knowledge is not obscured, the conscious knowledge of the human mind is naturally level and calm, and cannot fly off.

Then you use effort to harmonize, using the true fire inherent in the mind of Tao to burn away the false consciousness in the human mind, and return it to completely receptive consciousness, so that heaven and humanity work together, real knowledge and conscious knowledge become unified.

When knowledge arrives, the intent is sincere; this is called the yellow sprout. The yellow sprout is planted by real consciousness. When real consciousness has earth, it develops, like a plant in the ground; when sprouting, it is yellow (central), so it is called the yellow sprout. After real knowledge and conscious knowledge are harmonized by the strength of the fire, they return to balance in the proper place. Once they are in the central earth pot, then you apply true intent to nurture them. After ten months, the energy is sufficient, and they naturally mature and become free, transmuted.

5

On the true lead (4 verses)

SWALLOWING SALIVA AND DOING BREATHING EXERCISES ARE HUMAN ACTIONS; ONLY WHEN YOU HAVE THE ELIXIR CAN EVOLUTION OCCUR. IF THERE IS NO TRUE SEED IN THE CRUCIBLE, THAT IS LIKE TAKING WATER AND FIRE AND BOIL-ING AN EMPTY POT.

The real knowledge of the mind of Tao has in it the primordial true unified energy, which is symbolized by lead. This is the true seed of enlightenment. If you want to cultivate the great elixir, there is no substi-tute for this true seed. Ignorant and confused people of the world vainly cultivate the body in a physical sense, swallowing saliva and doing breath-ing exercises, thinking they are thus practicing the Tao. They still do not realize that what the body produces is all conditioned and polluted: how can that produce the primordial elixir of highest consciousness? This means that if you don't have the true seed in the crucible, it is like taking water and fire and boiling an empty pot.

6

HARMONIZATION OF LEAD AND MERCURY IS NEEDED TO PRODUCE THE ELIXIR; WITHOUT INJURY TO GREAT OR SMALL, BOTH COUNTRIES ARE SAFE. IF YOU WONDER WHAT THE TRUE LEAD IS, MOONLIGHT SHINES ON THE WEST RIVER ALL DAY.

The gold elixir is made by the true lead of real knowledge of the mind of Tao plus the true mercury of the conscious knowledge of the human mind. If you want to cultivate the gold elixir, first harmonize lead and mercury. The firmness of the mind of Tao belongs to yang; this is "great." The flexibility of the human mind belongs to yin; this is "small." If the human mind lacks the mind of Tao, it can defeat the Tao by using consciousness to produce illusion. If you govern it by the mind of Tao, the conscious light is clear and can thereby help the Tao. So the mind of Tao is not to be diminished, and yet the human mind is not to be annihilated— just don't let the human mind misuse its consciousness. When the ancients told people to kill the human mind, what they meant was to kill the false consciousness of the human mind, not to kill the true consciousness of the human mind.

If you do not distinguish true and false, and kill them both, you become indifferent and nihilistic; hurting the small, you injure the great. Yin and yang become isolated, and the breath of the living mechanism has not the means to produce the gold elixir. That is why the text says, "Without injury to great or small, both countries are safe." "Both countries are safe" means the conscious knowledge of the human mind and the real knowledge of the mind of Tao are unified, with real knowledge governing conscious knowledge, and conscious knowledge conforming to real knowledge. When reality and consciousness do not separate, innate knowledge and innate capacity integrate with the principles of nature, and the gold elixir of the round and luminous fundamental essence is attained.

After all, real knowledge and conscious knowledge are extensions of innate knowledge and innate capacity; in the primordial state they are called innate knowledge and innate capacity, in the temporal state they are called real knowledge and conscious knowledge. When the primordial is restored within the temporal, real knowledge is innate knowledge, conscious knowledge is innate capacity. Originally they are one, without duality, but because of mixture with the conditioned, the natural reality of innate knowledge is lost outside and becomes the property of another, and the consciousness of the innate capacity remaining within oneself is also adulterated and becomes unstable.

If you want to go back to the fundamental and return to the original, it is necessary to seek out reality from the midst of artificial knowledge, and recover it; only then can conscious knowledge be lucid. This real knowledge is something most firm and strong, so it is represented as true lead. As real knowledge contains the primordial truly unified energy, it is also represented as metal in water, and also represented as light in the moon. Metal in water and light in the moon both mean the presence of yang within yin.

However, as long as this real knowledge has not been recovered and restored, it still is in another's domain and is not one's own. Hence the saying, "Moonlight shines on the west river all day." Moonlight represents real knowledge being dark outside and light inside. Shining all day on the west river and not shining on the east means the shining of the light is elsewhere, in another. A later verse says, "The metal man is originally a child of the eastern house, sent to grow up in the western neighborhood." This is exactly what "moonlight shines on the west river all day" means. If people can know that moonlight shines on the west river all day, this is truly knowing where real knowledge rests, and they can thereby use it to shine on the east and meet with conscious knowledge.

Alas, going along to death, coming back to life, again and again having you seek, without finding—do you think real knowledge is easy to know?

7

DON'T GO INTO THE MOUNTAINS BEFORE YOU HAVE RE-FINED THE RESTORED ELIXIR; IN THE MOUNTAINS, INSIDE AND OUT, IS NOT LEAD. THIS SUPREME TREASURE IS IN EVERYONE'S HOUSE; IT'S JUST THAT IGNORANT PEOPLE DO NOT FULLY RECOGNIZE IT.

Retirement from the world and going into the mountains to cultivate tranquility is something that is properly done only after the restoration of the elixir. People who don't know this go into the mountains to cultivate tranquility and think they can thereby live forever. But the way of eternal life requires that one acquire pure true lead; only then can effect be obtained.

However, the true lead must be sought out in the midst of the social world; if you go into the mountains to cultivate the Tao, in the mountains, inside and outside is all yin energy—how can there be true lead, which is pure yang? The true lead is the primordial root of consciousness; it is also called the root of heaven, or the true unified vitality, or the true unified energy, or lead from the homeland of water, or metal within water, or black within white, or the yang soul within the yin soul, or the black tiger, or the metal man, or the method of immortality of that house: the ancients represented it symbolically in many ways, but when we get back to the important point, they are all just depicting the mind of Tao.

This mind of Tao, when active, is the subtle being of real knowledge; when latent, it is the true openness of total concentration. It is inherently complete in everyone, not more in sages or less in ordinary people. Everyone has it, but they do not possess it themselves; after all, when you view it you cannot use it, and when you use it you cannot view it. Because everyone has it but they do not possess it themselves, ignorant people do not recognize it when they encounter it, and stumble past it even though it is right before their eyes.

At the end of the Ming dynasty, P'eng Hao-ku, who didn't understand this principle, took the phrase "is in everybody's house" to refer to woman as the alchemical crucible, and in recent times I don't know how many people have explained it as referring to sexual practice. Nothing is more blameworthy than such ignoramuses misleading students.

8

WHEN BAMBOO BREAKS, YOU SHOULD USE BAMBOO TO REPAIR IT; TO HATCH A CHICKEN YOU NEED AN EGG. IT'S A WASTE OF EFFORT IF YOU'RE DEALING WITH DIFFERENT SPECIES; IT'S BETTER TO JOIN THE SPIRITUAL POTENTIAL WITH TRUE LEAD.

Broken bamboo is repaired with bamboo, chickens are hatched from eggs—you seek to accomplish something by what is homogeneous with it. The *Triple Analogue* says, "With the same species, it's easy to work; it's hard to work with different kinds. What is not of the same species is not the true seed; whatever you do with it is a waste of effort." What this all means is that the great science of the gold elixir is the business of sages; if you want to learn sagehood, you must seek the seed of sagehood. The seed of sagehood is the real knowledge which is referred to as true lead. If you use real knowledge to practice and maintain the great Tao, you will surely accord with the potential of sagehood. The potential of sagehood is simply the integral principle of nature. With real knowledge there is nothing you do not know, nothing that is not real. You can thereby return to the principle of nature; so the text speaks of joining the spiritual potential. Once you accord with the spiritual potential, you become a sage—why are students recalcitrant?

9

On using lead

"EMPTY THE MIND, FILL THE BELLY"—THE MEANINGS ARE BOTH PROFOUND. IT IS PRECISELY IN ORDER TO EMPTY THE MIND THAT IT IS NECESSARY TO KNOW THE MIND. IT IS BEST WHEN REFINING THE LEAD TO FIRST FILL THE BELLY, AND CAUSE THE GATHERING IN OF THE GOLD THAT FILLS THE ROOM.

Alchemy involves two tasks, to empty the mind and fill the belly. Emptying the mind means to empty the human mind; this is the task of cultivating essence. To fill the belly means to fulfill the mind of Tao; this is the task of cultivating life. The two matters of emptying the mind and filling the belly, dealing with essence and life, are both of profound meaning.

If you want to empty the mind, it is necessary to know the mind. In the mind there is the human mind and there is the mind of Tao. The human mind should be empty, not full, and the mind of Tao should be full, not empty. If you do not distinguish true and false, right and wrong, in the mind, and empty both, not only can you not comprehend life, you cannot even comprehend essence.

If you know the mind, you do not need to empty the human mind; first you should refine the mind of Tao, the true lead, to fill the belly. When the belly is full, sane energy arises through accumulation of right action, and the energy of conditioning dissolves of itself. The human mind will spontaneously become empty, the four forms will be in harmony, the five elements will aggregate, gold and jade will fill the room, the jewel of life will be in your hands. With this you can empty the human mind and nurture the mind of Tao, understand the essential source, and return to the homeland of nothingness.

10

On not using lead

IN USING LEAD, YOU MUST NOT USE ORDINARY LEAD. EVEN TRUE LEAD IS ABANDONED AFTER ITS USE IS FINISHED. THIS IS THE TRUE SECRET OF USING LEAD. USING LEAD AND NOT USING IT—THESE ARE VERACIOUS WORDS.

In cultivating the elixir, it is essential to gather true lead. There is also a difference in lead—there is ordinary lead, and there is true lead. Ordinary lead is extracted from mines, and is a gross material substance, and a pollutant. It has no sympathy with ourselves. True lead is produced in one's own home; it is the formless mind of Tao, and is of a kind with ourselves. The immortals since antiquity who have been able to transcend the ordinary and enter into sagehood have all relied on the work of the true lead, the mind of Tao. So the text says not to use ordinary lead.

However, though the mind of Tao is the primordial jewel of reality, it is produced from within the temporal; there is a time to use it, and a time not to use it. Before you have crystallized the elixir, you need to use the real knowledge of the mind of Tao to govern the conscious knowledge of the human mind. When the human mind has been stabilized, conscious knowledge is lucid; the mind of Tao and the human mind are as one in action and stillness, real knowledge and conscious knowledge correspond in openness and fulfillment.

When the spiritual embryo has formed, you should hasten to extract the hardness of the mind of Tao, and incubate the embryonic breath. The use of the mind of Tao is to govern the human mind; after the human mind is quiet, and discriminatory awareness is extinguished, innate knowledge and innate capacity are tranquil and unstirring yet sensitive and effective. Real consciousness exists independently, bright and lucid, the mind of Tao then has no function; it is thus possible to not set up either being or nonbeing, so things and self all return to emptiness. One alchemist said, "The rule of using lead is that it is like a trap to catch game, the game being caught by means of the trap; once you've caught the game, the trap has no further use." Herein lies the real secret of using the lead. If you don't know the secret of using the lead, when the elixir has crystallized, yet you still are concerned about the mind of Tao, you will not avoid using the mind of Tao to reactivate the human mind. Real consciousness will again scatter, and the gold elixir, once gained, will be lost again. Therefore the text says, "After its use is finished, the true lead too is abandoned." The secret of using the lead and not using it can be known from this.

11

On lead and mercury

IN A DREAM I VISITED THE SUBLIME ENERGY AND REACHED THE NINE HEAVENS; A REAL PERSON GAVE ME A BOOK POINTING TO THE ORIGIN. THE BOOK IS SIMPLE, WITHOUT MANY WORDS; IT JUST TEACHES PEOPLE TO REFINE MERCURY AND LEAD.

The science of the gold elixir is most simple, without much talk—it is not more than refining the real knowledge in the mind of Tao and the conscious knowledge in the human mind. When the firm strength of the mind of Tao is centrally balanced, the mind of Tao is always present, governing conscious knowledge by real knowledge. When the flexible receptivity of the human mind is centrally balanced, the human mind is always calm, with conscious knowledge cleaving to real knowledge. When firmness and flexibility match each other, and reality and consciousness are united, this is called lead and mercury mixing and the gold elixir crystallizing. The method is very simple and uncomplicated; even ordinary people can rise directly to sagehood if they accomplish it.

However, most people are lacking in character, so they cannot attain it easily. If people are rich in virtue and get to meet real people who will show them the method of simple spiritual sublimation, it is like waking up from a dream, finally to realize the great medicine is in oneself, not gotten from another, and may be taken and used at will.

There is certainly a deep meaning in the author's saying that he visited the sublime energy in a dream and received a transmission. This is not made up. The sublime energy is where the true gold is produced, representing the radiance of pure light of true gold. The "nine heavens" is the realm of pure yang with no yin.

True gold is a representation of real knowledge: in the midst of yin darkness, suddenly the yang light of real knowledge appears; take this real knowledge and bring it home, mix it with conscious knowledge, cook it with fire, until there is pure yang with no yin—this is called the great elixir of gold liquid, reverted seven times and restored nine times. Is it a dream, after all?

12

On the one energy of nothingness

THE TAO PRODUCES ONE ENERGY FROM NOTHINGNESS, THEN FROM ONE ENERGY GIVES BIRTH TO YIN AND YANG. YIN AND YANG THEN COMBINE TO FORM THREE BODIES; THE THREE BODIES REPRODUCE, AND MYRIAD THINGS GROW.

The Tao of essence and life is the Tao of creative evolution; the Tao of creative evolution is the Tao which produces and reproduces unceasingly. When we investigate the source of the Tao, we find it produces one energy from nothingness, and from the one energy produces heaven, produces earth, gives birth to yin and yang. Yin and yang recombine therein, and while containing the one energy produce three bodies. Once the three bodies are formed, the one energy goes into motion, from yin to yang, yang to yin; thus myriad things and beings are born.

So this is like the growth of plants and trees: first one sprout grows from the earth—this is one energy born from nothingness. Once the sprout has emerged from the ground, it opens into two leaves—this is producing yin and yang from one energy. Then a stem grows up from between the two leaves—this is yin and yang combining to form three bodies. From this branches and leaves grow—this is the three bodies reproducing so that myriad things grow.

Everything in the world, sentient or insentient, grows out of this one single energy of nothingness; but then all follow the course of creation. If practitioners of the Tao know about following the course of creation, they practice it in reverse, returning the myriad to three, returning the three to two, returning the two to one, returning the one to nothingness. Then that which is beyond the senses is reached.

13

On water and fire

WATER LIGHTNING BOILS AND THUNDERS IN THE REGION OF METAL WATER; FIRE ARISES IN THE K'UN-LUN, YIN AND YANG. IF THE TWO THINGS ARE RESTORED AND MIXED TO-GETHER, NATURALLY THE ELIXIR DEVELOPS, FRAGRANT THROUGHOUT THE BODY.

Water lightning represents producing fire in water, a metaphor for the real knowledge of the mind of Tao appearing in utter darkness. When it appears is the "living midnight" in our bodies. "Boiling and thundering" represents the vacillation of rapture.

As for the "region of metal water," the real knowledge of the mind of Tao is the true sense of total concentration, which contains the two energies of "metal" and "water."

The K'un-lun mountains are in the west, and are the mountain range from which myriad mountains stem, the place where true metal is produced.

When the real knowledge of the mind of Tao appears in the midst of utter darkness, it is like flashing lightning; all of a sudden it is light, then at once it is dark. The rapture vacillates; it is hard to get and easy to lose. Quickly use the fire of open awareness to meet it; then real knowledge and conscious knowledge, essence and sense, will cleave to one another, yin and yang will join. Therein is produced the primordial spiritual elixir: then activate the natural real fire and burn away conditioned polluted energy. When the slag is gone, the gold is pure, and the gold elixir is perfected. Ingest this, and you are released from what encloses you and you become transformed, revealing the pure spiritual body. Then a fragrant breeze fills the world—not only is the body filled with fragrance.

14

On heaven-earth and earth-earth

IF *FIRE* AND *WATER* ARE RETURNED WITHOUT HEAVEN-
EARTH AND EARTH-EARTH, THOUGH THEY CONTAIN THE
FOUR FORMS, THEY WILL NOT MAKE ELIXIR. IT IS ONLY
THROUGH THESE LATTER TWO, EMBRACING TRUE EARTH,
THAT THE GOLD ELIXIR CAN BE RESTORED.

Water in humans is the original vitality, which manifests as knowledge.
Within water is hidden metal; in humans it is true sense, which manifests
as justice. *Fire* in humans is the original spirit, which manifests as courtesy. Fire produces wood; in humans this is the original essence, which
manifests as benevolence. The mind of Tao has the form of *water,* the
human mind has the form of *fire;* so the mind of Tao and the human
mind contain the four natures of metal, wood, water, and fire.

But the four natures are separate; if you want one energy to produce
them, this depends wholly on the work of heaven-earth and earth-earth.
Heaven-earth is yang earth; it is the original energy, which manifests as
truthfulness. Earth-earth is yin earth; it is intention, which manifests as
desire. *Water* takes in heaven-earth; in the mind of Tao this is truthfulness. *Fire* takes in earth-earth; in the human mind, this is intent. If you
want to rectify your mind, first make intent sincere. Once intent is sincere, earth-earth is stabilized and the human mind is calm. If you want to
traverse the Tao, first establish truthfulness. Once truthfulness is established, heaven-earth appears and the mind of Tao manifests.

If the mind of Tao is without truthfulness and the human mind is
insincere, even if one has benevolence, justice, courtesy, and knowledge,
they do not relate to each other. How then could it be possible to crystallize the spiritual elixir of consummate awareness and wisdom?

Therefore those who practice the Tao must consider sincerity of intent
and truthfulness to be the main concern. With sincerity and truthfulness,
the mind of Tao is manifest and the human mind is correctly oriented.
When these two are joined harmoniously, yin and yang correspond, and
the primordial energy emerges from nothingness and crystallizes into a
black pearl; that which was scattered is reassembled, that which had gone
is restored. That is why the text says it is only through these two things,
embracing true earth, that the gold elixir can be restored. So the work of
heaven-earth and earth-earth is very great indeed.

15

On inverting water *and* fire

THE SUN, IN THE POSITION OF *FIRE,* TURNS INTO A WOMAN;
WATER, IN THE MOON PALACE, TURNS OUT TO BE A MAN. IF
YOU DO NOT KNOW THE MEANING OF INVERSION HEREIN,
STOP ENGAGING IN LOFTY DISCUSSION WITH YOUR RE-
STRICTED VIEWS.

Conscious knowledge is originally yang; but it is light outside yet dark
inside, and always draws external influences. This is like the sun being in
the position of *fire* ☲ , yang outside, yin inside, yet turning into a
female. Real knowledge is originally yin; but it is dark outside yet light
inside, and contains true energy. This is like *water* ☵ being in the palace
of the moon, yin outside, yang inside, yet after all being male.

The conditioned human mentality uses consciousness to create illusions, so the natural reality of the mind of Tao is buried away. This is also
like a woman taking over the home, whereat the man retreats from his
position. The path of alchemy is to govern the human mind of conscious
knowledge by means of the mind of Tao with real knowledge, to follow
the mind of Tao of real knowledge with the human mind of conscious
knowledge. When the man (real knowledge) is firm and the woman (conscious knowledge) is flexible, the man taking charge of things and the
woman obeying directions, there is no great work that cannot succeed.

"If you don't know the meaning of inversion herein" refers to not perceiving the real knowledge of the mind of Tao and not recognizing the
conscious knowledge of the human mind, resulting in confusion, in both
cases taking the false for the true; "stop engaging in lofty discussion with
your narrow views," or you'll fool yourself and deceive others.

16

TAKE THE SOLID IN THE HEART OF THE POSITION OF *WATER,*
AND CHANGE THE YIN IN THE INNARDS OF THE PALACE OF
FIRE: FROM THIS TRANSFORMATION COMES THE SOUND
BODY OF *HEAVEN*—TO LIE HIDDEN OR TO FLY AND LEAP IS
ALL UP TO THE MIND.

The solid in the heart of the position of *water* ☵ is the real knowledge in the mind of Tao; the yin in the innards of the palace of *fire* ☲ is the conscious knowledge of the human mind. Take out the reality-knowing mind of Tao that has fallen into water and with it replace the consciously knowing mind in the palace of fire. In a short time the yin energy will dissolve and the yang energy will return, and you will again see the original face of *heaven* ☰, recovering your original nature of innate knowledge and innate capacity, tranquil and unperturbed yet sensitive and effective, sensitive and effective yet tranquil and undisturbed. Therefore it says, "From this transformation comes the sound body of heaven—to lie hidden or to fly and leap is all up to the mind."

This "body" is not the material substance of the ephemeral mortal body; it is the real body of the spiritual being. The spiritual being, or spiritual body, is the original essence. At the start of human life, the original essence of real consciousness is round and bright and lucid; firm strength is balanced, and it is unadulterated, pure, without a trace of pollution: this is like the three whole lines of the trigram *heaven* ☰, the image of pure yang without yin.

Subsequently, upon mixture with acquired conditioning, natural goodness is obscured, and there is artificiality in conscious energy. This is like the center of the *heaven* trigram becoming hollowed, forming *fire* ☲, the center of the *earth* ☷ becoming solid, forming *water* ☵. The hollow in the center means the real has left *fire;* the solid in the center means the real has fallen into *water:* taking from *water* to fill in *fire* means restoring natural reality, recovering the original nature of real consciousness. This is likened to the *fire* trigram again changing into the *heaven* trigram.

Once real consciousness is restored, it is at your command, always responsive yet always calm, able to adapt appropriately to any situation. Whether to lie hidden or fly and leap—whether to act or not—is all up to the mind.

People of later times have thought taking from *water* to fill in *fire* means taking the energy in the genitals and mixing it with the heart. There are also those who take the genital energy, make it rise up the spine, then draw it down the front of the body into the solar plexus. Indeed, there is something else, wonder of wonders. The heart and genitals are actually not *fire* and *water;* those who consider *fire* and *water* the heart and genitals are very foolish.

17

On the five elements

THE *THUNDER* DRAGON MERCURY COMES FROM THE LAND
OF *FIRE;* THE *LAKE* TIGER LEAD IS BORN IN THE REGION OF
WATER. THE TWO THINGS BOTH ARE BASED ON THE CHILD
GIVING BIRTH TO THE MOTHER; THE WHOLE ESSENCE OF
THE FIVE ELEMENTS ENTERS THE MIDDLE.

Thunder ☳ is a dragon, and is mercury associated with wood. *Lake* ☱
is a tiger, and is lead associated with metal. "Dragon mercury comes from
the land of *fire*" is producing wood in fire. "Tiger lead is born in the
region of water" is producing metal in water. The wood produced in fire is
wood that never rots; the metal produced in water is metal that never rusts.

Wood originally produces fire, yet fire paradoxically produces wood;
metal originally produces water, yet water paradoxically produces metal—
this is called the child giving birth to the mother. This is what an old classic means when it says, "When the five elements do not go in the usual
order, the dragon emerges from the fire; when the five elements go in
reverse, the tiger is born in water."

The temperament of humans is easily stirred, and is likened to the natural buoyancy of wood and mercury; if you use the fire of the original
spirit to burn away pollutants, the temperament is converted and the true
nature becomes manifest, as a nature which is permanently stable.

The arbitrary feelings of humans are very heavy, like the density of
metal, lead; if you use the water of total concentration to wash away the
dust and dirt, then arbitrary feelings will vanish and true sense will solidify, becoming permanent unemotional sense.

Furthermore, when the temperament is transmuted, there is no fire in
one's nature; the spirit of discrimination dies out and the original spirit
lives permanently. When emotional desires vanish, there are no thoughts
of lust; polluted vitality is sublimated and the original vitality does not
leak out.

When true nature is manifest, true sense is solidified, the original spirit
is alive, and the original vitality is stable, then essence, sense, vitality, and
spirit return to one energy; benevolence, justice, courtesy, and knowledge
return to one truthfulness. This is called the wholeness of the five elements. Once the five elements are whole, they merge in the center of
unity; this is called the five elements entering the center.

When the five elements enter the center, without imbalance, and yin and yang join, this is called the crystallization of the gold elixir. If you look for medicinal ingredients other than these elements to form the elixir, it will be impossible. The most important part of this section is the line "the whole essence of the five elements enters the middle." If the five elements are not in the center, they will separate, and the gold elixir will not form. If the five elements go into the center, then they are one energy, and the elixir naturally crystallizes. So students should first understand the five elements.

18

On the two poles

AS SOON AS THE HALF MOON IS BRIGHT ON THE HORIZON, ALREADY THERE IS THE SOUND OF THE DRAGON'S HOWL AND THE TIGER'S ROAR. THEN ONE SHOULD APPLY EFFORT TO CULTIVATE THE TWO EIGHTS; WITHIN AN HOUR SEE THE ELIXIR FORM.

The gold elixir is produced by the mixture of the energy of the two poles of the dragon-essence and the tiger-sense. First take "eight ounces" of the "metal" of the upper pole, for the matrix of the elixir; then take "half a pound" of the "wood" of the lower pole, to form the spiritual embryo.

What are the poles? From the third day of the lunar month the first yang is born; by the eighth, there is half yang within yin, so that the edge of the moon is flat as a stretched rope, and the moon looks like a strung bow. Because the yang light is above, this is called the upper pole. On the fifteenth, the moon is full; on the sixteenth, the first yin is latent, and on the eighteenth the first yin appears. On the twenty-third, there is half yin within yang, so that the edge of the moon is flat as a stretched rope, and the moon looks like a strung bow. Because the yang light is below, this is called the lower pole.

The yang light of the moon gives birth to the tiger from the west, in the province of metal, which is in the west; therefore the moon on the eighth day of the lunar month is called the polar energy of the tiger. The yin body of the moon produces the dragon from the east, in the province of wood, which is in the east; therefore the moon on the twenty-third day of the lunar month is called the polar energy of the dragon.

The sense of real knowledge is firm; represented as a tiger, it is like the yang light of the moon. The essence of conscious knowledge is flexible; represented as a dragon, it is like the yin body of the moon. The firm sense of real knowledge progressing to correct balance is like the yang light produced by the upper pole of the moon. This is "eight ounces of metal." The flexible essence of conscious knowledge withdrawing to correct balance is like the yin body of the waning moon at the lower pole. This is "eight ounces of wood."

"As soon as the half moon is bright on the horizon" is when the firm sense of real knowledge advances to correct balance. When real knowledge advances to correct balance, there is firmness within flexibility; conscious knowledge is governed by real knowledge and cannot become flighty. Yang controls yin, and yin follows yang; so there is the effect of the dragon's howl and the tiger's roar responding to each other with the same energy.

At this point, one should apply effort in cultivation, using yang to equalize yin, causing the flexible essence of conscious knowledge also to revert to correct balance. When conscious knowledge reverts to correct balance, there is firmness within flexibility. When real knowledge and conscious knowledge are both restored to correct balance, the "two eights," the twin polar energies, are present in sufficient quantity; yin and yang balance each other, firmness and flexibility are united—in an hour's time you can see the elixir form.

However, if you do not reach sufficiency of the two eights, and have too much yang with too little yin, or too little yang with too much yin, neither can form the elixir. It is only when yin and yang are matched, evenly balanced, that you can see the elixir form in an hour. Do you think the work of that hour is easy to do? If you do not put in decades of dedicated effort, you cannot all at once reach this realm.

19

On harmonization (2 verses)

ON THE TOP OF FLOWER CRAG MOUNTAIN, THE MALE TIGER ROARS; AT THE BOTTOM OF SACRED TREE OCEAN, THE FEMALE DRAGON HOWLS. THE YELLOW FEMALE NATURALLY KNOWS HOW TO GET THEM TOGETHER, SO THEY BECOME MAN AND WIFE AND SHARE THE SAME MIND.

The "flower crag" is in the west, the "sacred tree" is in the east; the tiger is metal, sense, the dragon is wood, essence. In the beginning of life, essence and sense are combined, metal and wood are together; after mixture with acquired conditioning, the artificial comes and the real is obscured—essence and sense separate, like the dragon going east and the tiger west.

The tiger is called male because "metal" sense is firm; the dragon is called female because "wood" essence is flexible. Even though true sense is blocked by artificial feelings, and true essence is covered by artificial nature, true sense and true essence always want to meet. The male tiger roaring on the mountain and the female dragon howling in the ocean represents subtle communication of separated yin and yang.

Since there is subtle communication through the barrier separating them, it is possible for them to meet; it is just because there is no harmonizing agent between them that they cannot meet. "The yellow female" or "yellow woman" is also called true earth, true intent, true sincerity. Once true sincerity appears, the intent is truthful, and the mind is right; the false leaves and the real comes, sense returns to essence. In a short time essence and sense join, like an engagement joining two families, sending them to become man and wife and share the same mind.

20

THE RED DRAGON AND BLACK TIGER TAKE TO THE WEST AND EAST; THE FOUR FORMS MIX WITH THE TWO EARTHS IN THE CENTER. RESTORATION AND BEAUTY HENCEFORTH GO INTO OPERATION; WHO SAYS THE GOLD ELIXIR WILL NOT BE ACHIEVED?

Wood can produce fire; fire and wood are in the same house, so they are called the red dragon. Metal can produce water; metal and water are in the same house, so they are called the black tiger. Metal, wood, water, and fire are the four forms: earth can combine the four forms, and when earth is added to the four forms they make the five elements.

When the five elements proceed in order, the universe is a pit of fire; when the five elements are reversed, the world is made of jewels. The only question is how this operates in people. When the sense of real knowledge in the mind of Tao is active, this is called restoration; one should properly advance the yang fire to make the elixir. When the essence of conscious knowledge in the human mind is still, this is called beauty; one should retreat into yin convergence to incubate.

Using yang when yang should be used, using yin when yin should be used, yang is strong and yin receptive; use of yang and use of yin each according to the time, real knowledge and conscious knowledge unite and go into the center. The five elements aggregate, and the golden elixir is formed, as a natural process.

21

On the dragon and tiger

JUST WHEN THE WHITE TIGER ON THE WEST MOUNTAIN GOES WILD, THE BLUE DRAGON IN THE EAST SEA CANNOT HANDLE IT. CATCHING THEM BOTH, HAVE THEM FIGHT TO THE DEATH, AND THEY WILL TURN INTO A MASS OF VIOLET GOLD FROST.

Although the sense of real knowledge and the essence of conscious knowledge are primordial things, yet when they fall into temporal conditioning, reason and desire get mixed up together, and reality and artificiality get confused. When reality and consciousness have been separated for a long time, they cannot be immediately reconciled; this is why the text says "Just when the white tiger on the west mountain goes wild, the blue dragon in the east sea cannot handle it."

But in spiritual alchemy there is a method of using the artificial to cultivate the real, using the real to convert the artificial. The method is to go along with what one desires, gradually guiding desires, making dedicated effort on one level to lead from disharmony to harmony, so that after a long process of gradually increasing one's strength, arbitrary feelings will spontaneously vanish and true sense will spontaneously arise, temperament will dissolve and true essence will be exposed, the false will die out and the true will remain.

Only unemotional sense is true sense, only impersonal essence is true essence. When true sense and true essence unite, the mind dies while the spirit lives; unconsciously following the laws of God, they change into a mass of violet gold frost. Gold is something stable and incorruptible: when gold reaches violet, coming from smelting in a great furnace, it is considered gold in full hue. Violet gold becoming frost represents the

psycho-physiological being melting into one unified energy, transcending
beyond yin and yang.

22

On cultivating the self (3 verses)

FIRST OBSERVE HEAVEN AND UNDERSTAND THE FIVE BAN-
DITS; THEN EXAMINE EARTH, TO PACIFY THE PEOPLE. WHEN
THE PEOPLE ARE SETTLED AND THE COUNTRY RICH, YOU
SHOULD SEEK WAR; WHEN THE WAR IS OVER, THEN ALONE
CAN YOU SEE THE SAGE.

Observing heaven means observing our own celestial essence. Understanding the five bandits means understanding how the five elements of
metal, wood, water, fire, and earth overcome one another. Examining
earth means examining the ground of our mind. Pacifying the people
means settling vitality, spirit, yang-soul, yin-soul, and intent, each in its
own place.

In the path of spiritual alchemy, nothing takes precedence over cultivation of the self, refinement of the self. The essential point of refining the
self is first to observe the celestial essence. When the celestial essence is
not obscured, the five bandits cannot fool you. Next one should examine
the mind ground; when the mind ground is clear and clean, the five
things are all settled. When the five things are settled, the vitality is firm,
the yang soul is stable, the yin soul is calm, the intent is sincere. This is
called the richness of the country.

At this point one should battle the five bandits and repel all negativi-
ties; when negative energy turns into positive energy, the killing potential
transmutes into the enlivening potential, and one can thereby see the
sage.

The sage is the original aspect of innate knowledge and innate capacity.
It is also called the spiritual embryo. When the five bandits are overcome,
they change into the five bases, which in action become the five virtues.
Tranquil and unstirring, yet sensitive and effective, unconsciously obeying the laws of God, is this not the spiritual embryo?

The word "war" in the text has a profound meaning. The five bandits
are in the mind, and they go into action in heaven; if you do not have the
great spiritual power to be a match for heaven, you cannot conquer them.

C *J*ing battle with them is precisely how to activate great function and bring forth great potential, progressing vigorously, growing stronger as time goes on, not letting yourself give up halfway along. An ancient immortal said, "As long as there is even the slightest positive energy left, you do not die; as long as there is even the slightest negative energy left, you do not become immortal." In refining oneself it is necessary to refine oneself until there is no more negative energy, so that the five elements fuse and transmute, the slag is gone and the gold is pure.

23

IN EMPLOYING GENERALS, YOU SHOULD DIVIDE LEFT AND RIGHT ARMIES; LET THE OTHER BE THE HOST AND YOU BE THE GUEST. BRINGING THE RULER TO THE BATTLE LINE, DO NOT TAKE THE ADVERSARY LIGHTLY; YOU MAY LOSE THE PRICELESS TREASURE OF YOUR OWN HOUSE.

In refining oneself, one cannot achieve success immediately; it is necessary to concede to desires, gradually guiding them in the right direction. In most people, the opening of real consciousness has been locked up tight for a long time; their accumulated habits are deep-seated, and the five bandits have been causing afflictions for a long time, so they are most difficult to exterminate.

"In employing generals, you should divide right and left armies; let the other be the host, and you be the guest" means when you want to get you must first give. "Bringing the ruler to the battle line, do not take the adversary lightly; you may lose the priceless treasure of your own house" means that you do not lose yourself in desiring to get from the other. By inwardly forestalling danger, wary of perils, and outwardly working on refinement, the false can be removed and the real can be preserved; why worry that the great Tao will not be achieved?

24

FIRE ARISING IN WOOD INHERENTLY CONTAINS DANGER; IF YOU DO NOT KNOW HOW TO INVESTIGATE, DO NOT FORCE THE ISSUE. THE OCCURRENCE OF CALAMITY IS ALL DUE TO

THE HARM OF THIS; IT IS NECESSARY TO CONTROL IT AND
SEEK THE METAL MAN.

When people act from acquired conditioning and the spirit of discrimination rules, the afflictive perceptions borne all along by the energies of
the conditioned five elements in the body, as well as the pollution of
present habits, are active all at once; if you haven't great spiritual power
and great method, how can you overcome them? If you do not know how
to investigate true principle, and start out impetuously to control mind
by mind, attacking them too fiercely, sometimes the fire of the ruler and
the fire of the minister flare up at once, and not only are you unable to
attack the bandits, you are even attacked by the bandits. It is not only not
beneficial, it is even harmful. It is like fire arising in wood; when the
calamity arises, it will overcome—the wood is burnt by the fire, destroying its life.

The *Ts'an T'ung Ch'i* says, "The flowing pearl of the sun always wants
to leave people; finally finding the golden flower, they change and stay
by each other." The golden flower is the mind of Tao. The mind of Tao is
mind which is not mind; it originally emerges from the body of natural
reality and is imbued with the sense of real knowledge. It has indestructible true energy, and nothing can deceive it. Once the light of the mind of
Tao appears, all falsehood retreats. Its efficacy and firm resolution are like
sharp metal, so the mind of Tao is called the metal man. Investigating
true principle is simple investigating the true principle of using metal to
control wood.

Over all, the "metal man" is the master of spiritual alchemy: if you
want to refine yourself without the metal man, you will merely bring on
calamity. Therefore Chang San-feng said, "When refining the self, you
must use true lead." True lead and the metal man are both names for the
mind of Tao.

25

On the metal man

THE METAL MAN IS ORIGINALLY THE SON OF THE FAMILY TO
THE EAST, LIVING INSTEAD AT THE NEIGHBORS' TO THE
WEST. RECOGNIZED, HE IS CALLED BACK HOME TO GROW
UP, AND ESPOUSED TO A BEAUTIFUL GIRL, BECOMING INTI-
MATE.

The metal man is the real knowledge of the mind of Tao, as mentioned before. Real knowledge constitutes true sense. In human life originally essence and sense are one and not separate: in terms of substance, it is called essence; in terms of function, it is called sense—sense is essence, essence is sense; they have the same origin but different names, yet they are not two.

Mixing with acquired conditioning, sense and essence change; true sense becomes obscured and arbitrary feelings arise. The indestructible true energy is covered by external influences, and is no longer at one's command. This is likened to the son of the family to the east living at the neighbors' to the west. But though he be living at the neighbors' to the west, it is not that we never meet—yet when we see him we don't recognize him.

If one is determined and investigates truth penetratingly, when one recognizes real truth it comes when called, like an empty valley transmitting a voice, without using up any energy at all. Then one can nurture it in a closed room, always protecting and sustaining it. Wedding it to the "beautiful girl" of true essence, yin and yang are one energy, joining in intimacy. As before it is of the eastern house.

The beautiful girl is the essence of conscious knowledge. The reason why essence is called a girl even though it is originally yang is that essence commands flexibility. It is represented by wood. The reason sense is called male even though it is originally yin is that sense commands firmness. It is represented by metal. The metal man having been out for a long time, when one day he returns home and meets the beautiful girl, they become extraordinarily intimate, and unfailingly produce the elixir. Therefore the *Ts'an T'ung Ch'i* says, "When metal first comes back to essence, it can be called restored elixir." Metal and wood joining—sense and essence merging—is the restored elixir. There is no other restored elixir.

26

On the beautiful girl

THE BEAUTIFUL GIRL TRAVELING HAS HER OWN DIRECTION; THE FIRST TRIP SHOULD BE SHORT, THE NEXT TRIP LONG. COMING BACK, SHE GOES INTO THE YELLOW WOMAN'S HOUSE, MARRIES THE METAL MAN AND MAKES HIM HER OLD MAN.

The beautiful woman is the essence of conscious knowledge, as explained in the preceding section. When it goes into temporal conditioning, there is the spirit of discrimination of the human mind which dwells there, so there is artificiality within the real. Producing illusion by consciousness, seeing fire it flies and wanders unsettled; this is what is called going out and in irregularly, not knowing where home is. If you want to practice spiritual alchemy, you must first cause this conscious essence to travel in the direction it should go, opening the awareness up and not obscuring that consciousness, so that it returns to real consciousness.

"The first trip should be short" refers to seeking sense through essence; "the next trip should be long" refers to nurturing reality through consciousness. Seeking sense through essence is the subtlety of the momentary congealing of the elixir, so it is said to be short. Nurturing reality through consciousness is the work of the ten months of incubation, so it is said to be long. Short when short is appropriate, long when long is appropriate—this is referred to by the line "she has her own direction." If you go in the right direction, the alchemy can succeed.

But you must first dismiss intellectualism and turn your attention inward: take this point of conscious essence and place it in the center. This is called "coming back and going into the yellow woman's house." The yellow woman's house is the abode of balance, without bias or inclination. When the conscious essence is correctly balanced, the mind is straightforward and the intent is sincere. When the intent is sincere, truthfulness is real; when truthfulness is real, it does not meander outside. Thereby one seeks sense through essence; when sense returns to essence, essence and sense become attached to each other and join into one energy. This is referred to here as "marrying the metal man and making him her old man."

"Making him her old man" is not an ordinary expression—it has a deep meaning. Generally speaking, spiritual alchemy begins with summoning true sense through conscious essence. When true sense returns, the conscious essence is no more disturbed or agitated, and it also returns to reality. Once the conscious essence is linked to true sense, it is necessary to nurture true sense in the realm of pure yang with no yin. This is likened to husband and wife growing old together, not letting there be any rift between them along the way. This is in fact the meaning of "the latter trip should be long." Students should study this deeply.

27

On the firing process (2 verses)

EVEN IF YOU KNOW THE RED CINNABAR AND BLACK LEAD,
IT IS USELESS IF YOU DO NOT KNOW THE FIRING PROCESS.
THE WHOLE THING DEPENDS ON THE POWER OF PRACTICE;
IF YOU DEVIATE EVEN SLIGHTLY, YOU WILL NOT FORM THE
ELIXIR.

The science of the elixir of restoration is simply to take the two medicinal materials, red cinnabar and black lead, and forge them into a jewel,
with which to extend the life of the essence. The cinnabar is the energy of
open consciousness within *fire* $\equiv$; this is conscious knowledge, which is
the realm of the human mind. The lead is the energy of firm rectitude
within *water* $\equiv\equiv$; this is real knowledge, which is in the province of the
mind of Tao. Because the conscious knowledge of the human mind is
light outside and dark inside, and light belongs to fire, which is red, it is
symbolized by red cinnabar. Because the real knowledge of the mind of
Tao is dark outside and light inside, and darkness belongs to water, which
is dark, it is symbolized by black lead. These are immaterial formless cinnabar and lead, not the material cinnabar and lead of the world.

Once you know the cinnabar and lead of real knowledge and conscious
knowledge, you can freely gather them without difficulty. However,
when you gather them you must refine them, and if you know the medicines but not the method of refining them, it is the same as if you didn't
know them. Therefore the text says, "Even if you know the red cinnabar
and black lead, it is useless if you don't know the firing process." The formation of the gold elixir totally depends on the practice of the firing process. The "fire" is the power of effort in practice, the "process" is the
order of procedure of practice.

In gathering the medicines, one must know their levels of gravity and
energy; in refining the medicines, one must know the proper timing.
There is a firing process of "cultural" cooking, and a firing process of
"martial" refining; there is a firing process of getting started, and a firing
process of stopping. There is a firing process of advancing yang, and a firing process of withdrawing yin; there is a firing process of restored elixir,
and a firing process of great elixir. There is a firing process of increasing
and decreasing, and a firing process of incubation. There are many processes of firing, which must be thoroughly understood from beginning to

end before it is possible to succeed in the work. A slight deviation produces a great loss, making it impossible to form elixir.

28

TREATISES, CLASSICS, AND SONGS EXPOUND ULTIMATE REAL-ITY, BUT DO NOT EXPRESS THE FIRING PROCESS CLEARLY IN WRITING. IF YOU WANT TO KNOW THE ORALLY TRANSMIT-TED TEACHINGS AND PENETRATE THE ARCANA, THIS RE-QUIRES CAREFUL DISCUSSION WITH THE SPIRITUAL IMMOR-TALS.

Since ancient times the writings of the immortals and real people have meticulously discussed the medicinal substances and firing process of cultivating reality. What they have said is true and not false, but though they discuss it, discussion cannot reach it; though they speak of it, speech cannot exhaust it. It is not that they haven't written about the firing process, but the meanings of the writings are deep and mysterious. Some say essence, some say life, some say medicine, some say fire; some speak of the firing process of cultivating life, some speak of the firing process of cultivating essence, some speak of an external firing process, some speak of an internal firing process.

So it is not that they haven't spoken of the firing process, but what they say is not organized. If you do not meet an illumined teacher, who will indicate the order for you, you will not be able to know it. That is why the text says they haven't expressed the firing process clearly in words, and it also says it is necessary to discuss it carefully with spiritual immortals. This is telling people to study the writings and also seek illumined teachers for certainty. One should not just seek a teacher without reading texts, and one should not take the writings as one's own understanding and fail to seek a teacher.

If there were no firing process in the writings—the treatises, classics, and songs—why would it say the writings expound ultimate reality? Generally speaking, students should both read the alchemical writings and seek enlightened teachers too. By reading the texts they can distinguish false and true, genuine and bogus, and can extend their knowledge and perspective; calling on enlightened teachers, they can ascertain the verity of the principles they have discerned. Study on one's own and finding a teacher are both necessary.

29

On the firing process of gathering the medicine

ON THE FIFTEENTH DAY OF THE EIGHTH MONTH, ENJOYING THE MOONLIGHT, THIS IS PRECISELY WHEN THE GOLD ESSENCE IS IN ITS PRIME. WHEN YOU REACH THE POINT WHERE ONE YANG BEGINS TO MOVE, THEN YOU SHOULD ADVANCE THE FIRE, WITHOUT DELAY.

When the moon comes to mid-autumn, the gold essence is in its prime; when the path comes to proper balance of firm strength, the original nature is completely illumined, the achievement of complete illumination rests completely in the mind of Tao. The point where one yang begins to move is when the yang light of real knowledge of the mind of Tao stirs but is not yet very active; only then is a glimpse of the root of heaven revealed. At this time you should quickly set about increasing the fire, gathering the yang and putting it into the furnace of evolution, gradually gathering, gradually refining, from vagueness to clarity, from one yang to complete purity of six yangs. This is also like the mid-autumn moon, exceptionally bright, shining through the universe.

The words "without delay" express urgency; because the light of real knowledge of the mind of Tao is hard to find and easy to lose, if you hesitate and delay, the energy of the light will again dissipate, and you will miss it even though it is near at hand.

30

On the firing process of extraction and addition

WHEN ONE YANG STIRS, MAKING THE GOLD ELIXIR, THE LEAD CRUCIBLE, WARM, SHINES DAZZLINGLY. THE BEGINNING OF RECEPTION OF ENERGY IS EASILY GOTTEN; IN THE OPERATION OF EXTRACTION AND ADDITION, IT IS URGENT TO PREVENT DANGER.

This section follows up urgently on the preceding one. When one yang stirs, you gather it back into the crucible: the mind is peaceful, the energy harmonious; "brightness arises in the empty room," its radiance collecting inside, producing light from within darkness, shining dazzlingly.

Master Ts'ui said, "Receiving energy is auspicious; prevent it from becoming unfortunate." The return of one yang is easy; but pure completeness is most difficult. It is necessary to forestall danger, aware of perils, using the technique of extraction and addition, increase and reduction, in order to accomplish the work. Extraction means reduction of excess of the conscious knowledge of the human mind; addition means increasing real knowledge of the mind of Tao where it is lacking.

Extracting and extracting, adding and adding, until you reach the point where there can be no more extraction or addition, then the human mind does not arise, while the mind of Tao is always present; real knowledge and conscious knowledge conjoin, and inside and outside are illumined. Only then will you not be afflicted by "wind and thunder at midnight."

In particular, because when the mind of Tao first returns the yang energy is weak while yin energy is strong, if you do not work on extraction and addition, as soon as you slack off you lose what you have gained. Therefore the work of extraction and addition is important. This work of extraction and addition is the work of preventing danger. There is no preventing danger without this extraction and addition, and extraction and addition is not beyond preventing danger. Preventing danger is extraction and addition—the two are one thing. Students should pay attention to this.

31

On the firing process of incubation

THE MYSTIC PEARL TAKES ON FORM, BORN FOLLOWING YANG; WHEN YANG PEAKS, YIN GROWS, GRADUALLY STRIPPING AWAY GROSSNESS. IN TEN MONTHS THE FROST FLIES, AND THE ELIXIR IS NOW DEVELOPED; AT THIS TIME EVEN SPIRITS AND GHOSTS WILL BE SURPRISED.

The mystic pearl is the pearl of complete yang, something round and bright and unclouded; it is a different name for the gold elixir, and is the fundamental essence of innate knowledge and innate capacity which human beings originally have. This fundamental essence is silent and calm, yet sensitive and effective; it is represented as a mystic pearl. This pearl is the stable, strong real knowledge of the mind of Tao, which takes on form through correct concentration. When it grows and grows until its bountiful energy is all-pervasive and its shining light waxes full, this is the peak of yang.

When yang peaks, you should receive it with yin; yin growing and stripping away grossness is using yin to nurture yang, getting rid of the hot energy of the adamancy of yang. Gradual stripping away requires ten months of work: after ten months of incubation, the dross is gone and the gold is pure, transmuting into spiritual frost, really empty yet including subtle existence, wondrously existent yet containing true emptiness, unconsciously following the laws of God. Being like frost flying in the sky is a representation of not falling into being or nonbeing—now the elixir is developed. At this stage, creation cannot constrain you, myriad things cannot move you; your work is done in the human world, your name is recorded in heaven. How could the spirits and ghosts not be startled?

32

On the firing process of forming the embryo

AFTER THE PRIOR POLE, BEFORE THE LATTER POLE, THE TASTE OF THE HERB IS EVEN, THE FORM OF THE ENERGY IS COMPLETE. GATHERING IT, RETURN IT TO THE FURNACE AND REFINE IT; WHEN IT IS REFINED, KEEP IT WARM, AND IT WILL COOK BY ITSELF.

The prior pole is yang within yin, real knowledge reverting to correct balance. The latter pole is yin within yang, conscious knowledge returning to correct balance. When real knowledge and conscious knowledge both return to correct balance, firmness and flexibility match each other. Where they match is called "after the prior pole, before the latter pole." At this time, real knowledge and conscious knowledge, the great and the small, are free from defect—"both countries are whole." Therein is produced a primordial spiritual sprout; the taste of the herb is even—yin and yang are merged: quickly gather it and put it in the furnace of evolution, refining it into reality, consolidating it into the spiritual embryo. At this stage, the medicine is the fire, the fire is the medicine. Applying the work of ten months of incubation, there will spontaneously be natural true fire cooking, from vague to clear, producing form from no form.

33

On yin and yang returning to the center

JUST AS THE ELDEST SON DRINKS THE WINE OF THE WEST, THE YOUNGEST DAUGHTER FIRST OPENS THE FLOWER OF THE NORTH. AFTER THE MEETING WITH THE GREEN BEAUTY, LOCK THEM UP AT ONCE IN THE YELLOW HOUSE.

The eldest son is *thunder* ☳. The wine of the west is metal-water. On the third of the lunar month, the moon appears in the west; under yin, one yang arises—this is represented by the trigram *thunder.* Therefore it says, "Just as the eldest son drinks the wine of the west." The youngest daughter is *lake* ☱. The flower of the north means producing the flower of metal within water. The development of the moonlight goes to *lake* from *earth* ☷; within yin, yang appears. Therefore it says, "The youngest daughter first opens the flower of the north." The two lines both symbolize the arising of one yang. "Just as he drinks" means he has not drunk before, and now suddenly drinks. "First opens" means not having previously opened, only now opened. Both describe the sense of the real knowledge of the mind of Tao being easy to lose and hard to find. The mind of Tao having been long buried away, real knowledge is obscure; when suddenly, in the midst of utter quietude, it happens to become manifest, this is like just drinking wine, or first getting a flower to bloom. This is the opportunity for restoration, a fortunate encounter on a good night, not to be missed. You should take advantage of the opportunity to gather it, mating it with conscious knowledge, shutting them in the room of the central yellow court; husband and wife meet and naturally give birth to the elixir.

Conscious knowledge is essence, yin within yang. It is in the province of wood; because the color of wood is green, conscious knowledge is symbolized as a "green beauty." When real knowledge and conscious knowledge meet, with the same mind, one energy, they naturally return to the center. When they return they return, but if you do not know how to lock up, they may again separate after joining. Having shut the door, lock it: with the door locked tight, if they haven't joined they will join, and when they have joined they will stay together always. This is what Chang San-feng meant when he said, "The woman of the eastern house and the man of the western house mate as husband and wife and enter the empty room. The yellow woman urges them to drink wine of the finest flavor, and they revel in intoxication."

The words "lock up" convey the work of forestalling danger. When yin and yang first meet, essence and feeling are not yet pure and simple. It is essential not to forget, yet not to force. Only if you guard strictly can you avoid leakage. The gold elixir crystallizes from within nothingness. This is the celestial mechanism, which cannot be known without a teacher.

34

On bathing

WHEN THE MOON IN THE EAST AND WEST REACHES ITS SEA-SON, PUNISHMENT AND REWARD ARE AT HAND; THE MEDI-CINE IS PATTERNED ON THIS. AT THIS POINT THE GOLD ELIX-IR SHOULD BE BATHED; IF INSTEAD YOU INCREASE THE FIRE, THAT IS DANGEROUS.

The moon in the east is the spring equinox, when yang energy rises between heaven and earth. The moon in the west is the autumn equinox, when yin energy rises between heaven and earth. The spring equinox, in the sphere of wood, is the enlivening energy, which is "reward." The autumn equinox, in the sphere of metal, is the killing energy, which is "punishment." Reward is that whereby to enliven people, punishment is that whereby to mature people. Without punishment, reward is not perfect; without reward, punishment is not complete. When there is both punishment and reward, the evolution of heaven and earth can circulate unceasingly by the flow of one energy.

In practitioners of the Tao, the return of the firmness of real knowledge to proper balance is like the autumn solstice; the return of the flexibility of conscious knowledge to proper balance is like the spring solstice. The reversion of both real knowledge and conscious knowledge to proper balance is like the reward of spring and the punishment of autumn. The

firm strength of real knowledge is that whereby to control the deviant
energy of the human mind; the flexible receptivity of conscious knowledge is that whereby to nurture the right energy of the mind of Tao.

Being firm when it is appropriate to be firm, being flexible when it is
appropriate to be flexible, not missing the time, firmness and flexibility
then are balanced, like the spring and autumn equinoxes each coming in
their time. Therefore the text says the moon in the east and west reaches
its season. When there is flexibility in firmness, and firmness in flexibility, firmness and flexibility are as one; then reality and consciousness are
not disparate. It is like spring reward and autumn punishment alternat-
ing in course; therefore the text says punishment and reward are at hand,
the medicine being patterned on this.

When the path reaches correct balance of firmness and flexibility, the
mind of Tao is always present, and the human mind is utterly quiet; real
knowledge is completely conscious, and conscious knowledge is completely real. When reality and knowledge are united, and innate knowledge and capacity take form in the gold elixir, one should bathe it and
keep it warm, taking the firewood out from below the furnace. Otherwise, if one does not know when enough is enough, and still adds fire,
then firmness is excessive and flexibility insufficient; so firmness and flexibility are not balanced, the medicine dries out and the elixir is damaged
—how can danger be avoided?

35

On cultural cooking and martial refining

THE SUN AND MOON MEET ONCE IN THIRTY DAYS; EX-
CHANGING HOURS FOR DAYS IS THE PATTERN OF THE SPIRI-
TUAL WORK. GUARDING THE CASTLE, BATTLING IN THE
FIELD, KNOWING BAD AND GOOD, YOU INCREASE THE SPIR-
ITUAL CINNABAR, FILLING THE CRUCIBLE, RED.

The moon originally has no light; its light depends on the sun. In one
year it meets the sun twelve times. In one month, thirty days, they meet
once between the beginning and end of the month. People's real knowledge is hidden away, pure yin without yang, like the moon's having no
light; it needs conscious knowledge before it can produce light. When

real knowledge and conscious knowledge meet, it is like the sun and moon meeting in thirty days.

Developed people, emulating the image of sun and moon meeting, place thirty days within one day, and also place one day within one hour: in one hour activating strong energy, they use the human mind to produce the mind of Tao, use the mind of Tao to govern the human mind, produce real knowledge by conscious knowledge, and purge conscious knowledge by real knowledge; they gather the undifferentiated primal energy for the mother of the elixir, and follow the spiritual mechanism of the transformations of yin and yang as the firing process.

This path has cultural cooking and martial refining. "Guarding the castle" is cultural cooking; "battling in the field" is martial refining. To apply the cultural when it is appropriate and the martial when it is appropriate is good; to apply the martial when the cultural is appropriate or the cultural when the martial is appropriate is bad. The cultural fire is turning the attention within, dismissing intellection, nurturing the true energy single-mindedly, like guarding a castle. The martial fire is controlling anger and desire, getting rid of falsehood and maintaining truth, forcefully removing acquired energies, like battling in the field.

Knowing the cultural and the martial clearly, understanding good and bad clearly, when there is some matter, use the martial fire, and when there is no matter use the cultural fire. Culturally cooking and martially refining, yin energy is exhausted and yang energy is purified; real knowledge and conscious knowledge join, and turn into innate knowledge and innate capacity—the original nature of ineffable awareness is round and bright, clean and naked, tranquil and unstirring yet sensitive and effective, sensitive and effective yet tranquil and unstirring. Integrating with the celestial design, there is no human desire. This is like "spiritual cinnabar filling the crucible, red."

When the cinnabar is spiritualized, the substance of energy changes; being neither material nor immaterial, neither existent nor nonexistent, it is wholly the energy of pure yang. By ingesting this one can get rid of illness and extend life, nullify calamity and avoid problems. Restoring one's original nature, open awareness without obscurity, truly empty yet subtly existing, creation cannot limit one, yin and yang cannot constrain one, myriad things cannot hurt one. And yet, there are also people in the world who know good and bad but still will not do the spiritual work.

36

On the meanings of hexagrams (2 verses)

WHEN *OBSTRUCTION* AND *TRANQUILITY* MIX, MYRIAD
THINGS ARE FULL; THE TWO HEXAGRAMS *DIFFICULTY* AND
DARKNESS RECEIVE LIFE AND GROWTH. GETTING THE
MEANING HEREIN, STOP SEEKING SYMBOLS; IF YOU STUDY
THE LINES, YOU USE THE MIND IN VAIN.

With *heaven* ☰ above and *earth* ☷ below, the celestial energy
descends from above, while the terrestrial energy ascends from below; yin
and yang do not mix, so this is *obstruction*. With *earth* above and *heaven*
below, the terrestrial energy descends from above, while the celestial
energy rises from below; yin and yang mix, so this is *tranquility*. When
obstruction ends, tranquility comes; as soon as yin and yang mix, myriad
things are born, filling the universe.

Difficulty has *water* ☵ above and *thunder* ☳ below; within water
there is thunder—yang arises within yin, thereby dissolving yin and giving birth to things. *Darkness* has *mountain* ☶ above and *water* ☵
below; under the mountain is water—yang falls into yin, thereby nurturing yang and developing things.

Obstruction and *tranquility* refer to the flow or blockage of myriad
things; *difficulty* and *darkness* refer to the birth and development of myriad things. Flow or blockage, birth and development, are all operated by
the coming and going of yin and yang. The coming and going of yin and
yang, the flow and blockage, birth and development of myriad things, all
come about naturally and are not forced.

In the path of cultivation of reality, when firmness and flexibility are
not yet joined, this is *obstruction:* when firmness and flexibility join, this
is *tranquility*. When firmness is appropriate, to promote firmness to cultivate reality is *difficulty;* when flexibility is appropriate, to use flexibility
to nurture reality is *darkness*. When firmness and flexibility are used
according to the appropriate timing, their variations produce the sixty-
four hexagrams; this is within our own mind.

Generally speaking, the way the hexagram symbols produce meanings,
we can forget the symbol when we have grasped the meaning. If one does
not know the intent of the hexagram and just clings to the form of the
hexagram, one will want one yang, two yangs, three yangs to effect *tranquility,* and will want one yin, two yins, three yins to prevent *obstruction*.

To produce three yangs to effect *tranquility* is somewhat close to the principle, but when it comes to producing three yins to prevent *obstruction*, that would be impossible. Furthermore, one might take the midnight hour as yang energy stirring within *water*, focusing the mind on the genital region at midnight, and considering this *"difficulty* in the morning," then take the noon hour as yang energy having a limit and stopping, focusing the mind on the heart at noon, and considering this *"darkness* in the evening." If you take these to be *tranquility, obstruction, difficulty,* and *darkness,* how can you align all the lines of the sixty-four hexagrams in practice? If you study all the lines and try to align them all, would that not be a vain use of mind?

An ancient immortal said, "It is not necessary to seek midnight and noon in the sky; in the body one yang naturally arises." This can be a clear testimony for those who work on the lines of the hexagrams—students should think it over carefully.

37

SETTING UP SYMBOLS IN THE HEXAGRAMS IS BASED ON DESCRIPTIONS OF THE MODES; UNDERSTANDING THE SYMBOL, FORGET THE WORDS—THE IDEA IS CLEAR OF ITSELF. THE WHOLE WORLD IS ASTRAY, ONLY CLINGING TO SYMBOLS, ACTING OUT THE ENERGIES OF THE HEXAGRAMS, HOPING TO FLY ALOFT.

The sixty-four hexagrams of the *I Ching,* with three hundred and eighty-four lines, only elucidate the modes of yin and yang, and the representations of balance and imbalance. If you understand the meaning of balance and imbalance of yin and yang, you can harmonize yin and yang, spontaneously fitting in with the symbols of the hexagrams.

Nevertheless, the deluded who do not investigate this meaning instead cling to the symbols; they intend to act out the energies of the hexagrams by practicing *difficulty* in the morning and practicing *darkness* at night, beginning with *difficulty* and *darkness* and ending with *settled* and *unsettled,* hoping thereby to attain the Tao and fly aloft. They do not know that when the adepts have spoken of *"difficulty* in the morning, *darkness* at night," this is to teach people that the arising of yang is difficult and the falling of yang is darkness.

The rising of yang is like the morning of the day, the falling of yang is like the evening of the night. To advance the yang fire to gather yang when yang arises is called "*difficulty* in the morning." To operate the yin convergence to nurture yang when yang falls is called "*darkness* at night." *Settled* and *unsettled* teach people that when yin and yang are joined, that is being settled, and when yin and yang have not yet joined, that is being unsettled. Once yin and yang are joined, the gold elixir crystallizes, and the work of the yang fire is finished. Once settled, it is necessary to prevent unsettling, for which the work of yin convergence is required. If yin and yang have not joined, and the gold elixir is not crystallized, yin convergence is no use—what is unsettled should speedily be settled, and for this the work of the yang fire must be used.

The meanings concealed in these hexagrams are the meanings of these four hexagrams; considered in this light, the other sixty hexagrams are all permutations of yin and yang. That is why the text says, "Understanding the symbol, forget the words—the idea is clear of itself." If you understand the meaning of the hexagram symbols, the pivot of heaven is in your hand, the axis of earth depends on your mind. Wherever you go, everywhere is the Tao—there is no need to cling to the hexagram symbols, for you spontaneously accord with them.

38

On the beginning of yang and culmination of yin

THE FILLING AND EMPTYING OF HEAVEN AND EARTH HAVE THEIR OWN TIMES: IF YOU ARE DISCERNING AND CAPABLE OF DISSOLVING AND GENERATING, THEN YOU WILL KNOW THE MECHANISM. BASED ON THE BEGINNING OF YANG AND CULMINATION OF YIN MAKING PLAIN THE ORDER, KILLING OFF THE THREE VERMIN, THERE IS HOPE OF ATTAINING THE TAO.

The Tao of heaven and earth is the Tao of filling and emptying. When filling culminates, then there is emptying; when emptying culminates, then there is filling—each has its time. If practitioners of the Tao can clearly discern the true principle of fullness and emptiness, and also can dissolve their yin and generate their yang, only then can they be said to know the mechanism of filling and emptying, dissolving and generating.

Overcoming and dissolving the yin is the mechanism of emptying, generating and expanding the yang is the mechanism of filling. But dissolving and generating are not apart from the sense of real knowledge and the essence of conscious knowledge. The sense of real knowledge is firm, and is in the realm of the beginning of yang, associated with metal. The essence of conscious knowledge is flexible, and is in the realm of the culmination of yin, associated with wood. Using firmness to govern the external, overcoming acquired energies from outside influences, using flexibility to deal with the internal, quietly nurturing natural reality, firmness and flexibility are both employed, the inner and outer are both cultivated—this is called "the beginning of yang and culmination of yin making plain the order."

When the order is clear, firmness and flexibility are in their proper places, dissolving and generating accord with the time; the true energy prevails and false energy is transformed. Inwardly thoughts do not emerge, while external things do not get in. There are no accretions defiling the sense faculties; one is naked and clean. This is called "killing off the three vermin." Once the three vermin are killed off, all negative elements are transmuted, and there is hope of attaining the great Tao.

The important point of this section is in the line "If you are discerning and capable of dissolving and generating, then you will know the mechanism." Discernment involves thorough consideration, penetrating every subtlety. Only after profound work over a long period of time can one see reality. When one can see reality, only after attaining correspondence of understanding and action is one able to dissolve and generate. When one can dissolve and generate, only then is this knowing the mechanism. If one cannot dissolve and generate, one still cannot be said to know the mechanism; this means one has not thoroughly discerned the principles —how can one then make the order plain and kill the three vermin? Therefore the study of correcting the mind and making the intent sincere is all a matter of investigating things and attaining knowledge.

39

On the mysterious female (2 verses)

IF YOU WANT TO ATTAIN THE ETERNAL IMMORTALITY OF THE VALLEY SPIRIT, YOU MUST SET THE FOUNDATION ON THE

MYSTERIOUS FEMALE. ONCE THE TRUE VITALITY HAS RE-
TURNED TO THE ROOM OF YELLOW GOLD, THE GLOBE OF
SPIRITUAL LIGHT NEVER PARTS.

The valley spirit is the unique energy of primordial nothingness; this is
what is called the spiritual embryo. This energy is not matter or emptiness, yet is both material and empty at the same time. It is in the darkness
of profound abstraction—when you look for it you cannot see it, when
you listen for it you cannot hear it, when you try to grasp it you cannot
find it. It is the border of the mind of Tao and the human mind, the root
of real knowledge and conscious knowledge, the basis of firm sense and
flexible essence. It gives birth to heaven, gives birth to earth, gives birth
to humanity: Confucians call it the Great Ultimate, or ultimate good, or
ultimate truth; Buddhists call it complete awareness, or the body of reality, or the relic of Buddha; Taoists call it the gold elixir, or the spiritual
embryo, or the valley spirit. In reality it is the innate knowledge and
innate capacity fundamental to human life, the spirit of open consciousness like an empty valley.

When this valley spirit falls into temporal conditioning, yin and yang
separate; the artificial acts while the real recedes, and the valley spirit is
buried away, as though dead. If you want to cultivate the gold elixir, it is
necessary to revive this valley spirit; if you want to enliven the valley
spirit, it is first necessary to harmonize yin and yang. If yin and yang are
not in harmony, the gold elixir will not crystallize.

The "mystery" is yang, which is firm strong sense. The "female" is
yin, which is flexible receptive essence. When there is both firmness and
flexibility, the valley spirit lives forever, and the foundation of immortality is established. The valley spirit consists of the combination of polar
energies, with firmness and flexibility in proper balance. When the poles
combine, in the darkness of transic abstraction there is something which
is called the vitality of the real unity. The vitality of the real unity is
another term for the valley spirit. Before cultivation and refinement, it
appears and disappears—then it is called true vitality; after cultivation
and refinement it solidifies and does not dissolve—then it is called the
valley spirit.

Once true vitality has been returned to the room of yellow gold, mental focus is restored to central balance, and the valley spirit stabilizes.
When the valley spirit is stable, the mind of Tao is always there, and the
human mind obeys it docilely: real knowledge and conscious knowledge
unite, and innate knowledge and capacity integrate completely with the

celestial design, tranquil and unperturbed yet sensitive and effective, sensitive and effective yet tranquil and unperturbed. Always responsive, yet always calm, the globe of spiritual light never parts. When the spiritual light never parts, this is the immortality of the valley spirit. This is what the author is referring to in the statement, "When you have ingested a grain of the gold elixir, then you will know your destiny doesn't depend on heaven." The valley spirit, true vitality, and the spiritual light are one thing: the only difference is whether or not one has developed it in oneself. Students should be aware that they are not three different things.

40

RARE ARE THOSE IN THE WORLD WHO KNOW THE OPENING OF THE MYSTERIOUS FEMALE; STOP FOOLING AROUND WITH MOUTH AND NOSE. EVEN IF YOU DO BREATHING EXERCISES FOR MANY YEARS, HOW CAN YOU GET THE GOLDEN RAVEN TO CATCH THE RABBIT?

Lao-tzu said, "The valley spirit doesn't die; this is called the mysterious female. The opening of the mysterious female is called the root of heaven and earth." The "mystery" is *heaven,* yang, the quality of firm strength; the "female" is *earth,* yin, the quality of flexible receptivity. Yang rules movement, yin rules stillness; the movement and stillness of the valley spirit is the opening of the mysterious female.

This opening gives birth to heaven, earth, humans and other beings; it is ultimately nonexistent yet contains ultimate existence, it is ultimately empty yet contains ultimate fulfillment. In the human body it is the place where the physical elements do not adhere; right in the middle of heaven and earth, one hole hangs in space, opening and closing at particular times, moving and resting spontaneously. Fundamentally it has no fixed position, and no form or shape; it is also called the aperture of the mysterious pass. The mysterious pass is utterly empty and utterly inconceivable; being and nonbeing have no place there. It is also called the door of all marvels. "All marvels" means that it includes all principles and contains all virtues.

If you take the mouth and nose to be the mysterious female and do breathing exercises with polluted air, how can you chase the golden raven and jade rabbit back into the yellow path and solidify them into the elixir of supreme consciousness? The golden raven is a symbol for the sun;

within yang there is yin, in humans the quality of correct balance of flexible receptivity, which is the spiritual essence of conscious knowledge. The jade rabbit is a symbol for the moon; within yin there is yang, in humans the quality of correct balance of firm strength, which is the true sense of real knowledge.

The quality of correct balance of conscious knowledge and real knowledge is the energy of the twin poles of the yang mystery and the yin female; the valley spirit is formed by the consolidation of the energies of the two poles. If you do not know the mysterious female, how can you know the raven and rabbit? If you do not know the raven and rabbit, how can you be capable of the immortality of the valley spirit? What opening is this? If you go along, you die; if you come back, you live. Time and again it has had you seek without finding—how could the mysterious female be easy to know?

41

On essence and sense

FEW PEOPLE KNOW THESE ARE DIFFERENT NAMES FROM THE SAME SOURCE; BOTH OF THEM, MYSTERIOUS, ARE THE ESSENTIAL KEY. PRESERVING LIFE, MAKING THE PHYSICAL BEING WHOLE, CLARIFYING ENHANCEMENT AND REDUCTION, THE PURPLE GOLD ELIXIR IS MOST MARVELOUS.

Spiritual alchemy is accomplished by two medicinal ingredients, one firm, one flexible—nothing else. Firmness belongs to the sense of real knowledge; flexibility belongs to the essence of conscious knowledge. Though essence and sense have different names, really they both come from the primordial energy of true unity in nonbeing. This is what is called the mysterious female in the preceding verse. Mystery and femaleness, mystery upon mystery, are the essential key of the undying valley spirit.

In the primordial spontaneous Tao, the valley spirit gives birth to the mysterious female; in the temporal restorative Tao, the mysterious female becomes the valley spirit. If mystery and receptivity do not combine, openness and consciousness do not join: the reason the mysterious female is the essential key is simply that it is that whereby to form the valley spirit.

When the mysterious female is established, the valley spirit forms; thereby can life be preserved and the physical being made whole, and also enhancement by advancing yang and reduction by repelling yin is clarified.

When yang is increased until it cannot be increased any further, and yin is reduced until it cannot be reduced any further, when yin is exhausted and yang is pure, the valley spirit lives forever, merged into one energy, without any polluting substance, round and bright, clean, naked, free, unconstrained by creation, unharmed by myriad things. It is like the firing process forging purple gold elixir, restoring life from death, most marvelous.

42

On doing

STARTING WITH DOING, PEOPLE CAN HARDLY SEE; THEN WHEN NONDOING IS REACHED, EVERYONE KNOWS. IF YOU ONLY SEE NONDOING AS THE ESSENTIAL MARVEL, HOW CAN YOU KNOW THAT DOING IS THE FOUNDATION?

The real people of ancient times said that essence and life should both be cultivated; so the work requires two stages. One of the paths of spiritual alchemy is cultivating life, one is cultivating essence. The path of cultivating life is the path of doing; the path of cultivating essence is the path of nondoing. The path of doing is prolonging life by certain arts; the path of nondoing is making the being whole by the Tao.

"Starting with doing" means the path of doing is used to build life. The science of building life is carried out entirely according to rules, the essential path of snatching the primal energy before the differentiation of chaos, gripping the mainspring of evolution, turning back the process of time. Heaven and earth cannot know it, ghosts and spirits cannot fathom it, divination cannot figure it out; since even heaven and earth, ghosts and spirits, and divination cannot know it, how can people know?

Ending up in nondoing means the path of nondoing is used to cultivate essence. The path of cultivating essence is embracing the fundamental, keeping to unity, all things empty, like a hen incubating an egg, like an oyster embracing a pearl. When this work reaches its consummation, one becomes ultimately truthful and has prescience; the mind of wisdom opens up, and one develops instantaneous comprehension. One has prior understanding of good and bad consequences, so everyone knows.

However, if people only know the path of nondoing is the essential marvel and do not know the path of doing is the foundation, not knowing doing, only nondoing, they are not only unable to cultivate life, they are also unable to cultivate essence. Even if they have some cultivation, this is only cultivation of the acquired nature—how can they cultivate the primordial fundamental essence?

The fundamental essence is the essence of the life bestowed by heaven; originally essence and life are one, with no duality. Due to mixture with temporal conditioning, yin and yang separate, and one becomes two— essence and life differentiate. When essence and life are separate, then essence cannot attend to life and life cannot attend to essence: life is usurped by things and cannot be autonomous; essence too is disturbed by this. When essence is disturbed and life shaken, false and true are lumped together, reason and desire get mixed up; the artificial handles affairs while the real recedes from its position. Day by day, year by year, negative energy strips away the positive until it is exhausted, so essence and life inevitably break down and perish.

Therefore spiritual alchemy must start with doing, restoring the primordial while in the midst of the temporal, recovering one's original jewel of life. When the jewel of life is in the hand, its control depends on oneself, and it is not moved by creation. At that point one embraces the fundamental and preserves unity, traveling the path of nondoing, thereby realizing the original essence of real emptiness, directly transcending to the marvelous path of the supreme one vehicle. What can be done for all the quietists who only know nondoing and do not know doing?

43

On female and male

WITHIN BLACK THERE IS WHITE, WHICH IS THE MATRIX OF THE ELIXIR; WITHIN THE MALE IS ENCLOSED THE FEMALE, WHICH IS THE SPIRITUAL EMBRYO. WHEN THE ABSOLUTE ONE IS IN THE FURNACE, IT SHOULD BE CAREFULLY WATCHED; GATHERED JEWELS IN THE THREE FIELDS CORRESPOND TO THE THREE TREASURES.

"Within black there is white" is the real knowledge awakened by the mind of Tao; it is the path of correct balance of firm strength, so it is called the matrix of the elixir. "Within the male is enclosed the female" refers to the original conscious knowledge of the human mind; it is the quality of correct balance of flexible receptivity, so it is called the spiritual embryo. When strength and receptivity are joined in one, and firmness and flexibility are one energy, the human mind changes into the mind of Tao, and conscious knowledge returns to real knowledge. This is called the absolute one, containing true energy.

The absolute one is pure unified spirit in which yin and yang are merged together; it is a different name for the gold elixir. Putting this true energy of absolute unity into the furnace of evolution, incubating and nurturing it, carefully keeping it securely sealed, watching over it and not losing it, will result in wholeness of vitality, wholeness of energy, and wholeness of spirit. These jewels gathered in the three fields are like the "three terraces," the three stars that surround the star representing the lord of the heavens. Then evolution is in your hands.

These three fields do not refer to the perineum, center of the torso, or center of the brain, nor to the umbilical region, solar plexus, or center of the brow, or to the coccyx, center of the spine, or back of the brain; they are the places where the three great medicines—primordial vitality, primordial energy, and primordial spirit are produced. They are formless and have no location, but because they are where the vitality, energy, and spirit are produced, they are called fields, and because vitality, energy, and spirit are spoken of separately they are called three fields.

In reality, the three fields are all one field, and the three jewels are all one jewel. Because there are three levels of work—refining vitality into energy, refining energy into spirit, and refining spirit into space—three fields are spoken of separately; but when you reach refinement of spirit into space, there is only one space, and vitality, energy, and spirit too return to tracklessness—how can there be any more talk of three fields?

44

On being and nonbeing

SEEKING WITHIN ABSTRACTION FOR THE IMPRESSION OF BEING, LOOKING WITHIN TRANCE FOR THE TRUE VITALITY,

FROM THIS BEING AND NONBEING INTERPENETRATE—WITH-
OUT HAVING SEEN IT, HOW CAN YOU IMAGINE IT?

Abstraction is an indefinable impression which is neither formal nor
void; trance is an invisible realm which is utterly silent and tranquil. The
impression of being within ecstasy is conscious knowledge; the true vitality in trance is real knowledge. Conscious knowledge is light outside and
dark inside—this is nonbeing within being. Real knowledge is dark outside and light inside—this is being within nonbeing. If practitioners of
the Tao want to make the gold elixir, they must seek conscious knowledge
in abstraction and seek real knowledge in trance. If they can actually
attain intellectual understanding and spiritual realization, and find the
real truth, this is called having seen. Once one has seen clearly, one controls conscious knowledge by real knowledge, and nurtures real knowledge by conscious knowledge. Then being and nonbeing are henceforth
wed, interpenetrating and communing. The gold elixir is thereupon
formed. Otherwise, if you don't know the impression within abstraction
or the vitality within trance, you have not seen what the medicinal ingredients of the gold elixir are; if you try to form the elixir according to arbitrary ideas, how can you even imagine it?

45

On ingestion of the elixir (2 verses)

WHEN THE FOUR FORMS MEET, THE MYSTIC BODY IS MADE;
WHERE THE FIVE ELEMENTS ARE COMPLETE, THE VIOLET
GOLD IS BRIGHT. FREEING IT FROM THE MATRIX AND IN-
GESTING IT, THE BODY REACHES SAGEHOOD; LIMITLESS DRA-
GONS AND SPIRITS ALL BECOME LOST IN AMAZEMENT.

The path of spiritual alchemy lies entirely in aggregating the five elements and combining the four forms. If the four forms are joined, then
essence, sense, vitality, and spirit unite; thus the mystic body is made. If
one can then go on to truly keep balance, and use the fire of natural reality to refine it, this is called the completeness of the five elements.

Once the five elements are complete, benevolence, justice, courtesy,
and wisdom all return to one truthfulness; essence and sense, vitality and
spirit all transmute into one energy. Strength and receptivity combine,

firmness and flexibility are traceless; real knowledge and conscious knowledge also turn into innate knowledge and innate capacity, ultimately good without evil, integrated with the celestial design, all-pervasive, unobstructed. Open awareness unobscured, it includes all principles and responds to myriad things. This is like yellow gold refined into violet gold, its light radiant. When you ingest this, it dissolves acquired mundanity and exposes the primordial spiritual body. Entering into the foundation of sages, one's fate depends on oneself and not on heaven. How can dragons and spirits not be amazed?

The meaning of ingestion is sudden enlightenment; it does not mean swallowing something. When the primordial energy has been refined to perfection, there is an abrupt shift from a gradual process to a sudden realization, from clarification to truth. This is like myriad diseases vanishing when medicinal elixir is ingested. Therefore the body can reach sagehood. Students should clearly understand the intent which is outside the words: if you look upon "ingesting" as swallowing, think carefully about the primordial energy—it has no substance, no form; what would one swallow? This should clarify the matter.

46

WHEN THE PARTY IS ENDED AT THE FLOWER POND, THE MOON SHINES CLEAR; ASTRIDE A GOLDEN DRAGON, ONE VISITS THE STAR OF THE LORD OF HEAVEN. HENCEFORTH, AFTER THE MEETING OF THE IMMORTALS, LET THE OCEANS, HILLS AND VALES, MOVE AS THEY MAY.

"The party ended at the flower pond" refers to taking the true yang within *water* ☵ and putting it in the furnace of evolution; the mind of Tao peacefully settles and "fills the belly." "The moon shines clear" means the mind of Tao is always present, the light of real knowledge shines clearly, without concealment or deception. As for "astride a golden dragon," *heaven* ☰ is represented by gold and by a dragon: taking the mind of Tao within *water* ☵, the one yang of real knowledge, filling in the human mind within *fire* ☲, the one yin of conscious knowledge, conscious knowledge then also transmutes into real knowledge, and *fire* ☲ again becomes *heaven* ☰. The original self becomes completely manifest, wholly integrated with the celestial design, round and bright, pure yang with no yin.

As for "visiting the star of the lord of heaven," the lord of heaven is the lord of creation; when practice of reality reaches the point of restoration of the body of heaven, the lord is in oneself, the key of heaven is in the hand, the axis of earth depends on the mind. Then creation cannot constrain you, myriad things cannot move you; you visit the lord of heaven and become a companion of heaven. Your work is accomplished in the human world, your fame is proclaimed in heaven above. Henceforth you meet with the immortals; even if the oceans should overturn and the hills and valleys shift, the spiritual body is permanently indestructible.

47

On the elixir crystallizing from within

IF YOU WANT TO KNOW THE METHOD OF RECOVERING ELIXIR OF GOLD LIQUID, YOU MUST CULTIVATE YOUR OWN GARDEN. IT DOES NOT REQUIRE HUFFING AND PUFFING OR APPLICATION OF FORCE; SPONTANEOUSLY THE ELIXIR MATURES AND IS RELEASED FROM THE MATRIX OF REALITY.

In the method of recovering elixir of gold liquid, the great medicine is extremely close at hand, not far away; the work is simple, not complicated. Your garden naturally has the herbs; you can cultivate it any time. You don't need an external furnace and crucible, or effort to operate the fire, huffing and puffing; the elixir naturally develops to maturity and comes out.

The "elixir" is the energy of true unity, of primordial nothingness; in connection with the root of consciousness when chaos first becomes differentiated, it acts as the generative energy which produces beings. Latent, it is true emptiness; apparent, it is ineffable existence. Functioning, it is the mind of Tao; nurturing, it is the valley spirit. It is ultimate nonbeing, yet contains ultimate being; it is utterly empty, yet contains complete fulfillment. In it are the energies of the five elements, but not the substances of the five elements. It is immanent in the five elements, but not trapped in the five elements. Becoming sage, becoming wise, becoming enlightened, becoming immortal—all are based on this.

This is nothing else but our original, inherent endowment, which is neither material nor void. It is just because of involvement with acquired conditioning, working with the spirit of discrimination, that it is buried and not apparent. If you meet a genuine teacher who points it out to you, for the first time you realize it is already in your own garden, and is not obtained from another. The seed is then settled, and gradually grows, naturally developing to maturity. The author says, "You should cultivate your own garden"—maybe this will wake up those on deviated paths who seek outside themselves and change their minds.

48

On medicine coming from without

STOP APPLYING CLEVER ARTIFICE AT WORK, AND RECOGNIZE THE OTHER'S METHOD OF NOT DYING. ADD LIFE-EXTEND-ING WINE TO THE POT; GATHER SOUL-RESTORING BROTH IN THE CRUCIBLE.

The preceding section said to cultivate your own garden; lest people cling to the individual body in practice, this section immediately follows up by saying, "Stop applying clever artifice at work, and recognize the other's method of not dying." The statement "cultivate your own garden" refers to the fact that the medicinal substance of the gold elixir is not more in sages or less in ordinary people but complete in everyone, not needing to be sought from another but inherent in oneself. The expression "the other's method of not dying" refers to the fact that the primal energy mixes with temporal conditioning, so that the spirit of discrimination does things and yang is trapped by yin, like something of one's own becoming the possession of another.

If you want to return to the basis and restore the fundamental, it is necessary to use the method of pursuit and incorporation, so that the primordial true yang which is gone can come back: when it returns, it is as before one's own. Before it has come back, it belongs to other; once it has come back, it belongs to self. There is a distinction between other and self because there are times when it has not come back and when it has come back. Therefore in the future it is necessary to tread on the ground of reality, gradually gathering, gradually refining, adding more and more, collecting more and more, thereby carrying out work in which there is striving. But though we say there is striving, in reality there is no striving. To say there is striving is in reference to appropriating yin and yang and taking over evolution; it does not refer to all the other clever artifices. It is all natural function.

"Adding life-extending wine" means adding the real knowledge of
the mind of Tao, so as to stabilize life. "Gathering soul-restoring broth"
means emptying the conscious knowledge of the human mind, so as to
nurture essence. The life-extending wine is metal juice; the soul-restoring
broth is wood liquid. Adding the metal, gathering the wood, metal and
wood join—sense and essence unite—and real knowledge and conscious
knowledge solidify, and the basis of the elixir takes form.

The words "adding" and "gathering" have a most deep meaning. As
yin and yang have been long fragmented, without adding and gathering,
progressively advancing, metal and wood cannot join, sense and essence
cannot unite. Adding and gathering, working hard by day and being
careful by night, neither forgetting nor forcing, the accomplishment
deepening as time goes on, metal and wood naturally join, sense and
essence naturally combine; only then can one extend life, restore the soul,
and enter the realm of immortality.

49

On the two elixirs, inner and outer

THE FINE GHEE OF THE SNOWY MOUNTAINS, OF ONE FLA-
VOR, POURS INTO THE EASTERN SUN'S FURNACE OF EVOLU-
TION. IF HE CROSSES THE K'UN-LUN, GOING NORTHWEST,
CHANG CHIEN WILL FINALLY GET TO SEE MA KU.

The snowy mountains (Himalayas) are in the west; they stand for
metal, representing basic sense. Ghee stands for water, representing basic
vitality. The eastern sun stands for wood, representing basic essence. The
furnace of evolution stands for fire, representing basic spirit. Taking the
metal and water of basic sense and basic vitality and pouring them into
the wood and fire of basic essence and basic spirit, use the wood and fire
to refine the metal and water, use the metal and water to control the
wood and fire. Using discipline to perfect award, using award to complete
discipline, when discipline and award are both employed, metal and
wood join, water and fire balance each other; the four elements are harmoniously combined, and the elixir is recovered. This is the model of the
outer elixir.

The K'un-lun mountains are in the northwest; as the mountain range
from which myriad mountains extend, it is compared to the energy of the

primordial true unity, which is the generative energy that gives birth to beings. Northwest is the province of *heaven* ☰, the highest place on earth. Height stands for yang. Chang Chien, the famous traveler, is yang; Ma Ku, a female immortal, is yin. When the restored elixir has crystallized and transmuted into the true unitive energy, going from vagueness to clarity, yang energy is replete and the great medicine arises; wholly integrated with the celestial design, firm strength balanced correctly, it frees a grain of elixir of pure positive energy. With this elixir one sublimates the body's acquired force of mundanity, like a cat catching a mouse; false yin vanishes and true yin appears. Yin and yang merge and coalesce into the spiritual embryo. Therefore the text says that if he crosses the K'un-lun, going northwest, Chang Chien will finally get to see Ma Ku.

The words "will finally get to see" contain the stages of the work. Before this restored elixir reaches the peak of yang, "Chang Chien" cannot yet see "Ma Ku." Only when it is developed to the peak of yang will "Chang Chien" get to see "Ma Ku." When true yin and true yang meet, the mind of Tao and the human mind both transform into the original mind; real knowledge and conscious knowledge transform into innate knowledge. A tiny black pearl hangs in the middle of nothingness, neither material nor immaterial, illumining the universe to view, with no obstruction whatsoever. This is the model of the inner elixir.

The outer elixir is a matter of regaining what has been lost, returned inside from outside. This is the "restored" or "recovered" elixir. The inner elixir is a matter of refining away the force of mundanity from the elixir once it has been recovered, manifesting the true light from within. This is the "great" elixir. When the outer elixir is complete and the inner elixir perfected, one roams in the land of nothing-whatsoever.

50

On positive vitality

WITHOUT KNOWING THE POSITIVE VITALITY, AS WELL AS HOST AND GUEST, WHO KNOWS WHICH IS NEAR, WHICH FAR? VAINLY SHUTTING THE COCCYX OPENING IN THE BEDROOM HAS THOROUGHLY DELUDED SO MANY PEOPLE ON EARTH.

Yuan-tu-tzu said, "A point of positive vitality is hidden in the physical body: it is not in the heart or genitals, but in the aperture of the mysterious pass." Positive vitality is so called because it is completely positive and pure, without a trace of mundane polluted energy. This is the original pure vitality, firm, strong, balanced correctly: latent, it is true emptiness; active, it is ineffable existence. This is what is called the innate good mind; it is also called the mind of Tao. It cannot be compared with the conditioned mundane polluted vitality.

In the human body, the positive vitality governs creation and gets rid of aberrations. Ancients called it the vitality of true unity, the water of true unity, and the energy of true unity. In reality, these are all one thing, the positive vitality of the mind of Tao.

The positive vitality is primordial, and is the "host." The mundane vitality is acquired, and is the "guest." The host is close to the self, the guest is far from the self. If you mistake the mundane vitality for the positive vitality, practice the art of sexual yoga, shut your coccyx and control the sexual fluid, imagining you will thereby form the elixir, how can you accomplish it?

Though the positive energy is obtained in a "room," this does not mean an actual bedroom, but rather the "room" of the body. Similar expressions, like "house" and "garden," are also used with the same meaning—how can you take it to mean an actual room? If students want to know the positive vitality, first seek the mysterious pass. When you know the mysterious pass, the positive vitality is herein.

51

On returning to the root

MYRIAD BEINGS, IN ALL THEIR MULTIPLICITY, EACH RETURN TO THE ROOT; RETURNING TO THE ROOT, RESTORING LIFE, THEY THEN EXIST FOREVER. PEOPLE CAN HARDLY UNDERSTAND KNOWING ETERNITY AND RETURNING TO THE ROOT; AGAIN AND AGAIN WE HEAR OF FALSE PRACTICES BRINGING ON MISFORTUNE.

Myriad beings are born in spring, grow in summer, are gathered in autumn, and stored in winter: this is the constant Tao. Having produced and fostered them, then to gather and store them, is called returning to the root. Returning them to the root is called restoring life. Restoring life means restoring the living energy of the natural order. Once the living energy is restored, it again emerges from the root and therefore can exist forever without dying. If people can know the natural mechanism of eternal existence of all beings, and can return to the root and restore life, then they also can exist forever and be immortals.

However, the principle of the path of knowledge of eternity and returning to the root is very profound, and its practice is very subtle. There is the matter of the density and energy level of the medicines, and the matter of the degrees of intensity of the firing process. There are inner medicine and outer medicine, inner firing and outer firing. There is gentle firing and intense firing, there is a process of culling medicine, there is a process of refinement, there is a process of crystallizing the elixir, there is a process of freeing the elixir, there is a process of cultivating life, there is a process of cultivating essence.

These steps each must be transmitted by a genuine teacher before they can be put into practice. Otherwise, if you don't know to seek and inquire from others, you just rely on your own intelligence and perception, making your own personal assessments and taking your private guesswork to be understanding, impetuously setting about the task, still unaware that the slightest deviation produces tremendous error. It is inevitable that false practice, arbitrary action, will bring on disaster.

52

On the sword of wisdom

OU-YEH PERSONALLY TRANSMITTED A METHOD FOR CAST-ING A SWORD; MO-YEH, WITH METAL AND WATER, ALLOYED FLEXIBILITY AND STRENGTH. WHEN THE FORGING IS COM-PLETE, IT CAN READ PEOPLE'S MINDS, A FLASH OF LIGHT-NING SLAYING DEMONS FOR TEN THOUSAND MILES.

A sword is something to protect the body; here it means the tool of wisdom to become enlightened and immortal, the means to become a sage. This is what is called the restored elixir; there is no "sword" other than the restored elixir. The "restored elixir" means restoration of the original innate knowledge and innate capacity, the true consciousness in which strength and flexibility are combined. "Casting the sword" means casting this tool of wisdom of innate knowledge and capacity in which strength and flexibility are united. In terms of substance, it is called elixir; in terms of function it is called a sword. In reality the sword and elixir are one.

In ancient times there was a smith named Ou-yeh: as he was casting a sword, it repeatedly failed to turn out; his wife, Mo-yeh, jumped into the forge, and the work was accomplished in one firing. People called it the precious sword of Mo-yeh; it was incomparably sharp. In practicing the Tao, casting the sword is first: taking energy with a proper balance of strength and flexibility, using water and fire to forge it into a masterpiece, it is called the sword of wisdom. Wearing it at one's side, using it at will, in a flash of lightning it cuts through demons for ten thousand miles.

The author uses Ou-yeh and Mo-yeh to symbolize the combination of strength and flexibility—indeed there is a subtle meaning in this. Practitioners of the Tao need to know strength and flexibility must both be properly balanced before it is possible to transmute the mundanity of acquired conditioning. If one yields when it is appropriate to be firm, or is adamant when it is appropriate to be flexible, or is strong but too aggressive, or flexible but too weak, this is not correct balance, and so the casting of the sword will not succeed. If the casting of the sword is unsuccessful, inwardly one has no mastery, and will get bogged down every step of the way—how can one complete the great Path then?

But the method of casting the sword is not easy to know; the combination of strength and flexibility is most difficult to understand. If you do not meet a genuine teacher and get personal instruction, you will just be indulging in vain guesswork.

53

On harmonious combination of essence and sense

DRUM ON BAMBOO TO CALL THE TORTOISE TO SWALLOW THE JADE MUSHROOM; STRUM A LUTE TO SUMMON THE PHOENIX TO DRINK FROM THE ALCHEMICAL CRUCIBLE. SHORTLY A GOLDEN LIGHT PERVADING THE BODY WILL APPEAR; DO NOT SPEAK OF THIS RULE TO ORDINARY PEOPLE.

Bamboo is something empty inside; it sounds when you drum on it. A lute is something musical; tune it and it is harmonious. A tortoise is a being that nurtures breath energy. A phoenix is a concretization of civilization. A jade mushroom is something soft and tender with a long life. An alchemical crucible is something pure and unadulterated. The tortoise and crucible belong to yang, the phoenix and jade mushroom belong to yin.

Spiritual alchemy involves two things, "emptying the mind" and "filling the belly." There is nothing else besides this. When the human mind is emptied, the mind of Tao arises and fills the belly; this is like drumming bamboo to call the tortoise. Once the belly is full, the flexibility of the human mind is governed by the firmness of the mind of Tao; this is like the tortoise swallowing the jade mushroom. When real knowledge becomes manifest, conscious knowledge is quiet and the mind is clear; this is like strumming the lute and summoning the phoenix. Once the mind is clear, the essence of conscious knowledge is used to nurture the sense of real knowledge; this is like the phoenix drinking from the alchemical crucible.

When the emptiness and fullness of the real knowledge of the Tao mind and the conscious knowledge of the human mind correspond, firmness and flexibility are united; always responsive yet always calm, round and bright, clean and naked, bare and untrammeled, the whole being is crystal clear, inside and out illumined, and one enters the sages' realm of equanimous serenity on the middle way. This is a matter of the path of appropriating yin and yang, taking over evolution, revolving heaven and earth, controlling potential and energy, primordial and unopposed by nature; how could it be discussed with ordinary people?

54

On gradual and sudden

WHEN THE MEDICINES MEET IN ENERGY AND KIND, ONLY THEN DO THEY TAKE ON FORM; THE TAO IS IN IMPERCEPTIBLE SUBTLETY, MERGING WITH NATURE. WHEN ONE GRAIN OF SPIRITUAL ELIXIR IS SWALLOWED INTO THE BELLY, FOR THE FIRST TIME YOU KNOW ONE'S DESTINY DOES NOT DEPEND ON HEAVEN.

The medicines which are of the same energy and same kind are the true yang of real knowledge and the true yin of conscious knowledge. Only when they conjoin is it possible to crystallize form from formlessness. What cannot be seen or heard is called imperceptibly subtle; unseen and unheard, the Tao returns to emptiness, one energy undifferentiated, lively and active, without thought, without contrivance, silent and unstirring, yet sensitive and effective, not depending on forced effort for any reason in the world, merging with nature, for the first time yin and yang congeal.

Once yin and yang merge, a grain of spiritual elixir hangs in space, illumining the whole world. If you ingest this, light arises within, dissolving aggregated conditioning, changing acquired characteristics. Then for the first time you know one's destiny depends on oneself, not on heaven.

The first two lines speak of ending up at naturalness by way of effort; the third phrase speaks of ending up at sudden enlightenment by way of naturalness. The spiritual elixir entering the belly means sudden enlightenment. When practice of Tao reaches sudden enlightenment, neither being nor nonbeing stand, and the universe returns to emptiness. Leaping beyond yin and yang, not constrained by yin and yang, one's destiny depends on oneself, not on heaven. Before you have reached sudden enlightenment, when you are still within yin and yang, destiny still depends on nature; this can be known by considering the words of the text, "for the first time."

55

On the supreme ease of crystallizing the elixir

SHINING BRIGHT, THE GOLD ELIXIR IS MADE IN ONE DAY; WHAT THE ANCIENT IMMORTALS SAID IS TRULY WORTH LISTENING TO. THOSE WHO SPEAK OF NINE YEARS AND THREE YEARS ARE ALL DELAYING AND WASTING TIME.

The great medicine of the gold elixir is inherent in everyone: if you can thoroughly investigate the true principle, call on enlightened teachers, know the two medicines of real knowledge and conscious knowledge, find the opening of the mysterious pass, and actually plunge in without reservation to climb directly up onto the other shore, in one day of work you can make the shining elixir of pure yang—what's the necessity of three years and nine years?

This saying of ancient immortals is true indeed, but while the crystallization of the elixir is done at once, incubation to develop it requires ten months. Without incubation, the gold elixir is not stabilized, and will surely be lost again after having been obtained. The statement that it is completed in one day only refers to the blending of yin and yang, not to the complete maturation of the gold elixir.

Complete maturation requires the work of yin convergence and yang fire, withdrawing and adding, increasing and decreasing. Increasing and increasing, decreasing and decreasing, until no more increase or decrease is possible, only then do you get a complete elixir of brilliant pure yang. If it is really completely developed elixir, how could it be completed in a day? A previous section of the text said, "Even if you know the cinnabar and lead, if you do not know the firing process, it's of no use: it all depends on the power of practice—the slightest deviation, and you will fail to crystallize the elixir." Later on it says, "If you want to cultivate the nine transmutations, first you must refine yourself and control the mind." Here we can see the meaning of the gold elixir being made in one day.

56

On difficulty and ease

THERE IS DIFFICULTY AND EASE IN CULTIVATING THE GREAT MEDICINE; AND IT IS KNOWN TO DEPEND ON ONESELF AS WELL AS ON HEAVEN. IF YOU DO NOT CULTIVATE ACTION TO ACCUMULATE HIDDEN VIRTUE, THERE ARE APT TO BE DEMONS TO CAUSE OBSTRUCTION.

The preceding section said the elixir is made in one day; this is not difficult. But this section teaches virtuous action, lest students take the great Tao lightly and improperly desire the path of immortality without cultivating virtuous action. What heaven enjoins on people is virtue; and virtue is also that whereby people requite heaven. If you have virtue, heaven is glad; then carrying out this mandate is very easy, and depends on oneself. If you have no virtue, heaven is angry; then practicing this path is very difficult, and depends on heaven. Why is this? Without vir-

tue and application, one will not be countenanced by the spirits, and
there are apt to be demons which cause obstruction; suffering difficulty
and sickness, one will inevitably give up along the way. Therefore, those
who practice the Tao must make it a priority to cultivate virtue. When
one studies and practices the Tao rich in virtue, the Tao is easy to learn
and practice, particularly because heaven is glad and the obstacles of
demons spontaneously vanish.

57

On the mechanism of takeover

THE THREE COMPONENTS TAKE EACH OTHER OVER WHEN
THE TIME COMES; THE SPIRITUAL IMMORTALS CONCEAL THIS
MECHANISM. WHEN MYRIAD TRANSFORMATIONS REST, ALL
THOUGHTS CEASE; THE WHOLE BODY IS IN ORDER, AND
NONSTRIVING IS REALIZED.

"The three components take each other over" means heaven and earth
take over myriad things, myriad things take over people, and people take
over myriad things. As for "when the time comes," myriad things flourish by taking the energy of heaven and earth; through the flourishing of
myriad things, heaven and earth absorb them when the time comes—so
heaven and earth take over myriad things. People see things and give rise
to greed and folly; through people's greed and folly, when the time
comes things steal people's vital spirit—so things take over people.
Things come to fruition through people's care and cultivation; when the
time comes, as things are developed, people take and use them—so people also take over things.

"Takeover in time" has the meaning of taking before and after. Over
the ages, spiritual immortals have hidden and not come out in the open;
their hiding is because of the mechanism of timely takeover—appropriating yin and yang, taking over evolution, turning over enlivening and killing, controlling the workings of energy, they dissolve acquired influences and foster sane energy. Therefore myriad transformations rest, all
thoughts cease, the whole body is in order, and they realize the Tao of
nonstriving spontaneity.

The important point in this section is "when the time comes." If you
take it when the time is right, the energy of heaven, earth, and myriad

things becomes your own; if you try taking at the wrong time, your energy will be snatched away by heaven, earth, and myriad things. When the time comes, it is a takeover; when the time is not right, it's not a takeover. The word "time" is very subtle.

58

On thorough investigation of principle

THE PRECIOUS WORDS OF THE YIN CONVERGENCE EXCEED THREE HUNDRED, THE SPIRITUAL WORDS OF THE POWER OF TAO ARE FULLY FIVE THOUSAND: THE SUPERIOR IMMORTALS OF PAST AND PRESENT HAVE ALL ARRIVED AT THE TRUE EX-PLANATION HEREIN.

The two books *Yin Convergence* and *Power of Tao* are basic books for practice of Tao: they divulge the mechanism of creation and evolution of the universe, and reveal the opening of yin and yang, enlivening and kill-ing. From ancient times to the present, the adepts have all investigated the true principles in these two classics and arrived at the real explana-tion, whereby they have comprehended essence and life. This book, *Understanding Reality,* is also composed based on the *Yin Convergence* and *Power of Tao;* if students can understand this book, they will also be able to understand the meanings of the *Yin Convergence* and the *Power of Tao.*

59

On seeking a teacher

EVEN IF YOU ARE INTELLECTUALLY BRIGHT, IF YOU HAVE NOT MET A REAL TEACHER, DO NOT INDULGE IN GUESS-WORK. AS LONG AS YOU DO NOT HAVE PERSONAL INSTRUC-TION IN THE GOLD ELIXIR, WHERE CAN YOU LEARN TO FORM THE SPIRITUAL EMBRYO?

The preceding section mentioned the *Yin Convergence* and *Power of Tao* classics as precious and spiritual writings, which students should thoroughly examine. However, lest students cling to the alchemical classics, consider these enough and not seek realized persons, this section tells people to call on true teachers without delay.

The alchemical classics and books of the adepts tell about the medicines and the firing processes, with many metaphors, all enabling people to understand these principles and know this path. However, the science of essence and life is occult and profound; it is not easy to discern the reality. Whatever you may perceive or understand, you should seek a teacher for verification. If you do not seek a teacher but rely on your intelligence to guess and make your own interpretations, aren't you taking on the burden of essence and life? Therefore the text says, "Even if you are intellectually bright, if you haven't met a real teacher, don't indulge in guesswork."

The quintessence of the science of essence and life is to gather primal energy. But primal energy is formless, imperceptible, ungraspable—how can it be cultivated, how can it be recovered? The alchemical classics and works of the adepts all speak of this energy, all speak of cultivation, all speak of recovery; but no matter how much they say, words cannot describe it. It is necessary to rely on the personal instruction and mental transmission of a true teacher to be able to recognize the medicines, understand the firing process, and go straight forward without impediment.

Otherwise, if you don't seek the personal instruction of a true teacher, and only rely on the words of the alchemical classics, thinking you're enlightened as soon as you distinguish some minor points, and immediately act on your ideas, either clinging to emptiness or sticking to forms, where will you form the spiritual embryo? The personal instruction of a real teacher should be sought without delay.

60

On stopping machination

THOROUGHLY UNDERSTANDING THE MIND-MONKEY, THE MACHINATIONS IN THE HEART, BY THREE THOUSAND ACHIEVEMENTS ONE BECOMES A PEER OF HEAVEN. THERE NATURALLY IS A CRUCIBLE TO COOK THE DRAGON AND TIGER; WHY IS IT NECESSARY TO SUPPORT A HOUSEHOLD AND BE ATTACHED TO SPOUSE AND CHILDREN?

Students' failure to understand the Tao and attain the Tao is all due to instability of mind and insubstantiality of approach. If you succeed in emptying all objects, being aloof of everything, reducing and reducing until you reach nondoing and your heart is clear and calm, then the inner work is done. When you then go on to build up virtue and cultivate action, taking hardship on yourself for the benefit of others, doing what is necessary in each situation, unaffected by wealth, poverty, authority, or power, walking the earth unattached, passing the days according to conditions, all psychological afflictions gone, then the outer work is done.

When the inner work is done and the outer work is done, "three thousand achievements are fulfilled," and one's virtue is on a par with heaven. Then it is possible for the life span to be equal to heaven. As it is said, those with great virtue will attain corresponding longevity.

Not a mote of dust is to be allowed into the human mind; as soon as there is any defilement, essence and sense do not join, the dragon and tiger are out of harmony, and various ills occur. If you succeed in getting rid of the machinations of mind so that it is open and clear, it is not necessary to seek a crucible besides this—this itself is the crucible. Once the crucible is set up, action and stillness unconsciously accord with the laws of God, essence and sense join into one, and harmonious energy pervades you. This itself is the cooking of the dragon and tiger—it is not necessary to ask further about cooking the dragon and tiger.

This is the path: the medicinal substances are at hand, the crucible is there of itself; if those who know this practice it diligently, even be they ordinary ignorant people, they can ascend to the ranks of sages. But worldly people do not see through things of the world; accepting unreal nature and life, they are attached to their spouses and children and do not sever the bonds that entangle them. Expending all their mental potential, when the oil is exhausted the lamp goes out, when the marrow dries up the person dies. What a pity!

61

On stopping at sufficiency

IF YOU HAVE NOT YET REFINED AND RESTORED THE ELIXIR, THEN QUICKLY REFINE IT; WHEN YOU HAVE REFINED IT, THEN YOU SHOULD KNOW TO STOP AT SUFFICIENCY. IF YOU

KEEP THE MIND GOING AT FULL BLAST, YOU WILL NOT
ESCAPE DANGER AND DEGRADATION ONE DAY.

Restoring the elixir means restoring innate knowledge and capacity, in
which strength and flexibility are unified, the fundamental essence of
true consciousness. After yang culminates in people, giving birth to yin,
the primordial enters into the acquired, innate knowledge turns into artificial knowledge, innate capacity turns into artificial capacity, strength
and flexibility do not match, and true consciousness is obscured. It is as if
something of one's own were lost outside. Restoring means recovering
what was originally there, like regaining something that was lost, returning something that had gone.

Generally speaking, the method of restoring the elixir involves a process of advance and withdrawal, intensification and relaxation, cultivation and cessation: it is necessary to operate it with correct timing, regu-
lating it properly depending on events. It will not do to go too far, it will
not do to fail to go far enough. So before the elixir is restored, one proceeds energetically, gradually culling and refining, urgently seeking its
recovery. Once the elixir has been restored, it is as before innate knowledge and capacity, with strength and flexibility joined into one true consciousness without obscurity; the labor is done, the medicinal energy is
replete, striving is finished, and nonstriving comes to the fore. At this
point one should quickly stop the fire, take the fuel out from under the
stove, and apply incubation, gentle nurturing, guarding against danger,
preserving this bit of true consciousness; in the furnace of evolution the
natural fire of reality will spontaneously cook and simmer it, dissipating
all mundanities, extracting something indestructible; only then is there
complete success.

Otherwise, if you do not know to stop at sufficiency once the elixir has
been restored, and keep going at full blast, continuing to pour on the
fire, the yang energy will dry up and the medicine will go stale; the real
will leave and the false will arise—what was gained will be lost. One day
danger and degradation will be unavoidable. There are cases of ancient
adepts failing in their early efforts because of this.

Generally speaking, "cultural cooking" and "martial firing" each has
its proper time; the yang fire and yin convergence each has a subtle function. Even a slight deviation will result in a great loss, so practitioners of
the Tao must be careful.

62

On life and death (2 verses)

TAKE THE DOOR OF DEATH FOR THE DOOR OF LIFE; DO NOT TAKE THE GATE OF LIFE AS THE GATE OF DEATH. IF YOU COMPREHEND THE KILLING MECHANISM AND UNDERSTAND REVERSAL, THEN YOU WILL KNOW THAT BLESSING IS BORN WITHIN INJURY.

The gate of life and the door of death are basically one; that is, the gate and door of the aperture of the mysterious pass. In this gate and door, if you go along with the energies of the five elements in the internal organs, then the five elements destroy each other, so each one is isolated, and the five virtues turn into the five thieves; then the door of life is the door of death, the gate of life is the gate of death. If you reverse this, the five elements give rise to each other, all return to the same one energy, and the five thieves become the five virtues. Then the door of death is the door of life, the gate of death is the gate of life. The mechanism of life and death is simply in going along or reversing this.

If you understand how to seek the mechanism of life in the killing mechanism, using it in reverse, then blessing is born within injury; the gate of death and the door of death can become the gate of life and the door of life. This is eternal life. "Door" is odd-numbered, "gate" is even-numbered: the door of death turning into the door of life is false yang leaving and true yang arising; the gate of death turning into the gate of life is false yin retreating and true yin arising. When true yin and true yang arise, both joining into one, this is the original self which is completely good without evil, fully integrated into the celestial design, flowing without cease, the mechanism of life subsisting eternally—how could it not extend one's life?

63

THE ORIGINS OF CALAMITY AND FORTUNE DEPEND ON AND INHERE IN EACH OTHER, JUST AS SHADOWS AND ECHOES FOLLOW FORMS AND SOUNDS. IF YOU CAN REVERSE THIS MECHANISM OF ENLIVENING AND KILLING, CALAMITY WILL

TURN TO FORTUNE IN THE TIME IT TAKES TO TURN OVER
YOUR HAND.

The way of reaction in the world is that calamity comes when fortune
goes, fortune comes when calamity goes; calamity and fortune are inter-
dependent, much as shadows go along with forms and echoes follow
sounds. If practitioners of Tao know calamity and fortune depend on and
inhere in each other, then they can know that the enlivening and killing
of their own bodies are dependent on and inherent in each other. If you
can reverse this mechanism of enlivening and killing, seeking enlivening
within killing, then in the time it takes to turn over your hand calamity
will turn to fortune, without expending any energy.

The mechanism of enlivening and killing is the energies of the five elements in the body. If you go along with the energies of the five elements,
there is punishment within reward, and it is the killing mechanism; if
you reverse this, there is reward within punishment, and it becomes the
enlivening mechanism. With the enlivening mechanism one subsists;
with the killing mechanism one perishes. A classic says, "When the five
elements go along in order, the universe is a pit of fire; when the five elements are reversed, the world is made of jewels." The difference between
going along and reversing is a matter of life and death; so there is great
power in "reversal."

This reversal is only possible for those who share the virtues of heaven
and earth, who share the illumination of sun and moon, who share the
order of the four seasons, who share the fortune and misfortune of ghosts
and spirits, who are aloof of everything and see all as void, who take the
Tao as their own responsibility. It is not difficult to know this; what is difficult is to carry it out. The mechanism of enlivening and killing is not
easy to reverse.

64

On mixing with ordinary society and integrating illumination

CULTIVATING SPIRITUAL PRACTICE INVOLVES MIXING WITH
ORDINARY SOCIETY AND INTEGRATING ILLUMINATION,
ADAPTING TO FIT SITUATIONS. NOW APPEARING, NOW CON-

CEALED, NOW OPPOSING, NOW CONFORMING, INCOMPRE-
HENSIBLE TO OTHERS—HOW COULD PEOPLE BE ABLE TO PER-
CEIVE HOW ONE ACTS OR REMAINS HIDDEN?

The light of spiritual alchemy, the great path of the gold elixir, is truly
magnificent; it is practiced in the world, within society, and is not a small
path of solitary quietism in which one avoids the world and leaves society.
It is necessary to mix with ordinary society and integrate illumination
before one can adapt perfectly to the world, now appearing, now concealed, now opposing, now conforming, now active, now hidden, now
passive, now effective, being unpredictable. Only this is great activity,
great work.

As for occultists, who sit in meditation halls, contemplate emptiness
and fix the mind, or circulate energy and practice visualizations, or
manipulate vitality, or get involved in other extraneous practices like
material alchemy and sexual alchemy, how can they dare do what they do
out in the open? If you dare not do it out in the open, it is destructive
practice, not spiritual practice—how could you be able to comprehend
essence and life thereby?

In ancient times, Bodhidharma observed that China had the atmo-
sphere for the Great Vehicle, came to China, and thus completed the
great task. Once Hui-neng had gotten the transmission of the fifth patriarch of Ch'an, he disappeared among hunters in Ssu-hui, thus perfecting
true realization. Once Tzu-hsien had gotten Hsing-lin's transmission, he
went to the city and was supported by a powerful family, and thus perfected essence and life. These three sages all mixed with the ordinary
world and integrated illumination; therefore they were able to become
Buddhas and immortals.

If you reject the world, there is no Tao, and if there is no Tao, what can
be practiced to return to the fundamental and revert to the origin, to preserve life and make the being complete? The celestial mechanism of mixing with the ordinary world and integrating illumination can be spoken
of to those who know, but it is hard to tell those who do not know.

III

One verse
representing the Great One
engulfing true energy

THE WOMAN PUTS ON A GREEN ROBE, THE MAN DONS PLAIN SILK. WHAT YOU SEE IS NOT TO BE USED; WHAT IS USED CANNOT BE SEEN. MEETING IN ECSTASY, THERE IS CONJURATION WITHIN TRANCE. IN A MOMENT FLAMES FLY, AND THE TRUE PERSON SPONTANEOUSLY EMERGES.

Conscious knowledge is yin within yang. It contains the essence of flexibility; essence governs lifegiving, and is associated with wood, which is green, so the verse says "The woman puts on a green robe." Real knowledge is yang within yin. It contains the sense of firmness; sense governs killing, and is associated with metal, which is white, so the verse says "The man dons plain silk."

However, essence and sense are divided into primordial and acquired. That which is acquired is temperament and emotion, which are the nature and feelings of the psycho-physical constitution. These have form and appearance, and are visible; these are not to be used. The primordial is fundamental essence and fundamental sense, which are the essence and sense of true emptiness. Having no form or appearance, that which is to be used is invisible.

Being invisible, that which is to be used exists in ecstasy and trance, in profound abstraction. Ecstasy and trance means there is energy but no materiality; it is imperceptible, ungraspable. How then is it possible to crystallize the elixir? Even though imperceptible and ungraspable, the essence of conscious knowledge and the sense of real knowledge are sometimes encountered in ecstasy, conjured up in trance. At this time of encounter and conjuration, spiritual illumination silently operates, bringing them into the furnace of creative evolution, refining them with fire; in a while the primal energy comes from nothingness and crystallizes into form, whereat the true person in a dark room emerges. This representation of the method of restoring the elixir is referred to in the saying, "In an hour, watch the elixir form." This appearance of the true person is the appearance of the living potential when true yin and true yang merge within; it is what is called the "spiritual embryo," and is not the appearance of the "body outside the body," which emerges after ten months when the embryo is fully developed. As for the emergence of the "body outside the body," how could the release and transmutation resulting in the body outside the body be accomplished in a short time?

This poem represents the Great One engulfing true energy: if someone asks me the meaning of the appearance of the true person, I would say it is precisely the Great One engulfing true energy.

IV

Twelve verses
on the moon over the West River,
representing the twelve months.

The author, Tzu-yang, says,
"The west is the direction of metal,
the river is a body of water;
the moon is the function of the elixir."

1

THE INNER MEDICINE IS AFTER ALL THE SAME AS THE OUTER
MEDICINE; WHEN THE INNER IS MASTERED, THE OUTER
SHOULD BE MASTERED TOO. IN THE COMPOUNDING OF THE
ELIXIR, THE INGREDIENTS ARE OF THE SAME TYPE; THE IN-
CUBATION INVOLVES TWO KINDS OF OPERATION. INSIDE
THERE IS NATURAL REAL FIRE, BRIGHT IN THE FURNACE,
EVER CRIMSON. THE ADJUSTMENT OF THE OUTER FURNACE
REQUIRES DILIGENT WORK. NOTHING IS MORE SUBLIME
THAN THE TRUE SEED.

The inner medicine is the spiritual essence of conscious knowledge; the
outer medicine is the true sense of real knowledge. Because that conscious
knowledge is hidden in the human mind, and the human mentality takes
charge of affairs, using consciousness to create illusion, therefore it is
called inner medicine. Because real knowledge is inherent in the mind of
Tao, and as the mind of Tao recedes real knowledge is not manifest, therefore it is called outer medicine. Real knowledge and conscious knowledge
are originally of one family—they come from the same source but have
different names. Therefore the verse says, "The inner medicine is after all
the same as the outer medicine."

The inner medicine is that whereby one cultivates essence, so of course
it should be understood; the outer medicine is that whereby one cultivates life, so it too should be understood. An ancient classic says, "To cultivate life without cultivating essence is the number one disease of practice; if you cultivate essence without cultivating life, the yin spirit will
never enter sagehood." Therefore the text says, "When the inner is mastered, the outer should be mastered too."

Essence is yin, life is yang: the great elixir of gold syrup is made by taking the polar energies of true yin and true yang, which are of the same
type, and blending them together. If you cultivate life and not essence, or
cultivate essence and not life, this is solitary yin or isolated yang, and the
great elixir will not form. This is what is meant by the saying that essence
and life must be cultivated together.

However, for essence there is the operation of essence, and for life there
is the operation of life. Essence is a matter of the spiritual body, while life
is a matter of the ephemeral body. The two kinds of operation of incubation are quite different. That is to say, the work must be of two kinds.

The path of cultivating essence is the path of nonstriving, or nondoing. Nonstriving is based on stillness, and doesn't involve any action; "keeping to the middle, embracing oneness," the "inner furnace" has of itself a real "fire" which ever glows crimson. This is using the "cultural fire" for "incubation."

As for the path of cultivating life, this is the path of striving, doing. Striving is based on action, and requires adjustment of the "outer furnace," diligent effort at refinement. This is using the "martial fire" for "cooking." Adjustment means increasing and decreasing: increasing means increasing real knowledge where it is insufficient, picking out the good and cleaving to it; decreasing means decreasing the excess of conscious knowledge, getting rid of intellectualism.

When increase reaches the point where there can be no more increase, and decrease reaches the point where there can be no more decrease, essence is stabilized, life is solidified, and the "true seed" is obtained. Only this is to be considered sublime. When these two kinds of operation, of essence and life, and the outer elixir, are completed, when brought into the "crucible," this is the inner elixir. That is, before it has come it is called outer, once it has come it is called inner. This is what is meant by the saying that when metal first comes back to essence, then it can be called restored elixir.

2

THIS PATH IS MOST SPIRITUAL AND WISE; BUT I FEAR YOUR ENDOWMENT IS MEAGER AND YOU WILL HAVE TROUBLE DIGESTING IT. BLENDING LEAD AND MERCURY DOES NOT TAKE ALL DAY; YOU SOON SEE THE FORM OF THE ORIGINAL JEWEL APPEAR. IF DETERMINED PEOPLE CAN PRACTICE CULTIVATION, WHAT DOES IT MATTER IF THEY LIVE IN THE CITY? THE WORK IS EASY, THE MEDICINE IS NOT FAR OFF—IF I TOLD ALL, PEOPLE WOULD SURELY LAUGH.

The preceding verse brought up understanding both the inner and outer medicines; this one speaks of the application of the outer elixir. The path of the gold elixir is most spiritual and wise; those who practice are guided by its standards and climb straight up to the ranks of sages. However, it may be that people's endowments are shallow and slight, so they are hardly able to digest and absorb the teaching.

What is difficult to obtain for the gold elixir is the true lead of real knowledge and the true mercury of conscious knowledge. If you discern real knowledge and conscious knowledge and blend them, then strength and flexibility balance each other, essence and sense are as one; the form of innate knowledge and innate capacity will soon appear, without taking all day. This is also like the original jewel producing light in the dark.

Because the spiritual root of innate knowledge and innate capacity has been buried for a long time, it cannot emerge of itself: now with real knowledge and conscious knowledge uniting, though the spiritual root of innate knowledge and innate capacity cannot become pure and complete immediately, yet its point of living potential has already taken on form in abstract trance. Once there is the point of living potential, from vagueness it becomes clear, and gradually can be restored to pure completeness. The "appearance of the form" is the foretaste of pure completeness.

If there are people of determination who can diligently practice this, it is not necessary for them to leave society—there is no harm in living in the city. This is especially so since in the path of the gold elixir the medicine is at hand and the work is simple. It needn't be sought outside, being in the individual. If it were all told, it would make people laugh. The laugh is that ordinary people and sages are on the same road, there is one principle for heaven and earth—the only difference is in going along or going in reverse.

3

THE START OF THE COURSE OF THE WHITE TIGER IS MOST PRECIOUS; THE SPIRITUAL WATER OF THE FLOWER POND IS REAL GOLD. HIGHER GOOD IS BENEFICIAL AS THE WELL-SPRING IS DEEP; IT IS NOT COMPARABLE TO ORDINARY MEDICINES. IF YOU WANT TO ACCOMPLISH THE NINE TRANSMUTATIONS, FIRST YOU SHOULD REFINE YOURSELF AND CONTROL THE MIND. EXTRACTING AT THE RIGHT TIME, STABILIZING FLOATING AND SINKING, AS YOU ADVANCE THE FIRE YOU SHOULD FORESTALL DANGER.

The previous verse said when you blend lead and mercury you can form the elixir. But if you want to blend lead and mercury, first you must perceive the homogeneous great medicine of real knowledge which is the true lead; only then can you start work. Real knowledge is true sense; in the symbols of this science it is called the start of the path of the white tiger, and also called the spiritual water of the flower pond.

True sense is hidden by random feelings; since sense is associated with metal, it is called the white tiger. But though true sense is hidden by random feelings, sometimes it appears, and the mind of heaven and earth is again manifest, the living potential sprouts. Therefore it is called the start of the path. The start is the beginning, and the course is the eternal path. The start of the path is producing being within nonbeing, embracing yang within yin, as the mother of all things. This is the living potential. This bit of living potential is the root of attainment of sagehood and wisdom, the basis for realization of immortality and enlightenment; therefore it is called precious.

This living potential is also called the spiritual water of the flower pond. The flower pond is the opening of the mysterious pass, the door of all wonders. Because it stores the living potential, it is called the flower pond; because that living potential orders the physical constitution and washes the internal organs, it is called spiritual water. Because that living potential also goes through refinement by fire and crystallizes so that it does not disperse but remains stable, it is also called real gold.

The start of the course, the spiritual water, the true gold, are all one thing, the living potential; this is also called the essence of higher good. Higher good is ultimately good. Being ultimately good, without evil, embodying all truths and dealing with all events, it is like water having a source. When the wellspring is deep, the flow is long, benefiting all beings without exhaustion. This is the most real medicine, which preserves life and completes the body; it is not comparable to ordinary mineral or vegetable medicines.

However, this medicine is hidden by acquired conditioning, only appearing occasionally; time and again it is lost as it is found, and cannot be kept for long. If you wish to accomplish the nine transmutations to stabilize it permanently, you must first refine yourself and control your mind, erasing acquired influences and feelings about objects, culling the medicine at the right time, thus stabilizing its floating and sinking.

Conscious knowledge is stored in the human mind; when the human mind stirs, conscious knowledge flies—it easily floats. Real knowledge is inherent in the mind of Tao; when the mind of Tao is obscured, real knowledge is concealed—it easily sinks. To refine the self and control the mind means to refine away the conscious knowledge of the human mind, making that which is floating sink. Culling at the right time means culling the real knowledge of the mind of Tao, making that which is sunken float.

Floating and sinking reversed, controlling the human mind by the mind of Tao, the human mind obeying the mind of Tao, governing conscious knowledge by real knowledge, nurturing real knowledge by conscious knowledge, the human mind is quiet and the mind of Tao is present; real knowledge and conscious knowledge are continuous branches of the same energy, and the gold elixir is within view.

However, the medicine may be easy to know, but the firing process is difficult. In working to advance the fire, it is necessary to know the level of gravity and energy of the medicinal substances, and when it is beneficial or harmful to hurry or relax. If you go to work impetuously, not only will there be no benefit, it will even cause harm. Therefore the text says, "When advancing the fire you should forestall danger."

4

IF YOU WANT THE TRUE LEAD TO STABILIZE THE MERCURY, KEEP NEAR THE CENTER AND DO NOT LEAVE THE SERVANT. WHEN WOOD AND METAL ARE SEPARATED, THEY HAVE NO MEANS OF MEETING; IT ALL DEPENDS ON THE INDUCEMENT OF A GO-BETWEEN. WOOD, THE ESSENCE, LOVES THE RIGHTEOUSNESS OF METAL; METAL, SENSE, LOVES THE BENEVOLENCE OF WOOD. WHEN THEY EMBRACE AND NURTURE EACH OTHER IN MUTUAL INTIMACY, THEN YOU REALIZE THE MAN HAS CONCEIVED.

The preceding verse said that culling the medicine depends on self-refinement; self-refinement aims at the meeting of vitality, energy, and spirit. Spiritual alchemy is just a matter of firmness and flexibility: balance and correct orientation of firmness is real knowledge, symbolized by true lead; balance and correct orientation of flexibility is conscious knowledge, symbolized by true mercury. Taking these two things and blending them makes the elixir.

However, when real knowledge is not manifest, conscious knowledge tends to be flighty, so real knowledge is what regulates conscious knowledge. And while real knowledge can regulate and stabilize conscious knowledge, conscious knowledge can also nurture real knowledge; so conscious knowledge is the servant of real knowledge. If you do not settle conscious knowledge first, real knowledge will not appear; therefore it says, "If you want the true lead to stabilize the mercury, keep near the center and do not leave the servant."

"Keeping near" means the combining of real knowledge and conscious knowledge, the firm and the flexible. Real knowledge is the master, conscious knowledge is the servant: if the servant is disobedient, the master has trouble acting. The difference between real knowledge and conscious knowledge is a fine line: if conscious knowledge is complete, real knowledge is manifest; if real knowledge is present, conscious knowledge is receptive. When real knowledge is present, one is firm and strong; when conscious knowledge is calm, one is flexible and receptive. Firm and strong, flexible and receptive, essence and sense join; therefore spiritual alchemy takes only two medicinal ingredients, true lead and true mercury.

The "lead" of real knowledge, sense, is associated with metal; the "mercury" of conscious knowledge, essence, is associated with wood. When you do things on the basis of acquired conditioning, sense and essence are disparate; this is likened to metal and wood being separated, each keeping to itself, unable to meet. Unless sense and essence commune, true sense and true essence do not manifest, and real knowledge and conscious knowledge do not combine.

Genuine truthfulness is called true intent; it is also called true earth. Once true earth appears, metal and wood spontaneously join; once genuine truthfulness comes through, essence and sense spontaneously unite. So genuine truthfulness is the go-between of true sense and true essence.

True essence is "wood," and it governs receptivity and benevolence; true sense is "metal," and it governs firmness and righteousness. With truthfulness, essence and sense are blended in the center; then "wood," the essence, loves "metal," sense, and accords with right; "metal," sense, loves the benevolence of "wood," the essence. When essence and sense unite, and firmness and flexibility correspond, benevolence and righteousness are both complete: real knowledge and conscious knowledge are the same energy, they embrace and nurture each other; the essence is stabilized, feelings are forgotten, and the primordial energy comes from nothingness and crystallizes into a black bead, the spiritual embryo takes on form—this is what is called "the man having conceived."

5

WHOSE DAUGHTERS ARE TWO AND EIGHT? WHERE ARE THE
MEN THREE AND NINE FROM? THEY CALL THEMSELVES WOOD
LIQUID AND METAL VITALITY; MEETING EARTH, THEY MAKE
THREE CLANS. GOING ON TO USE MR. FIRE FOR REFINING,
HUSBAND AND WIFE BEGIN THEIR CONNUBIAL BLISS. THE
WATERWHEEL DARE NOT BE STOPPED FOR A MOMENT, CON-
VEYING TO THE SUMMIT OF THE K'UN-LUN MOUNTAINS.

The preceding verse spoke of the meeting of vitality, energy, and spirit,
which forms the spiritual embryo. However, the spiritual embryo will not
form by the meeting of vitality, energy, and spirit without refinement by
the true fire. Two is the number of yin fire, eight is the number of yin
wood; therefore they are called women. Nine is the number of yang
metal, three is the number of yang wood; therefore they are called men.
The "liquid" of wood is fire; wood producing fire is one clan. The "vitality" of metal is water; metal producing water is one clan. Earth in the
center makes one clan itself. These five elements are divided into three
clans; when the three clans meet, they combine into one clan—this is
called the completion of the five elements.

This is a metaphor for practicing the Tao: original essence and original
spirit are the clan of wood and fire, original sense and original vitality are
the clan of metal and water, and the original energy is the earth clan.
These are the inner three clans. Benevolence and courtesy form a clan
associated with wood and fire, justice and wisdom form a clan associated
with metal and water, and truthfulness makes a clan associated with
earth. These are called the outer three clans. Practitioners of the Tao govern the outer three clans by the inner three clans, and complete the inner
three clans by the outer three clans. The final outcome is to make the
three clans into one clan.

However, these three clans require vigorous practice and intense work
before they can become one clan. The "refinement of Mr. Fire" is this
vigorous practice. By vigorous practice, those who are not benevolent will
reach benevolence, the unjust will reach justice, the uncourteous will
reach courtesy, the unwise will reach wisdom, the untruthful will reach
truthfulness. Benevolence, justice, courtesy, and wisdom all wind up in
one truthfulness, and essence, sense, vitality, and spirit all transmute into
one energy. The three clans merge, strength and flexibility correspond,

essence and sense unite, and "husband and wife begin their connubial bliss."

Once husband and wife are joined in bliss, the firing work continues steadily, the longer the stronger, one energy accomplishing the work, until you arrive at pure yang, beyond the realm of the senses. Therefore the text says, "The waterwheel dare not stop for a moment, conveying to the summit of the K'un-lun mountains." The "waterwheel" is the true energy, associated with the north: it does not refer to the yogic practice of conveying the genital energy into the spine and up to the top of the head. It means that the one energy accomplishes its work, dousing fire with water, water and fire steaming without interruption. It is like a water wheel in a river, carrying water up and sending it down, revolving day and night without stopping. The K'un-lun mountains are the source of myriad mountains: "conveying to the summit of the K'un-lun" is the state of "the three flowers gathered on the peak," "the five energies returning to the origin," entering into true emptiness and ineffable existence, unconsciously obeying the laws of God.

6

THE SEVEN-REVERTED CINNABAR REVERTS TO THE ORIGIN, THE NINE-RESTORED GOLD LIQUID RETURNS TO REALITY: STOP COUNTING FROM THREE TO NINE AND ONE TO NINE— IT ONLY REQUIRES THE FIVE ELEMENTS TO BE IN ORDER. THE BASIS IS PURE MERCURY, FLOWING THROUGHOUT THE TIMES: WHEN THE NUMBER OF YIN AND YANG IS COMPLETE, IT NATURALLY COMMUNES WITH THE SPIRIT; GOING IN AND OUT, IT DOES NOT LEAVE THE MYSTERIOUS FEMALE.

The preceding verse said that the work can be accomplished when the five elements are aggregated and the fire is operated to refine them; but the refinement requires knowledge of the true principle of seven-reversion and nine-restoration. Seven is the yang number of fire, nine is the yang number of metal. The essence of conscious knowledge is flexible, inside it harbors a false fire; when the false fire is extinguished, the true fire arises. This is like the mercury of consciousness solidifying into cinnabar, losing its volatility forever; fire reverts to the origin. The sense of real knowledge is firm, it has in it dry gold; when the dry gold melts, real gold is pure. This is like contaminated gold being liquified, permanently becoming most pure and bright gold; gold returns to reality. This is the meaning of seven-reversion and nine-restoration in the alchemical classics.

In aberrated schools, they count the zodiac signs from the first to the ninth as "nine restorations," and count from the third to the ninth as "seven reversions"—they do not know the meaning of seven-reversion and nine-restoration. If you do not know the meaning of seven-reversion and nine-restoration, how can you know the order of the five elements? As for the ordering of the five elements, when fire reverts to the origin, wood is produced in fire, and the spirit is aware; when the spirit is aware, conscious knowledge is not obscured. When metal returns to reality, metal is produced in water and the vitality is unified; when vitality is unified, real knowledge is ever present. Real knowledge being conscious knowledge, conscious knowledge being real knowledge, the four forms— metal, wood, water, and fire—are blended and return to the center; the five elements being one energy, perfectly balanced, wholly integrated with the celestial design, the five elements are in order.

However, the accomplishment of ordering the five elements is all carried out by the great medicine of metal in water. "Mercury" is "metal in water," which is the point of true sense of real knowledge. Real knowledge contains within it the primordial real unified energy, which is the root of the five elements, the basis of the four forms. In motion it produces yang, in stillness it produces yin, and flows throughout the times of the four forms and five elements. The path of restoration is to advance the yang fire when it is time for yang, thereby gathering this real knowledge, and to operate the yin convergence when it is time for yin, thereby nurturing this real knowledge. When the number of yin and yang is complete, the five elements merge, innate knowledge and innate capacity are tranquil and unstirring yet sensitive and effective, spontaneously communing with the spirit. The spirit refers to something that cannot be assessed in terms of yin and yang.

Unfathomable by yin and yang, the spiritual embryo coalesces; this is called "the valley spirit not dying." The valley spirit not dying is called the mysterious female. The opening of the mysterious female is called the root of heaven and earth. When the number of yin and yang is complete, this mysterious female has been established; when the mysterious female is established, the valley spirit goes in and out of the opening of the mysterious female, living forever, not dying. Then the path of reversion and restoration is complete. This is what is meant when it is said, "If you want to attain the immortality of the valley spirit, you must set up the basis on the mysterious female."

7

CONTAINING FEMALE SUBSTANCE WITHIN THE MALE, BEAR-ING YIN YET EMBRACING YANG, WHEN THE TWO ARE COM-BINED THE MEDICINE IS THEN PRODUCED, CHANGING THE SLIGHTNESS IN THE YIN SPIRIT AND THE PREDOMINANCE IN THE YANG SPIRIT. TRULY IT IS SAID OF A GRAIN OF THE GOLD ELIXIR THAT A SNAKE THAT SWALLOWS IT IS IMMEDI-ATELY TRANSFORMED INTO A DRAGON AND A CHICKEN THAT EATS IT IS THEN CHANGED INTO A PHOENIX, FLYING INTO THE PURE REALM OF TRUE YANG.

The preceding verse said the seven-reversion and nine-restoration require the completeness of the number of yin and yang; but to operate yin and yang requires that you recognize true yin and true yang. "Containing female substance within the male," in terms of the *I Ching* signs, is the emptiness in *fire* ☲; in people it is the conscious knowledge hidden in the human mind. "Bearing yin yet embracing yang," in terms of the signs, is the fullness in *water* ☵; in people it is the real knowledge inherent in the mind of Tao. Real knowledge and conscious knowledge, the two medicinal substances, must be combined before they can make the elixir.

The "yin spirit" has yang within yin, which is the "spirit" of real knowledge; the "yang spirit" has yin within yang, the "spirit" of conscious knowledge. "Slightness in the yin spirit" means slightness of yang; "predominance in the yang spirit" means excess of yin. When yang is slight and yin excessive, there is imbalance and the gold elixir does not form. Only when real knowledge and conscious knowledge join do the yin spirit and yang spirit return to correct balance, changing into true essence and true sense.

When yin and yang combine into one, the celestial order is clearly revealed; the innate knowledge and capacity which had been about to fade away in people is round and bright, clean and bare. A bead of gold elixir hangs in the center of vast space, lighting up the universe to view, unobstructed in all directions. When people ingest a grain of this elixir, they immediately become immortals; when snakes swallow a grain they become dragons, when chickens eat a grain they become phoenixes, and fly straight into the pure realm of true yang.

The "snake swallowing" and the "chicken eating" also fit the laws of alchemy: the snake is associated with fire, in the south, as *fire* ☲. The dragon is associated with wood, in the east, as *thunder* ☳. The chicken, in the west, associated with metal, is *lake* ☱. The phoenix is akin to water, in the north, as *water* ☵. The snake swallowing and becoming a dragon is producing wood in fire, the chicken eating and becoming a phoenix is the existence of metal in water. Producing wood in fire, producing metal in water, metal and wood join, water and fire balance each other; one energy undifferentiated, being and nonbeing do not stand, things and self return to emptiness, body and mind, both sublimated, enter sagehood, and their unknowability is called spirit. Escaping the ordinary world and living in the realm of pure yang are not empty words.

8

AS SOON AS HEAVEN AND EARTH INTERACT, WITH OBSTRUCTION OR TRANQUILITY, MORNING AND EVENING YOU WILL DISCERN DIFFICULTY AND DARKNESS. SPOKES COME TOGETHER AT THE HUB, WATER RETURNS TO THE SOURCE; THE WONDER LIES IN THE OPERATION OF EXTRACTION AND ADDITION. WHEN YOU GET THE ONE, THE MYRIAD ARE ALL DONE; STOP MAKING DIVISIONS INTO SOUTH, NORTH, EAST, WEST. REDUCING AND REDUCING, BE CAREFUL WITH THE FOREGOING ACHIEVEMENT; THE JEWEL OF LIFE IS NOT TO BE TREATED LIGHTLY.

The path of the gold elixir is the path of creation; the path of creation is the path of alternation of yin and yang. In the first month of the year, the energy of heaven rises and the energy of earth descends: this makes *tranquility* ䷊. In the sixth month, the energy of earth rises and the energy of heaven descends: this makes *obstruction* ䷋. In a day, midnight is the beginning of morning; at midnight the yang energy moves within and the yin energy goes outside: this makes *difficulty* ䷂. Noon is the beginning of evening; at noon the yang energy stops outside and the yin energy arises inside: this makes *darkness* ䷃. *Obstruction* and *tranquility* mean the rising and descending of the yin and yang of spring and autumn in a year; *difficulty* and *darkness* mean the coming and going of the yin and yang of morning and evening in a day.

Observing the vicissitudes of *obstruction* and *tranquility* as heaven and earth interact, one will recognize the process of *difficulty* in the morning and *darkness* at night. This is because the waxing and waning of yin and yang in a day is like the waxing and waning of yin and yang in a year. But the yin and yang of a year and the yin and yang of a day are all operated by one energy coming and going. Practitioners of the Tao are guided by the seasons of *obstruction* and *tranquility* of heaven and earth, and follow the mechanism of *difficulty* and *darkness* of morning and evening: when yang is appropriate, they advance the yang fire, when yin is appropriate they operate the yin convergence. When the firm strength of yang and the yielding flexibility of yin are properly timed, there grows an accumulation of good, aggregating the five elements and blending the four forms, like thirty spokes coming together at the hub, forming a wheel, like a thousand streams all returning to the source and entering the ocean, integrating into one energy, so the gold elixir crystallizes.

However, the marvel of the crystallization of the gold elixir is all a matter of the operation of extraction and addition. Extraction means removing false yin and false yang, addition means adding true yin and true yang. When false yin is gone, true yin appears; when false yang vanishes, true yang arises. When true yin and true yang return to central balance, two yet joined into one, real knowledge and conscious knowledge, essence and sense, merge and again you see the original face of innate knowledge and innate capacity. The accomplishment of extraction and addition is indeed a wonder.

Overall, cultivating the elixir requires recognition of true yin and true yang, and also requires recognition of the primordial truly unified energy. This energy exists prior to the differentiation of chaos, when yin and yang are still undivided; when absorbed it is true emptiness, when activated it is ineffable existence. It is symbolized by metal in water, embodied as innate natural goodness, and functions as the vital unified mind of Tao. The rule of alchemy is just to take the uniform great medicine of the mind of Tao. Though this mind of Tao is uniform, it governs the energies of the five elements and contains the qualities of the five elements. This is because the mind of Tao is the manifestation of true unity. One is the first number; the mind of Tao is one yet contains five, five yet ultimately one. In reality, when the point of ultimate oneness is reached, we cannot even say it is the mind of Tao; we can only call it integration with the celestial design. Thus Confucianism calls integration with the celestial design the Great Ultimate, Taoism calls it the gold elixir, Buddhism calls it complete awareness. This is what the classic means when it says, "When you get the one, the myriad are all done."

If you get the one, this means the jewel of life is already in your hand; there is no need to distinguish south, north, east, and west, and use the method of aggregating. Just use the mind of Tao to ward off the human mentality, reducing and reducing it, eventually causing all the acquired influences in the human mind to vanish: when it is purified into flexible, harmonious conscious knowledge, then the human mind too turns into the mind of Tao.

The reason for this is that there is discrimination in the human mind, which carries the energies of senses and objects since time immemorial plus the accumulated habits of personal history, all joined in the aberrations of the individual temperament. If you do not eliminate each of these roots of ill, even the slightest residue will at some time act up, given the appropriate circumstances. Then the jewel of life will leak away, and the foregoing work will all be in vain. Therefore the text says to be careful with the foregoing achievement, and not treat the jewel of life lightly. An ancient immortal said that as long as there is any positive energy left one does not die, while as long as there is any negative energy left one does not become immortal. Therefore, after obtaining the elixir, it is necessary to eradicate entirely the seeds of the vicious circles that have been going on since time immemorial; only then can the jewel of life be one's own, forever indestructible.

9

AT THE WINTER SOLSTICE ONE YANG RETURNS; THIRTY DAYS ADDS ONE YANG LINE. BETWEEN MOONS THE HEXAGRAM *RETURN* COMES IN ON THE TIDE OF THE MORNING OF THE FIRST DAY OF THE MONTH; AFTER THE FIFTEENTH, *HEAVEN* ENDS AND *MEETING* APPEARS. A DAY IS ALSO DIVIDED INTO COLD AND HOT: WHEN YANG IS BORN, *RETURN* ARISES IN THE MIDDLE OF THE NIGHT; AT NOON *MEETING* SYMBOLIZES THE ARRIVAL OF ONE YIN. WHEN YOU REFINE THE MEDICINE YOU MUST KNOW DUSK AND DAWN.

The preceding verse spoke of the work of extraction and addition; this teaches people to be guided by the evolution of dusk and dawn of heaven and earth. As for the dusk and dawn of a year, on the winter solstice, in the eleventh lunar month, one yang arises; each thirty days adds another yang line: so one yang arising in the eleventh month makes *return* ☷☳, the second yang arising in the twelfth month makes *overseeing* ☷☱, the third yang arising in the first month makes *tranquility* ☷☰, the fourth yang arising in the second month makes *great power* ☳☰, the fifth yang arising in the third month makes *parting* ☱☰, and the sixth yang arising in the fourth month makes *heaven* ☰☰. These are the six yang hexagrams.

In the fifth month, one yin arises, making *meeting* ☰☴, and the thirty days of each month add one yin line; in the sixth month the second yin arises, making *withdrawal* ☰☶, in the seventh month the third yin arises, making *obstruction* ☰☷, in the eighth month the fourth yin arises, making *observing* ☴☷, in the ninth month the fifth yin arises, making *stripping away* ☶☷, and in the tenth month the sixth yin arises, making *earth* ☷☷. These are the six yin hexagrams. The six yang months are the dawn, the six yin months are the dusk; this is the dusk and dawn of a year.

In between moons, in the interval of the ending of one month and the beginning of the next, sun and moon meet, the moon receives the sun's light, and on the third day the yang light first spews over the ocean; the tide responding to it makes *return*. Every two and a half days adds a yang line, until the fifteenth, when sun and moon face each other and the light is round and full, making *heaven*. From the first to the fifteenth days of the month are the six yang hexagrams. After the full moon, *heaven* ends, and from the sixteenth to the eighteenth one yin arises; the yang light has waned, and *meeting* appears. Every two and a half days adds another yin line, until the thirtieth, when the moon is dark and the yang light is all gone; there is only a dark mass, making *earth*. From the sixteenth to the thirtieth days are the six yin hexagrams. Two and a half days are an interval, twelve intervals go through the six yang and six yin hexagrams: this is the dusk and dawn of a month.

The interval of a day is also divided into cold and hot. In the middle of the night, one yang arises, making *return;* every two hours adds one yang line, until the sixth yang arises in the 10 am–12 noon interval, making *heaven*. At noon, one yin arises making *meeting;* every two hours adds a yin line, until the sixth yin arises in the 10 pm–12 midnight interval, making *earth*. The twenty-four hours go through twelve hexagrams, six yin and six yang; this is the dusk and dawn of a day.

Sages transfer a year's dusk and dawn of yin and yang into a month, transfer a month's dusk and dawn of yin and yang into a day, and transfer a day's dusk and dawn of yin and yang into an hour. An hour has eight intervals, and each interval has fifteen segments, so eight intervals has one hundred and twenty segments. The sixty segments of the first four intervals are the six yangs, the sixty segments of the last four intervals are the six yins. Also, the dusk and dawn of one hour is transferred into one interval, with fifteen segments; the first seven and a half segments are yang, the last seven and a half segments are yin.

In a single interval culling the great medicine, returning it to the crucible and furnace of evolution, operating the yang fire and yin convergence, refining it into elixir, is what is called "dividing midnight and noon in time without intervals, distinguishing *heaven* and *earth* in a hexagram without lines." It is only necessary to know the "dusk" and "dawn" which are the arising of yin and yang. When you know the dusk and dawn, then the evolution of a day, a month, a year is right in a single hour, a single interval. The blind of the world who practice sitting meditation at midnight and noon, or circulate energy at the new and full moon, or practice developmental exercises at the winter and summer solstices, do not know the principle of "dusk and dawn."

10

IF YOU DO NOT DISTINGUISH THE FIVE ELEMENTS AND FOUR FORMS, HOW CAN YOU DISTINGUISH THE CINNABAR AND MERCURY, LEAD AND QUICKSILVER? WITHOUT HAVING EVEN HEARD OF THE CULTIVATION OF THE ELIXIR AND THE FIRING PROCESS, YOU ALREADY CALL YOURSELF A HERMIT? IF YOU ARE UNWILLING TO REFLECT ON YOUR OWN ERRORS, AND EVEN TEACH OTHERS ERRONEOUS WAYS, YOU MISLEAD OTHERS INTO PERPETUAL CONFUSION; HOW CAN YOU TAKE SUCH A DECEIVING MIND LIGHTLY?

The preceding verse said that to refine the medicine requires knowledge of the dusk and dawn of yin and yang; this verse quickly follows up on the preceding, for those who don't know the dawn and dusk of yin and yang, bringing out the path of spiritual immortals. The basic aim is to develop others after developing oneself, to cultivate virtue after cultivating the Tao. People who are astray do not know the true principles of the five elements and four forms, do not understand the code words cinnabar, mercury, lead, and quicksilver, do not understand the medicinal substances, do not ask about the firing process; yet, having learned some minor teachings of sidetrack methods, they imagine they have the Tao, call themselves hermits, are unwilling to reflect on their own errors, and even teach others erroneous paths. This is the blind leading the blind, misleading others into confusion, never able to get out. This sort of deceiving, indulging mind will go to uninterrupted hell, never to emerge—how could there yet be any hope of attaining the Tao?

11

CULTIVATING OVER EIGHT HUNDRED VIRTUOUS PRACTICES, ACCUMULATING A FULL THREE THOUSAND HIDDEN DEEDS, EQUALLY SAVING SELF AND OTHERS, FRIEND AND FOE, ONLY THEN DO YOU ACCORD WITH THE ORIGINAL VOW OF SPIRITUAL MORTALS. THEN TIGERS AND RHINOS, SWORDS AND SOLDIERS, DO NOT INJURE YOU, THE BURNING HOUSE OF IMPERMANENCE CANNOT CONSTRAIN YOU; AFTER THE PRECIOUS DESCENDS, YOU GO PAY COURT TO HEAVEN, CALMLY RIDING A PHOENIX-DRAWN CHARIOT.

The preceding verse said that sidetracked methods and aberrant procedures do not clarify the great Path but only damage virtue, and cannot develop virtue; this verse speaks of the need to practice virtue after practicing the Path.

Practicing the Path is for oneself, practicing virtue is for others. Practice of the Path has an end, but practice of virtue has no end. Therefore after spiritual immortals completed the Path, they always fulfilled three thousand meritorious deeds and eight hundred practices, forgetting both others and self, equanimous towards friend and foe, becoming coextensive with the universe, containing myriad things, embodying all the qualities of the Tao, thus finally according with their original vow.

When one reaches this stage, all is empty, inside and out; neither existence nor nonexistence remains, body and mind are both sublimated—tigers and rhinos cannot harm you, weapons cannot get at you, the burning house of impermanence cannot constrain you. The precious talisman comes down to summon you, and riding peacefully in a phoenix chariot you ascend in broad daylight.

12

THE FEELINGS OF ALTAIR AND VEGA ARE JOINED, THEIR PATHS MEET; THE TORTOISE AND SNAKE ACT ACCORDING TO THEIR NATURE. THE MOON AND SUN JOIN THEIR CHARMS AT THE BEGINNING OF THE MONTH; THE TWO ENERGIES OPER-ATE SUSTAINED BY EACH OTHER. BASICALLY IT IS THE WON-DROUS FUNCTION OF HEAVEN AND EARTH; WHO CAN COM-PREHEND THIS TRUTH? IF YIN AND YANG ARE KEPT APART, THEY BECOME MALIGNANT; HOW CAN YOU HAVE THE ETER-NITY OF HEAVEN AND EARTH?

The preceding eleven verses all say the great way of cultivation of the gold elixir requires a combination of two medicines of the same kind, true yin and true yang, before the elixir can be made. People may wonder if it is made by forced effort, but it is not—it is all a natural operation. Therefore this verse sums up the meaning of the foregoing verses, to get students to thoroughly investigate the true principle.

It is like the stars Altair and Vega meeting on the seventh day of the seventh month, tortoise and snake associating through similarity, moon and sun meeting at the turn of the month—all of these represent the nat-ural commingling of the two energies of yin and yang as they interact. This is the wondrous function of the creative operation of heaven and earth. The course of creation in heaven and earth is the course of alterna-tion of yin and yang: yin and yang sustaining each other, one energy flows, yin to yang, yang to yin; as yin and yang come and go, the four sea-sons take place and all things grow. The mechanism of life never ceases, so it is always there, of old and now.

If practitioners of the Tao do not comprehend this truth, and abandon the principle of creation by yin and yang, they stick to emptiness or cling to forms, making forced endeavors which have the contrary effect of keeping yin and yang apart. This is not only of no help to essence and life, it even harms essence and life; malignancy cannot be avoided. Can you then still hope for the eternity of heaven and earth, to become an undying immortal?

The path of eternity of heaven and earth is the path of blending of true yin and true yang. When true yin and true yang are blended, the mecha-nism of life therein wells forth and congeals into a spiritual embryo, com-ing into being from nonbeing, from being into nonbeing, escaping the illusory body and bringing forth the real body: only then can one share the eternity of heaven and earth. If practitioners of Tao want to seek the eternity of heaven and earth, they will find no means without true yin and true yang.

There is one more poem on the moon over the West River, representing the intercalary month. According to the author's own preface, this verse and the following five verses are not part of the main body of *Understanding Reality*, but belong to the collection of additions; reflecting on the meaning of the words, this is the path of first cultivating life and afterwards cultivating essence. Three commentators include it in the main collection because it has an explanation of cultivating life, and I follow them here.

THE ELIXIR IS THE MOST PRECIOUS TREASURE OF THE PHYSI-CAL BODY; WHEN CULTIVATED TO PERFECTION, THE TRANS-MUTATIONS ARE ENDLESS. ONE CAN GO ON TO INVESTIGATE THE TRUE SOURCE IN THE REALM OF ESSENCE, AND ASCER-TAIN THE INEFFABLE FUNCTION OF THE BIRTHLESS. WITHOUT AWAITING ANOTHER BODY IN THE NEXT LIFE, ONE ATTAINS THE SPIRITUAL CAPACITIES OF A BUDDHA IN THE PRESENT; AFTER THE NAGA GIRL ACHIEVED THIS, WHO SINCE THEN HAS BEEN ABLE TO FOLLOW IN HER FOOTSTEPS?

Yuan-tu-tzu said, "A point of positive vitality is hidden in the physical body; it is not in the heart or genitals, but in the opening of the mysteri-ous pass." The point of positive vitality is the elixir; hidden in the physi-cal body, it is the most precious treasure of the body. The elixir is nothing but the vitality of the primordial point of complete yang; it is also called the energy of primordial real unity, and it is also called the abundant sane energy. In storage it is called true emptiness, in action it is called ineffable existence. Its substance is natural wholesomeness, its function is the mind of Tao. This most precious treasure in the human body does not belong to the heart or genitals; it is stored in the mysterious pass.

The opening of the mysterious pass has no location, no form; this elixir also has no location and no form. Being equanimous in action and still-ness, untrammeled by matter or voidness, lively and effervescent, if you operate the fire to forge it into something stable and solid, it is always responsive yet always tranquil, always tranquil yet always responsive, capable of endless transformations, with unfathomable spiritual marvels, unfathomable even to the spirits of heaven and earth. It abides in the physical body, yet can transform the physical body; this is what is called the spiritual body. Therefore the author says that the evolution of life is connected with the body, meaning connected with the spiritual body. When the spiritual body is achieved, the spiritual embryo is complete, the foundation of life is stable, striving ends and nonstriving appears, by which one can cultivate essence.

The true source of essence is the ineffable function of the birthless. Cultivation of life is the way to live long; cultivation of essence is the way to be birthless. With no birth there is no death; no birth, no death, united with Space, body and mind both sublimated, one is forever freed from transmigration, and transcends beyond heaven and earth. Without awaiting another body in the next life, one attains the spiritual capacities of a Buddha in the present. This is because the path of birthlessness is sudden enlightenment, completely pervading, all things empty, directly transcending to the beyond.

In ancient times when the Buddha was teaching at the assembly on the Spiritual Mountain, a seven-year-old Naga girl emerged from the earth, presented a jewel, and attained buddhahood on the spot. The author here cites this case of the Naga girl presenting a jewel to demonstrate cultivation of the essence of true emptiness. Cultivating the essence of true emptiness is the Naga girl presenting a jewel and realizing true emptiness, unborn and imperishable; this is attaining the spiritual capacities of a Buddha.

But before the principle of life has been practiced, the principle of essence is hard to comprehend. On the whole, if one can suddenly awaken to complete pervasion and can nurture the true essence, one still has not escaped coming and going within temporal conditioning; without having gone through the tempering of the great fire, as soon as there is any leak one can hardly avoid the trouble of reincarnation. If one cultivates essence after having cultivated life, one has already come forth from refinement in the furnace of the great fire, so that all pollution has been burnt away; proceeding from here to cultivate essence by practicing the path of nonstriving, going from gradual to sudden, one directly ascends to the stage of ineffable enlightenment of the supreme one vehicle. How can one be reincarnated then? This is why the text says one gains the spiritual capacities of a Buddha in the present, without awaiting another body in the next life. So we know the great path of the gold elixir first cultivates life before cultivating essence.

V

Five verses,
representing the five elements,
metal, wood, water, fire, earth

1

EVEN IF YOU UNDERSTAND THE ESSENCE OF TRUE THUS-
NESS, YOU STILL HAVE NOT ESCAPED REINCARNATION; IT IS
BETTER TO INCLUDE CULTIVATION OF THE GREAT MEDICINE,
IMMEDIATELY TRANSCEND TO NONLEAKING, AND BE A REAL
HUMAN.

The essence of true thusness is naturally real being as is—there is no
effort involved at all. It is not material, not void. It is what is called
unconsciously following the laws of God. If you want to cultivate this
essence, you must understand this essence; once you have understood this
essence, you must take this essence and refine it into something indestructible—only thus can you attain salvation. If in spite of having understood it you do not know how to cultivate and refine it, your life does not
depend on yourself and still depends on fate—when your time is up, you
have no support, and cannot escape death and reincarnation.

Not giving up the work of gradual cultivation after sudden enlightenment, using the yang fire and yin convergence to cook and refine the great
medicine, you dissolve aggregated conditioning, shed that which withers,
and bring forth the real body. Then you can go into water without drown-
ing, go into fire without getting burned; tigers and rhinos cannot injure
you, weapons cannot harm you. Then you are a nonleaking real human.

In ancient times, after the sixth patriarch of Ch'an Buddhism had gotten the transmission of the fifth patriarch, he hid among hunters, min-
gling with ordinary folk, integrating his illumination, thus perfecting
true attainment. Tzu-hsien realized complete pervasion suddenly, but he
knew in himself it wasn't the ultimate, and he needed the transmission of
Hsing-lin to attain the great achievement. People usually think it is just a
matter of cultivating the great medicine, or that if one realizes true thusness this itself is enlightenment. Then what did the fifth patriarch trans-
mit to the sixth patriarch, since the latter had already realized "there is
originally not a single thing"? And why did Tzu-hsien seek out Hsing-lin
after having suddenly realized complete pervasion?

So we know that all-at-once understanding and gradual cultivation are
both necessary. It may happen that one suddenly understands first and
then gradually practices, or one may first gradually cultivate and then
suddenly understand. Essence and life must both be cultivated; the work
requires two stages. This verse speaks of reaching life by way of essence,
practicing the gradual from the sudden.

2

ENTERING THE WOMB, USURPING THE HOUSE, MOVING THE ABODE, LIVING IN AN OLD RESIDENCE—THESE ARE CALLED FOLLOWERS OF THE FOUR FRUITS. IF YOU KNOW HOW TO CONQUER THE DRAGON AND SUBDUE THE TIGER, REAL GOLD WILL MAKE A DWELLING THAT WILL NEVER DECAY.

"Entering the womb" means first spotting a rich and noble family with a pregnant wife in her last month, so as to enter her womb. As for "usurping the house," when a pregnant woman is near delivery, there will always be a yin-soul waiting to enter an opening; to enter first, before the other does, is called usurping the house. "Moving the abode" means when the body declines and fails, to pick a vigorous living body and surreptitiously move into it. "Living in an old residence" means when a vigorous healthy person dies by violence, to borrow the still warm corpse, enter an opening, and live in this "old residence."

"Entering the womb" and "usurping the house" are more or less the same, "moving the abode" and "living in an old residence" are also more or less the same. All four refer to cultivating the yin spirit to be able to go in and out. Self-serving Buddhists are called followers of the four fruits; they are also called heretics. Derivatives of the teachings of the two lesser vehicles, they are not the supreme vehicle of Buddhism, which is realization of true thusness. They are only different from ordinary people in that transmigration is clear to them.

As for the great path of the gold elixir, this involves conquering the dragon of true essence in the eastern house, and subduing the tiger of true sense in the western house, returning sense to essence, nurturing sense by essence, so that sense and essence harmonize, dragon and tiger meet, producing the spiritual body, like building a house of real gold, which lasts as long as heaven and earth, never to decay. Then there is no transmigration.

3

THE METHODS OF MIRROR-GAZING, IMPRISONING BREATH, AND CONTEMPLATING THE SPIRIT ARE HARD FOR BEGINNERS, BUT LATER BECOME EASY. EVEN IF ONE CAN SUD-

DENLY ROAM MYRIAD LANDS, NEVERTHELESS WHEN THE
HOUSE GETS OLD ONE CHANGES THE ABODE.

Mirror gazing is done by hanging a mirror on the wall and keeping the
spirit in it; after a long time at this, the yin spirit comes out. Imprisoning
the breath starts by not letting out one breath, two breaths, then ten
breaths, a hundred breaths, gradually reaching the point where one never
lets out the breath-energy, which then circulates internally by itself. Contemplating the spirit may be done by silently paying court to the supreme
God, or climbing up into the clouds to discover the sages, or imagining
the spirit emerging from the top of the head, or imagining the spirit
going out from the "hall of brightness," an inch behind the middle of
the brows. There are very many such practices; for beginners they are
hard, but later the going is easy. After many years they enable one to
project the yin-spirit. But it is only solitary yin: when the physical constitution deteriorates, it leaves this body and enters another—what benefit
is this for essence and life?

4

BUDDHISTS TEACH PEOPLE TO CULTIVATE ULTIMATE BLISS:
JUST FOCUSING ON ULTIMATE BLISS IS THE DIRECTION OF
METAL. OF ALL MATTER AND FORM, ONLY THIS IS REAL; ANY
OTHER IS UNREAL AND VAIN TO ASSAY.

Ultimate Bliss is (the pure land) in the west; the west is the direction of
metal, which in people is the firm sense of real knowledge. This sense is
stable, uncompromising, perfectly pure, and cannot be moved by anything. It is like the hardness of metal, which never breaks down. Cultivating Ultimate Bliss is cultivating this true metal of real knowledge. When
the true metal is forged to perfection, it has both firmness and flexibility;
freed from all pollutants, it shines brightly and becomes a supreme treasure. In ancient times Dipankara cultivated this and made a clear jewel
tower; Shakyamuni cultivated this and made a sixteen-foot-tall gold
body. Of all matter and form, the only thing that is real is cultivating this
firm, strong sense of real knowledge; anything else is unreal, not worth
considering.

5

ORDINARY EXPRESSIONS AND COMMON SAYINGS ACCORD
WITH THE PATH OF SAGES; YOU SHOULD TURN TO THEM FOR
CAREFUL RESEARCH. IF YOU USE EVERYDAY ACTIVITIES TO
SEARCH IN REVERSE, EVERYTHING IN THE WORLD TURNS TO
JEWELS.

The Tao is not far from people; what people consider the Tao is far from
people. The Tao of essence and life is the eternal Tao, the eternal Tao is
the Tao of daily life; it's just that while people use it daily they do not
know it.

If you want to cultivate essence and life, you should thoroughly investigate the principles of the eternal Tao. If you can carefully investigate the
principles, you do not need to read a thousand classics and ten thousand
texts; there are great revelations of the celestial mechanism right in ordinary expressions and common sayings. For example, good people are
called really genuine, truthful, conscientious, reasonable, respectable,
aware of proper proportion, aware of when to go forward and when to
withdraw, circumspect, perceptive, having their feet on the ground; bad
people are said to be inhuman, lacking conscience, and unreasonable—
they hurt others to benefit themselves, are self-deceived, violate nature
and reason, take suffering for pleasure, take the false for the real, pick up
one thing and forget another, without knowing death and life, without
knowing good and bad, only knowing one and not two, only aware of the
existence of themselves and not that of others.

Expressions like these are meaningless when said, but flavorful when
reflected on. Why not pick out one or two of these common sayings and
bore into them; in your ordinary activities, seeking against the tide,
everything in the world is a jewel, everywhere is the Tao, everything is
useful in this.

Ordinary scholars say the Tao cannot be spoken, so they will not make
real efforts to examine the principles of essence and life. Also, they cannot humble themselves to ask help from teachers and friends; or if they
do ask for help, they still do not truly recognize reality, and speak of
searching for the treasure from nothing at all. Those who act like this will
never accomplish anything even if they leave home and spend their lives
traveling all over the world.

The Outer Collection

The outer collection of *Understanding Reality* is based
on essence. After the author wrote *Understanding Reality*,
he still feared that the essence of true awareness, which is the
original source, might not yet be fully explored, so he wrote
more poems and sayings and appended them as material for
the path of twin cultivation of essence and life.

I. Four four-line verses

1

THE SUBTLE BODY OF BUDDHA IS OMNIPRESENT; MYRIAD PHENOMENA PRESENT NO OBSTACLE. IF YOU UNDERSTAND THE TRUE REALITY-EYE WHICH IS COMPLETELY PERVASIVE, THEN YOU WILL KNOW THE TRIPLE WORLD IS YOUR HOUSE.

The Buddha is the essence of true emptiness which comes from nowhere and goes nowhere. True emptiness is not empty; so its body is most subtle. The essence of true emptiness basically has no body, but because it includes subtle existence, that subtlety is its body. Emptiness without this subtlety is nihilistic, indifferent emptiness; it is not the real essence of Buddha. How can it be omnipresent, how can myriad phenomena present no obstacle? Because of its subtle nonvoidness, the body is omnipresent, all-pervasive; because it is empty yet real, myriad phenomena cannot obstruct it. Because it is omnipresent and unobstructed, it is also called the completely pervasive reality eye. Completeness means there is no head or tail, no back or front, no before or after, no above or below, no inside or outside—this is realization of suchness. Pervasion means being present in all places, manifest in all times. It is so great it fills the universe, so fine it enters a hair; this is the subtle body. Only completeness can be pervasive, only by pervasion is it complete. The light shines clear and bright, invulnerable to all situations; therefore it is called the reality eye. This is why it is called the treasury of the eye of truth. To understand this completely pervasive reality eye is to actually perceive the subtle body of Buddha, which is neither material nor void, yet is both matter and emptiness. Heaven and hell both swept away, the triple world is one house, the ten directions are the whole body.

2

LOOKING AT IT, YOU CANNOT SEE ITS FORM; BUT WHEN YOU CALL, IT RESPONDS. DO NOT SAY THIS SOUND IS LIKE A VALLEY ECHO; IF THERE IS NO VALLEY, WHAT SOUND IS THERE?

"Looking at it, you cannot see its form" refers to emptiness; "call, and it responds" refers to existence. Because of emptiness there is existence, like an echo in a valley. Emptiness is not empty—such is the subtle body of Buddha. But the subtle body of Buddha is always empty, always existent, always existent, always empty—what need is there to call before there is response? Response to a call means there is still "emptiness," still "existence"—still constrained by emptiness, emptiness which is not pervasive does not equal the subtle body of Buddha. It is better to take this "empty" thing and smash it. Emptiness does not empty anything—where does the sound come from? Since there is no sound, there is naturally no emptiness. No emptiness, no sound, this is great liberation, which is fully alive. This is what is meant by the saying, "The man unmoving atop the hundred foot pole may have gained initiation, but it is not yet real: step forward from the hundred foot pole, and the universe is the whole body."

3

ONE THING CONTAINS SEEING, HEARING, PERCEPTION, AND COGNITION: THE SENSE OBJECTS REVEAL ITS WORKING. EVEN THE ONE THING EVER AWARE IS NOT EXISTENT; WHAT COULD THE FOUR BE BASED ON?

Seeing, hearing, perception, cognition—these four are all produced by one thing, the luminous aware discriminating mind. Since that one thing is ever aware, in the midst of sense data the four associate and activate one another, without a moment's rest. If one can eliminate the one thing which is ever aware, the four have no basis to rely on, and naturally vanish.

Deluded people cannot perceive the basic nature of enlightenment, which is truly empty yet subtly existent; they just take the luminous aware discriminating mind as real. They may empty this thing, or guard this thing, still not knowing this thing is the root of repeated birth and death, the seed of perpetual transmigration. If you don't root this out, how can you perceive the basic nature of enlightenment? This is what is meant by the saying, "The root of eons of birth and death, fools call the original Man."

4

REACHING INDIA WITHOUT MOVING A STEP, SITTING
STRAIGHT, ALL PLACES ARE PRESENT BEFORE THE EYES. A
HALO BEHIND THE HEAD IS STILL A PHANTOM; EVEN WHEN
CLOUDS RISE BENEATH YOUR FEET YOU ARE STILL NOT AN
IMMORTAL.

The fundamental nature of enlightenment has no head or tail, no back
or front; when you go toward it you do not see its head, when you follow
it you do not see its back. If you say it exists, yet it seems not to; if you say
it does not exist, yet it does. Not falling within descriptions in terms of
existence or nonexistence, its light penetrates the hidden and reaches the
revealed, able to illumine the universe. This is spontaneous ineffable
awareness. Basically it is not produced by sitting; all those who study
Ch'an and practice sitting, those who just play with the discriminating
consciousness, think they have actually attained buddhahood when they
see illusory scenes and unreal images, or dream they travel to India, or
produce lights from their heads, or see things in trance, or walk in the
clouds in ecstasy. They are far off. Those who aspire to the Tao should first
sweep away all sidetracks and aberrated paths, then seek out the true ineffable awareness where there is no form or appearance. Only then can the
fundamental nature be realized.

II. Verses on various themes

On the essential ground

THE ESSENCE OF BUDDHAHOOD IS NOT THE SAME OR
   DIFFERENT: A THOUSAND LAMPS ARE TOGETHER ONE
   LIGHT—
ADDING LAMPS DOES NOT MAKE MORE LIGHTS, REMOVING
   LAMPS DOES NOT DAMAGE THE LIGHT.
NEITHER GRASPING NOR REJECTION IMPINGES ON IT,
   NEITHER FIRE NOR WATER CAN OBSTRUCT IT,
NOTHING IN PERCEPTION OR COGNITION CAN ASSESS IT.

The verse uses the term "essential ground" because the body of true essence is unmoving like the ground; be there sameness or difference, though circumstances and events be manifold and various, dealing with them all with an equanimous mind is like the shining of a thousand lamps, shining on all with a single light, the lamps not one but the light one. This essence has no increase or decrease, it has nothing to grasp or reject, it cannot be obstructed by fire or water. Also, just as the ground can sustain the weight of the mountains, and can take the thrust of the rivers, and can endure the injuries of myriad things, just as the ground is like this, so too the essence is like this. Perception and cognition have no existence in it; if we force a name on it, it is just emptiness. Emptiness doesn't mean extinction, but flexible adaptivity applied without minding.

On birth and death

WHEN YOU SEEK LIFE, THERE IS FUNDAMENTALLY NO BIRTH;
IF YOU FEAR DEATH, WHEN HAS THERE EVER BEEN
   EXTINCTION?
SEEING WITH THE EYES IS NOT AS GOOD AS SEEING WITH
   THE EARS;
HOW CAN TALKING WITH THE MOUTH COMPARE TO
   TALKING WITH THE NOSE?

162

The essence of enlightenment fundamentally has no birth or death; as for those who insist on life and fear death, when has there ever been life without death? When there is birth, there is death; only the birthless is deathless. Because that essence is birthless and deathless, it cannot be seen with the eyes, it can only be seen by the ears; it cannot be spoken of by the mouth, it can only be spoken of by the nose. What can be seen by the eyes and spoken of by the mouth is the nature which has birth and death; what is seen by the ears and spoken of by the nose is the nature which has no birth or death. Whatever can be seen by the eyes and spoken of by the mouth is not essence; what can be seen by the ears and spoken of by the nose, that is essence. Nonseeing seeing—that is true seeing; nonspoken speech is better than that which is spoken. Since this birthless deathless essence has no head or tail and no back or front, is neither existent nor nonexistent, is neither void nor material, what is there to see or tell? If you can see it or verbalize it, it is not the essence of true emptiness.

The three realms are only mind

THE SUBTLE PRINCIPLE OF THE THREE REALMS AS ONLY
   MIND:
MYRIAD THINGS ARE NOT THIS, NOT THAT;
THERE IS NOT A THING THAT IS NOT MY MIND,
THERE IS NOT A THING THAT IS MY SELF.

The three realms are the realm of form, the realm of desire, and the realm of no form. The realms of form and desire are realms of minding, the realm of no form is the realm of mindlessness. Neither minding nor mindlessness is the essence of buddhahood. The title of the verse says the three realms are only mind, but what is to be called the true mind is the unminding mind which is neither existent nor nonexistent, in which neither being nor nonbeing stands, and things and self are all ultimately empty. In the mind of the true mind, myriad things are one body, without division into "this" and "that." "There is nothing that is not my mind" refers to not clinging to voidness; "there is nothing that is my self" refers to not sticking to forms. Not clinging to voidness, not sticking to forms, there is just one mind; one mind is one essence, mind is Buddha and Buddha is mind.

Seeing mind in things

SEEING THINGS, YOU SEE THE MIND; WITHOUT THINGS,
MIND DOES NOT APPEAR.
IN THE TEN DIRECTIONS, OPEN OR BLOCKED, THE TRUE
MIND IS OMNIPRESENT.
IF YOU CONCEIVE INTELLECTUAL INTERPRETATION, IT TURNS
INTO A FALSE VIEW.
IF YOU CAN SEE OBJECTS WITHOUT MINDING, THEN YOU
WILL SEE THE FACE OF ENLIGHTENMENT.

"Seeing things, you see the mind; without things, mind does not
appear" refers to the human mind with perception and cognition. "In
the ten directions, open or blocked, the true mind is omnipresent" refers
to the true mind without perception or cognition. The human mind
arises and vanishes according to the presence or absence of things; the
spiritual light of the true mind is always bright, the same whether there
are things or not—everywhere is it. It neither arises nor vanishes, and cannot be assessed by the human mind with its limited faculties of perception and cognition; if you try to understand the true mind by the intellect, you are recognizing a thief as your child—a false view and a serious
error.

The true mind is round and bright, naked and free, not divorced from
objects yet not attached to objects. If people can see objects without
minding, this is the true mind, this is the original face of enlightenment
—there is no need to seek the original face of enlightenment anywhere
else. In sum, when there is no human mind, only then can you see the
true mind. Once the true mind is seen, you immediately realize enlightenment and suddenly transcend to the beyond.

Equalizing beings

I AM NOT DIFFERENT FROM OTHER PEOPLE; PEOPLE'S MINDS
ARE THEMSELVES DIFFERENT.
FOR PEOPLE THERE ARE FRIENDS AND STRANGERS; FOR ME,
NO "THAT" OR "THIS."
CREATURES OF WATER, LAND, AND AIR, I VIEW EQUALLY AS
ONE BODY;

WHETHER PEOPLE ARE HIGH OR LOW IN RANK, THEIR
    HANDS AND FEET ARE THE SAME AS MINE.
I AM NOT EVEN ME; HOW COULD THERE EVEN BE YOU?
"THAT" AND "THIS" BOTH NONEXISTENT, MYRIAD BUBBLES
    RETURN TO WATER.

The title of this verse is "Equalizing beings," which means equally seeing others and self, friends and strangers, fish, animals, and birds, people
in high and low ranks, as one body alone. The important point of this
verse is in the line "I am not even me." The reason people of the world
cannot see beings as equal is because they are egotistic. If one can be self-
less, how can one know there is a second person? With "you" and "me"
both forgotten, myriad beings all empty, they are equal of themselves
without being equalized.

Mind itself is Buddha

BUDDHA IS MIND, MIND IS BUDDHA: "MIND" AND
    "BUDDHA" ARE BASICALLY ILLUSIONS.
IF YOU KNOW THERE IS NO BUDDHA AND NO MIND, THIS AT
    LAST IS THE REAL BUDDHA OF TRUE SUCHNESS.
THE REAL BUDDHA HAS NO LIKENESS; A SINGLE ROUND
    LIGHT ENGULFS MYRIAD FORMS.
THE BODYLESS BODY IS THE REAL BODY; THE FORMLESS
    FORM IS THE TRUE FORM.
NOT MATERIAL, NOT VOID, NOT NONVOID, NOT MOVING,
    NOT STILL, IT DOES NOT COME OR GO.
NO DIFFERENCES, NO SAMENESS, NO BEING OR NONBEING,
    IT CANNOT BE GRASPED OR ABANDONED, CANNOT BE
    LISTENED TO OR LOOKED AT.
INSIDE AND OUTSIDE ROUND AND BRIGHT, IT PERVADES
    EVERYWHERE:
ONE BUDDHA-LAND IS IN A GRAIN OF SAND, ONE GRAIN OF
    SAND CONTAINS A UNIVERSE;
ONE BODY AND MIND, TEN THOUSAND ARE THE SAME.
    KNOWING THIS, YOU SHOULD UNDERSTAND THE
    PRINCIPLE OF UNMINDING:

NOT BEING CONDITIONED OR OBSESSED IS PURE WORK, NOT
   DOING ANYTHING, GOOD OR BAD, IS PAYING HONOR TO
   KAŚYAPA.

The important point of this verse is in the line, "Knowing this, you
should understand the principle of unminding." Unminding does not
mean ignorance; if it were ignorant unminding, it would be the same as a
wood carving or clay statue—how could it be said mind is Buddha? Generally speaking, the meaning of unminding is simply not sticking to
forms and not sticking to voidness.

The true mind has no substance or form; originally there is not a single
thing in it, so what form could it have? The light of the true mind engulfs
myriad things, all-pervasive without obstruction—how could it be void?
Not form, not void, round and bright, clean and naked, mind is Buddha,
Buddha is mind, yet neither is "mind" or "Buddha." Therefore it says
"mind is Buddha, Buddha is mind," and it also says "mind and Buddha
are basically illusions." If you perceive mind is Buddha, and also know it
is neither mind nor Buddha, the principle of unminding can avoid falling
into nihilism.

Unminding

WHAT A LAUGH MY MIND IS—LIKE A DUNCE, LIKE A
   BUMPKIN,
NOW UNMOVING, NOW EBULLIENT, CALMLY LETTING THINGS
   BE AS THEY MAY.
I DO NOT KNOW HOW TO CULTIVATE SPIRITUAL PRACTICE,
   YET DO NOT DO ANYTHING WRONG.
I HAVE NEVER HELPED OTHER PEOPLE, YET AM NOT
   SELF-SERVING EITHER.
I DO NOT KEEP ANY RULES OF DISCIPLINE, NOR DO I
   FOLLOW TABOOS.
I DO NOT KNOW RITUAL OR MUSIC, I DO NOT PRACTICE
   BENEVOLENCE AND DUTY.
WHAT PEOPLE CAN DO I DO NOT UNDERSTAND AT ALL.
WHEN HUNGRY, I EAT, WHEN THIRSTY, I DRINK,
WHEN TIRED I SLEEP, WAKING, I ACT.

WHEN IT'S HOT I DRESS LIGHTLY, WHEN COLD, I PUT ON
MORE CLOTHES.

WITHOUT THOUGHT OR RUMINATION, WHAT SORROW,
WHAT JOY?

NO REGRET, NO AMBITION, NO MEMORIES, NO IDEAS.

THE UPS AND DOWNS OF ORDINARY LIFE ARE JUST INNS ON
A JOURNEY.

A TREE IN A FOREST WHERE BIRDS MAY PERCH ALSO CAN BE
A SIMILE;

IT DOES NOT TRY TO PREVENT THEIR COMING, AND DOES
NOT TRY TO STOP THEM WHEN THEY LEAVE.

NOT AVOIDING, NOT SEEKING, NO PRAISE, NO BLAME,

I DO NOT DISLIKE UGLINESS OR ENVY BEAUTY.

I DO NOT RUN FOR A QUIET ROOM, OR RUN AWAY FROM THE
BUSTLING CITY.

I DO NOT SPEAK OF OTHERS' WRONGS OR BOAST WHEN I
AM RIGHT.

I AM NOT SOLICITOUS OF THE HIGHLY PLACED, NOR DO I
SLIGHT THE LOWLY OR THE YOUNG.

FRIEND AND ENEMY, GREAT AND SMALL, INSIDE AND
OUTSIDE,

SADNESS AND HAPPINESS, GAIN AND LOSS, HONOR OR
INSULT, DANGER OR EASE—

MY MIND DOES NOT SEE DUALISTICALLY, BUT IS
EQUANIMOUS, ALL THE SAME.

IT DOES NOT LEAD TO FORTUNE, AND DOES NOT START
CALAMITY;

SENSING, IT RESPONDS, RETURNING, IT AGAIN ARISES.

I DO NOT FEAR WEAPONS, I AM NOT SCARED OF WILD
BEASTS.

I REFER TO WHATEVER IS AT HAND WITHOUT BEING
RESTRICTED BY NAMES.

MY EYES DO NOT GO TO FORMS, SOUNDS DO NOT ENTER
MY EARS.

WHATEVER APPEARANCES THERE MAY BE ALL BELONG TO
FALSITY.

THE FORMS AND VOICES OF MEN AND WOMEN ARE NOT
    FIXED ENTITIES.
MINDLESS OF PHYSICAL APPEARANCES, I AM NOT
    INFLUENCED OR ATTACHED;
WANDERING FREELY, NOTHING CAN GET ME DOWN.
THE SPHERE OF LIGHT OF INEFFABLE AWARENESS SHINES
    THROUGHOUT, INSIDE AND OUT,
ENFOLDING THE FOUR QUARTERS, WITHOUT FAR OR NEAR.
THE LIGHT IS NOT LIGHT—IT IS LIKE THE MOON IN THE
    WATER.
SINCE YOU CANNOT GRASP IT OR THROW IT OUT, HOW CAN
    YOU COMPARE IT TO ANYTHING?
WHEN YOU UNDERSTAND THIS SUBLIME FUNCTION, YOU
    TRANSCEND TO THE BEYOND.
IF ANYONE ASKS MY RELIGION, IT IS JUST THIS.

This lengthy poem just illustrates unminding. The marvel is in
unminding, by which one can be beyond the world while in the world,
roaming freely, untrammeled by things. Not a particle of dust is to be
admitted into people's hearts, for whenever there is any dust within,
endless human mentality emerges. Once human mentality arises, one
becomes capricious and loses autonomy and independence, taking the
servant for the master and considering the master a servant. How then can
one be free? If one can be totally unminding, imperturbable and unshak-
able, then one is independent. When independent, one is autonomous.
Myriad ruminations cease, entanglements do not arise; the sphere of light
of ineffable awareness is all-pervasive and all-embracing, without distinction of far or near. This is true attainment of freedom, the sublime function of unminding.

On the Heart Scripture

THE CLUSTERS, THE TRUTHS, SENSE FACULTIES AND OBJECTS,
    VOID AND FORM—
IN NONE OF THESE IS THERE A SINGLE THING WORTH
    SAYING.
WHEN PERVERTED VIEWS ARE ENDED,
THE BODY OF TRANQUILITY IS SERENE.

The clusters are the five clusters of matter, sensation, perception, patterning, and consciousness, which form the human being. The truths are the four truths of suffering, its cause, its end, and the way to end it. The sense faculties are the six organs of eyes, ears, nose, tongue, body, and intellect. The sense objects are the six fields of form, sound, smell, taste, tactile feeling, and phenomena. Voidness is extinction, form is attachment to appearances. The clusters, truths, sense faculties and objects, void and form are all phenomena projected by the mind, and all are related to perverted views. If you can sweep all away, then the body of mind is tranquil; this is the bodhisattva Independent Seer, this is nonbirth and nondeath. If anything among these remains, then there is birth and death, so you do not attain independence. If you arrive at constant independence with no birth and death, then everything is pure.

No sin or merit

WALKING ALL DAY WITHOUT EVER WALKING, SITTING ALL
    DAY WITHOUT EVER SITTING,
DOING GOOD DOES NOT MAKE MERIT, DOING EVIL INVOLVES
    NO SIN.
IF PEOPLE TODAY HAVE NOT CLARIFIED THE MIND, DO NOT
    ACT ARBITRARILY, CLINGING TO THESE WORDS:
AFTER DYING YOU WILL SEE THE KING OF THE
    UNDERWORLD, AND HAVE TROUBLE ESCAPING BEING
    BOILED OR MASHED.

The title says there is no sin or merit—what does this mean? Sin and merit both come from the mind: mindfully doing evil is mindfully committing sin; mindfully doing good is mindfully seeking merit. Good and evil, sin and merit, all exist dependent on mind; if you reach the state of mindlessness, you are not even conscious of walking or sitting—how could you be conscious of good and evil, sin and merit? This is why it says doing good does not make merit and doing evil does not involve sin. It is like a baby, unselfconsciously and unknowingly laughing happily and crying angrily, this all proceeding from mindlessness—what merit or sin is there?

Mindlessness means there is no human mentality; when there is no human mentality, there naturally is the true mind. The extent of the true mind is the same as the universe, containing everything; not thinking of good, not thinking of evil, it does not commit sin, does not seek merit. It does not conceive of merit or sin. If people have not clarified the true mind, and just let their ignorant, intransigent mind act up, doing all sorts of mischief, and tell themselves there is nothing wrong, how can they avoid being boiled or mashed as a result after they die?

Complete pervasion

WHEN YOU HAVE SEEN TRUE EMPTINESS, EMPTINESS IS NOT
    EMPTY;
COMPLETE ILLUMINATION PERVADES EVERYWHERE.
SENSES AND OBJECTS, MIND AND PHENOMENA—THERE IS
    NO THING AT ALL;
ONLY BY SUBTLE FUNCTION CAN YOU KNOW HOW TO
    ASSIMILATE.

The essence of true emptiness is all-pervasive, unobstructed; its light illumines everywhere, nothing can get by it. It is intrinsically empty without being emptied, empty yet not empty. It is just a matter of being ever responsive yet ever tranquil, ever tranquil yet ever responsive.

Going along with it

MYRIAD THINGS, EVERY WHICH WAY, CONFRONT US;
GO ALONG WITH THEM IN ACTION AND REPOSE, LEAVE
    THEM TO THEIR DEVICES:
ROUND AND BRIGHT STABILITY AND WISDOM ARE
    ULTIMATELY NEVER DEFILED,
JUST AS WATER PRODUCES LOTUSES, YET THE LOTUS ITSELF IS
    DRY.

Though this verse has four lines, really the meaning is in the one line "Round and bright stability and wisdom are ultimately never defiled." "Round and bright" means subtle being; "stability and wisdom" means true emptiness. True emptiness is naturally in myriad things, yet is not defiled by myriad things. Subtle being naturally encounters myriad things, and can respond to myriad things. Ever responsive, ever tranquil, going along yet at peace, one is like a lotus, which grows from the mud yet is not dirtied.

The jewel moon

THE BRIGHT ORB OF THE MOON IN THE SKY; ITS CLEAR
   LIGHT IS UNOBSTRUCTED IN MYRIAD LANDS.
IT CANNOT BE GATHERED OR DISPELLED, IT CANNOT BE
   PUSHED FORWARD OR BACKWARD.
"THERE" IS NOT FAR, "HERE" IS NOT NEAR; THE EXTERIOR IS
   NOT OUTSIDE, THE INTERIOR IS NOT INSIDE.
THERE IS DIFFERENCE IN SAMENESS, SAMENESS IN
   DIFFERENCE; I ASK YOU THE MECHANISM—DO YOU
   UNDERSTAND?

The essence of enlightenment, true emptiness, is complete pervasion of ineffable awareness, its light illumining all, like the bright moon in the sky shining everywhere equally. Gather it, and you do not see the light collect; dispel it, and you do not see the light disperse. Ahead, you do not see the light go forward; behind, you do not see the light recede. As it illumines "there" it does not seem far; as it illumines "here" it does not seem near. Illumining the exterior, the light is not outside; illumining the interior, the light is not inside. Gathering, dispelling, before, behind, forward, backward, there, here, far, near, exterior, interior, inside, outside—though there is difference in the illumination, the light is the same. There is difference in sameness, sameness in difference; one root ramifies into myriad differences, myriad differences return to the one root. Release it and it fills the universe, wrap it up and it hides in secrecy. Lively and active, it is like the mechanism of a marionette.

Picking up the pearl

THE PEARL IN THE POOR ONE'S CLOTHES IS ORIGINALLY
   ROUND AND BRIGHT;
IF ONE DOES NOT KNOW HOW TO FIND IT ONESELF, ONE
   WILL COUNT OTHERS' TREASURES INSTEAD.

COUNTING OTHERS' TREASURES IS AFTER ALL OF NO BENEFIT
  —IT JUST MAKES YOU EXPEND YOUR LABOR IN VAIN:
HOW CAN IT COMPARE TO RECOGNIZING YOUR OWN JEWEL,
  WHICH IS WORTH MORE THAN BILLIONS IN GOLD?
THE SHINE OF THIS PRECIOUS PEARL IS MOST GREAT, AS IT
  LIGHTS UP ALL WORLDS IN THE UNIVERSE.
IT HAS NEVER BEEN SUBJECT TO DIMINUTION, BUT HAS BEEN
  BLOCKED BY FLOATING CLOUDS.
AFTER HAVING RECOGNIZED THIS JEWEL, WHO WOULD CARE
  FOR EPHEMERAL ILLUSIONS ANYMORE?
THE PEARL OF BUDDHA IS THE SAME AS ONE'S OWN PEARL;
  ONE'S OWN ESSENCE RETURNS TO THE OCEAN OF THE
  ESSENCE OF BUDDHAHOOD.
THE PEARL IS NOT A PEARL, THE OCEAN IS NOT AN OCEAN.
  EQUANIMOUS, THE MEASURE OF MIND EMBRACES THE
  COSMOS.
LET THE DUST AND CLAMOR FILL YOUR PURVIEW—STABILITY
  AND WISDOM, ROUND AND BRIGHT, ARE ALWAYS FREE.
THIS IS NOT VOID, THIS IS NOT MATERIAL; INSIDE AND
  OUTSIDE ARE CLEAR, WITHOUT OBSTRUCTION.
THE SIX PSYCHIC POWERS ARE SUBTLE AND INEXHAUSTIBLE,
  HELPING SELF AND OTHERS WITHOUT ANY END.
SEE AND YOU UNDERSTAND, MYRIAD TASKS ARE DONE;
  BEYOND STUDY, YOU PASS THE DAYS WITHOUT
  CONTRIVANCE.
CALM AS AN INFANT WITHOUT A SET CHARACTER, ACTIVE
  OR STILL ACCORDING TO SITUATIONS, WITHOUT
  FIXATION,
NEITHER STOPPING ILLUSION NOR CULTIVATING TRUTH, THE
  IDEAS OF TRUTH AND FALSEHOOD ARE ALL IN THE
  REALM OF DUST.
MYRIAD THINGS HAVE ALWAYS BEEN SIGNLESS; IN
  SIGNLESSNESS THERE IS THE BODY OF REALITY.
THE BODY OF REALITY IS THE NATURALLY SO BUDDHA,
  NEITHER A PERSON NOR A THING.
SO VAST AS TO FILL THE UNIVERSE, IT IS RARIFIED AND
  UNGRASPABLE.

FILTH CANNOT DEFILE IT, ITS LIGHT IS INHERENTLY BRIGHT.
  THERE IS NOTHING THAT IS NOT BORN FROM MIND;
IF MIND IS UNBORN, THINGS PASS AWAY. THEN YOU KNOW
  SIN AND MERIT ARE BASICALLY FORMLESS.
THERE IS NO BUDDHAHOOD TO CULTIVATE, NO TEACHING
  TO PREACH. THE KNOWLEDGE AND INSIGHT OF GREAT
  PEOPLE IS NATURALLY DISTINCT;
WHEN THEY SPEAK, THEY MAKE THE ROAR OF A LION,
  UNLIKE JACKALS DISCUSSING BIRTH AND DEATH.

The important point in this poem is the line "If mind is unborn, things pass away." These "things" are the various thoughts and imaginations in the mind. If the mind is unborn, all things are empty, the pearl of essence is always shining, stability and wisdom are round and bright, inside and outside are clear; ephemeral illusions are not worthy of attachment, dust and clamor may fill the eyes but cannot be a hindrance. Beyond study, uncontrived, one is like an unformed infant, active or still according to circumstances, without illusory images of truth or falsehood, the body of reality always exposed, the naturally-so Buddha is manifest. Then it fills the universe, light shining on all worlds; what veil of floating clouds is there?

Pointing out errors in meditation

THE ESSENCE OF ENLIGHTENED MEDITATION IS LIKE WATER:
  THE SUBSTANCE STILL, THE RIPPLES ROUSED BY THE
  WIND SPONTANEOUSLY STOP;
IN ACTION AND REPOSE TRANQUIL AND EVER CLEAR, IT IS
  NOT ONLY THUS WHEN SITTING.
PEOPLE NOW SIT QUIETLY TO GET REALIZATION, AND DO
  NOT SAY IT IS ALL IN SEEING ESSENCE.
IF ESSENCE IS CLEAR IN SEEING, SEEING IS STABLE IN
  ESSENCE.
STABILITY MAKES WISDOM, ITS USE WITHOUT END; THIS IS
  CALLED THE SPIRITUAL POWER OF BUDDHAS.
IF YOU WANT TO STUDY THEIR SUBSTANCE AND FUNCTION,
  JUST SEE THE SPACE OF THE TEN DIRECTIONS:

IN SPACE THERE IS NOT A SINGLE THING, AND THERE IS NO
  SUBTLETY OR TRANCE.
SINCE SUBTLETY OR TRANCE CANNOT BE FOUND, TO LOOK
  FOR THEM THROWS YOU OFF THE TRACK.
BUT DO NOT GRASP "OFF THE TRACK" AS WORDS TO RELY
  ON; THE ORIGINAL MIND IS LIKE SPACE—WHAT HAS IT
  TO DO WITH GAIN OR LOSS?
JUST CLEAR AWAY MYRIAD THINGS, CLEAR THEM AWAY
  WITHOUT REMAINDER,
AND SUDDENLY COMPLETE ILLUMINATION WILL APPEAR OF
  ITSELF, NO DIFFERENT FROM THE BUDDHAS.
THE PHYSICAL BODY IS A FETTER TO US, BUT THUS WE MIX
  WITH THE ORDINARY WORLD.
TOTALLY UNMINDING IN ACTION, WHAT RIGHT OR WRONG,
  GLORY OR IGNOMINY, IS THERE TO CONTEST OVER?
THE BODY IS JUST A LODGING; THE INNKEEPER'S NAME IS
  ILLUMINATOR.
THE ILLUMINATOR NEITHER COMES NOR GOES, SO WE KNOW
  IT HAS NO MORE BIRTH OR DEATH.
IF YOU ASK WHAT THE ILLUMINATOR IS LIKE, ANY
  DESCRIPTION IS WRONG;
EVERY ACT AND EVERY THING WE SEE IS NEITHER THE SAME
  NOR DIFFERENT.
SEEING THESE ACTS AND THINGS, EACH ONE IS BUDDHA
  AND DISCIPLE.
IN TERMS OF DIFFERENCE, MYRIAD PIPES ALL SOUND; IN
  TERMS OF SAMENESS, ONE WIND ENVELOPS ALL.
IF YOU WANT TO RECOGNIZE THE JEWEL, DO NOT SAY YOU
  WILL KNOW WHEN YOU GET THE TEACHING:
WHEN THERE IS SICKNESS, YOU USE MEDICINE TO CURE IT;
  ONCE THE SICKNESS IS CURED, WHY SHOULD MEDICINE
  BE DISPENSED ANYMORE?
WHEN THE MIND IS DELUDED, USE THE TEACHING TO
  REVEAL THIS; ONCE THE MIND IS ENLIGHTENED, THE
  TEACHING IS NO MORE NECESSARY.
IT IS ALSO LIKE A CLOUDED MIRROR GETTING POLISHED,
  THE STAINS ENCRUSTING IT DISAPPEAR.

BASICALLY BECAUSE THINGS ARE DECEPTIVE, WE ARE TOLD
TO DETACH FROM APPEARANCES.
DETACHED FROM APPEARANCES, THEN WHAT? THIS IS
CALLED ULTIMATE REALITY, UNEXCELLED.
IF YOU WANT TO ADORN A BUDDHA LAND, PRACTICE
COMPASSION IMPARTIALLY, RESCUE THE SUFFERING.
THOUGH THE FUNDAMENTAL VOW OF ENLIGHTENMENT IS
DEEP, DO NOT GRASP WITHIN FORMS.
THIS IS TWIN FULFILLMENT OF VIRTUE AND WISDOM; THE
FUTURE ASSURANCE OF ENLIGHTENMENT TAKES PLACE
BEFOREHAND.
IF ONE IS AFFECTED BY ANY TRACE OF NIHILISM OR
ETERNALISM, ONE HAS NO AFFINITY WITH THE
BUDDHAS.
THINKING BACK TO THE DELUDED CLINGING OF THE
MUNDANE, ALL ARE HABITUATED TO SENSUAL
ATTACHMENTS;
BECAUSE THEIR FEELINGS OF CRAVING ARE MANY, THEY
REMAIN BOUND TO THE WORLD.
STUDY OF THE TAO REQUIRES FIERCENESS, AN
UNSENTIMENTAL MIND FIRM AS IRON.
EVEN OUR CHILDREN AND SPOUSES ARE NOT DIFFERENT
FROM OTHER PEOPLE.
ALWAYS MAINTAIN A SINGLE ROUND LIGHT, NOT SEEING
ANY FAVOR TO BE DESIRED;
ONCE YOU HAVE NO ATTACHMENTS TO ANYTHING, WHAT
HELL OR HEAVEN IS THERE TO SPEAK OF?
AFTER THAT, OUR DESTINY IS UP TO US—THERE IS NO
ASCENSION OR FALL IN EMPTINESS.
APPEARING AND DISAPPEARING IN THE BUDDHA
LANDS, NEVER APART FROM THE SEAT OF
ENLIGHTENMENT,
KUAN-YIN HAS THIRTY-TWO ADAPTATIONS, AND WE TOO
SHOULD REALIZE FROM THIS
THAT CREATIVE MANIFESTATIONS ARE INCONCEIVABLE, ALL
COMING FROM THE ESSENCE OF FREEDOM.
I AM A MINDLESS MEDITATOR, AND DO NOT KNOW HOW TO

JUDGE ORDINARY THINGS. THE BLACK OX OF BEFORE
NOW IS ALL WHITE.
SOMETIMES I SING AND LAUGH TO MYSELF, AND
BYSTANDERS SAY I AM A HALFWIT.
HOW CAN THEY KNOW THIS WOOL CLOAKED FIGURE
ENBOSOMS A PRICELESS JEWEL WITHIN?
AND IF YOU SEE ME TALKING ABOUT EMPTINESS, IT IS LIKE
SWALLOWING A DATE WHOLE;
ONLY BUDDHAS CAN KNOW THIS TRUTH—HOW CAN THE
IGNORANT EXPRESS IT?
THERE ARE ALSO PRACTITIONERS OF CH'AN WHO ONLY
LEARN TO ARGUE
AND BOAST OF THEIR SWIFTNESS IN REPARTEE, STILL
BASICALLY IGNORANT OF THE TRUE SELF.
IT IS BECAUSE THEY PURSUE THE BRANCHES AND PICK THE
LEAVES, NOT KNOWING HOW TO FIND OUT THE ROOT.
WHEN YOU GET THE ROOT, THE BRANCHES AND LEAVES
NATURALLY FLOURISH; WITHOUT THE ROOT, BRANCHES
AND LEAVES CANNOT SURVIVE.
IF THEY GO ON FLAUNTING THE SPIRITUAL PEARL IN THEIR
GRIP, IT TURNS INTO DISCRIMINATION BETWEEN SELF
AND OTHERS, HARD TO REMOVE:
THAT IS VERY FAR AWAY FROM THE INEFFABLE AWARENESS OF
OUR SPIRITUAL SOURCE.
THESE PEOPLE ARE PITIFUL, LAUGHABLE, VAINLY TALKING OF
YEARS OF STUDY,
TOO PROUD TO ASK OF OTHERS, WASTING THEIR WHOLE
LIVES UNFULFILLED.
THIS IS THE DULLNESS OF THE IGNORANT AND DELUDED,
CAUSED BY FALSE VIEWS AND DEEP HABITS.
IF YOU DO NOT WAKE UP IN THIS LIFE, HOW CAN YOU
AVOID SINKING IN THE NEXT?

The meaning of this whole poem is in the first four lines. The essence
of enlightened nature is thoroughly pure, its clarity is like water. Not
arousing waves, not being defiled, all action and repose is it; one is not
stable only when sitting. If you take sitting to be meditation, that is not

true meditation; it is nihilistic, indifferent meditation, and cannot match the essence of enlightened meditation. True meditation includes both stability and wisdom, subtly functioning endlessly; mind and phenomena both forgotten, detached from appearances, adorning a buddha land, impartially practicing compassion, harmonizing with ordinary society, in the world yet beyond the world, meditating without meditating, stable without stabilization. All those who sit quietly for realization and those who engage in verbal competition, wild foxes ignorant of the true self, who wake up after meditation stupor only to have their wakefulness cause confusion, cannot know there is a true essence of meditation, which is the ineffable awareness of the spiritual source.

Song on reading Ch'an master Hsueh-tou's Anthology on Eminent Adepts

THE ONE WATER OF CH'AN IS DIVIDED INTO A THOUSAND STREAMS,

ILLUMINING THE PAST AND CLARIFYING THE PRESENT, WITH NO STAGNATION OR BLOCKAGE.

STUDENTS THESE DAYS DO NOT SEARCH OUT THE SOURCE: THEY MISTAKENLY POINT TO A FOOTPRINT AND CALL IT THE OCEAN.

THE TEACHER HSUEH-TOU ARRIVED AT THE TRUE IMPORT; HE BEAT THE DRUM OF TRUTH WITH A THUNDEROUS SOUND:

WHEN THE LION KING COMES OUT OF THE CAVE AND ROARS, ALL THE BEASTS AND DEVIANTS TAKE FRIGHT.

WITH SONGS, POEMS, AND SAYINGS, HE CAREFULLY GUIDES PEOPLE WHO ARE LOST.

HIS MANNER OF EXPRESSION IS FREE, HIS MEANINGS ARE LOFTY AND PROFOUND; HIS STRIKINGLY MUSICAL NOTES ECHO OVER THE AGES.

NEVERTHELESS THE DELUDED STOP AT CHASING OBJECTS AND CONSIDER ONLY THE LITERARY STYLE.

THE TRUE CHARACTER OF REAL SUCHNESS BASICALLY HAS NO WORD—NO LOW, NO HIGH, IT HAS NO BOUNDS;

NOT FORM, NOT VOID, NOT DUAL IN SUBSTANCE, THE

COUNTLESS LANDS IN THE TEN DIRECTIONS ARE ITS
SINGLE ORB.

WHEN HAS TRUE STABILITY EVER DIVIDED SPEECH AND
SILENCE—IT CANNOT BE GRASPED, CANNOT BE
ABANDONED.

JUST DO NOT KEEP THE MIND ON APPEARANCES; THIS IS
THE TRUE GUIDELINE OF THE BUDDHA.

TO CLEAR AWAY FALSE IDEAS, HE COUNTERPOSED THE TRUE;
IF FALSEHOOD DOES NOT ARISE, "TRUTH" IS INVISIBLE
TOO.

IF YOU CAN KNOW TRUTH AND FALSEHOOD ARE BOTH NOT
SO, THEN YOU WILL ATTAIN REAL MIND WITHOUT
OBSTRUCTION.

WITH NO OBSTRUCTION, YOU CAN BE FREE; ONE
ENLIGHTENMENT ABRUPTLY DISSOLVES THE EVILS OF THE
AGES.

WITHOUT EXERTING EFFORT, YOU REALIZE ENLIGHTENMENT
AND HENCEFORTH ARE FOREVER REMOVED FROM THE
OCEAN OF BIRTH AND DEATH.

OUR TEACHER IS NEAR AND HIS WORDS ARE UPLIFTING, LEFT
IN THE WORLD AS A MODEL AND GUIDE.

LAST NIGHT HE WAS CALLED FORTH BY ME, GRABBED BY
THE NOSE AND STUCK ON A STAFF:

I ASKED HIM ABOUT THE ULTIMATE MEANING, AND HE SAID
ALL WORDS DENY IT.

Though this song is a eulogy of the book *Anthology on Eminent
Adepts,* in reality it is communicating characteristics of real suchness.
Where it says, "Just don't keep the mind on appearances; this is the true
guideline of the Buddha," these two phrases have already summed up the
great meaning in the anthology. Not fixing the mind on appearances is
unminding; when unminding, "true" and "false" do not arise. When
true and false do not arise, there is no obstruction; when there is no
obstruction, one attains freedom. When one attains freedom, reality is
everpresent, and one is forever removed from the ocean of birth and
death.

The line "Last night he was called forth by me, grabbed by the nose
and stuck on a staff" indicates the author's intent outside words. Stu-

dents are to think, in calling forth, what is called; and what does sticking the nose refer to? Calling forth means calling the essence of the true character of real suchness; piercing the nose means penetrating the mind which is neither form nor void. Understanding this essence, knowing this mind, the staff is in one's hands, supporting the heavens above and the earth below. No back, no front, round and bright, clean and bare, naked and free, this is the ultimate meaning of Ch'an—what more is there to say?

Interpretation of discipline, concentration, and wisdom

DISCIPLINE, CONCENTRATION, AND WISDOM ARE SUBTLE
   FUNCTIONS IN RELIGION;
THOUGH THE BUDDHAS AND CH'AN ADEPTS HAVE SPOKEN
   OF THEM, THOSE WHO DO NOT AS YET COMPREHEND
   THEM HAVE FIXATIONS:
SO NOW I WILL BRIEFLY TALK ABOUT THEM, TO HELP PEOPLE
   AWAKEN.
WHEN MIND AND OBJECTS ARE BOTH FORGOTTEN AND NOT
   A SINGLE THOUGHT STIRS, THIS IS CALLED DISCIPLINE.
AWARENESS BEING ROUND AND BRIGHT, THOROUGHLY
   CLEAR INSIDE AND OUT, IS CALLED CONCENTRATION.
DEALING WITH THINGS ACCORDING TO CIRCUMSTANCES,
   SUBTLE FUNCTION INEXHAUSTIBLE, IS CALLED WISDOM.
THESE THREE REQUIRE EACH OTHER TO DEVELOP, AND ACT
   AS SUBSTANCE AND FUNCTION TO ONE ANOTHER.
THE THREE HAVE NEVER BEEN SEPARATED: IT IS LIKE THE
   SUN BEING ABLE TO SHINE BY LIGHT, LIGHT BEING ABLE
   TO ILLUMINE BY SHINING—
IF NOT FOR LIGHT, THE SUN CANNOT SHINE, IF NOT FOR
   SHINING THE LIGHT CANNOT ILLUMINE.
WHEN WE LOOK INTO THE SOURCE OF DISCIPLINE,
   CONCENTRATION, AND WISDOM, THEY ARE BASED ON
   ONE ESSENCE;
LIGHT, SHINING, AND ILLUMINATION ARE BASED ON ONE
   SUN.

SINCE THE ONE IS NOT EVEN ONE, HOW COULD THE THREE
   BE THREE?
THREE AND ONE BOTH FORGOTTEN, THERE IS PROFOUNDLY
   CALM PURITY.

In this interpretation, the author has already entered absorption in discipline, concentration, and wisdom; the words are simple, the meaning
clear. If students can put this into practice, they can directly ascend to the
goal. However, though the author's words and meaning are clear, it may
be that students are not very perceptive or may lack the necessary power,
and be unable to proceed to understanding the fundamental, so I will
add some footnotes, to guide people on behalf of the author, enabling
them to enter from the shallows to the depths, and rise from lowliness to
the heights. I hope this will be possible.
   Discipline means to forget emotions when confronting experiences,
and not to be affected by objects. Concentration means utter sincerity
and truthfulness, without vagary, not moving or shifting. Wisdom means
adapting efficiently according to events, without partiality or bias. To be
disciplined, to be concentrated, to be wise, the three require one another.
Going from effort to end up in spontaneity, they merge into one essence,
ultimately leading to the state of nonconscious purity.
   In reality, when you arrive at purity, even one essence is not it—how
could there be three things, discipline, concentration, and wisdom?
Therefore it says, "Three and one both forgotten, there is profoundly
calm purity." Before arriving at purity, the three are necessary; having
arrived at purity, the three merge and sublimate spontaneously. If the
three and one are not forgotten, it still is not pure meditation. One of the
verses says, "When the mind is astray, the Teaching must be used to
reveal it; when the mind is enlightened, the Teaching is no longer necessary." It is so that mind and teaching both be forgotten that we are told to
detach from all appearances. This seems to be the meaning of "Three and
one both forgotten, there is profoundly calm purity."

The moon on the West River
—twelve verses

1

ERRANT THOUGHT IS NOT TO BE FORCIBLY ANNIHILATED;
  WHY SHOULD TRUE SUCHNESS BE SOUGHT?
BUDDHAS EQUALLY ACT ON THE FUNDAMENTAL ESSENCE;
  DELUSION AND ENLIGHTENMENT ARE NOT CONFINED TO
  BEFORE AND AFTER.
WHEN ENLIGHTENED, YOU BECOME A BUDDHA INSTANTLY;
  WHEN DELUDED, YOU SINK IN THE FLOW FOR MYRIAD
  EONS.
IF YOU CAN ACCORD WITH TRUE PRACTICE FOR A MOMENT,
  YOU ANNIHILATE THE DEFILEMENT OF COUNTLESS
  WRONGS.

The fundamental essence is the essence of enlightenment, in which
there is no errant thought, and no true suchness. It is only because people
of the world have delusion and enlightenment that there are the terms
"errant thought" and "true suchness." When you are deluded about
essence, you conceive erroneous thoughts; when you realize essence, you
return to true suchness. When you awaken to suchness, you instantly
become a Buddha; when you conceive errant thoughts, you sink in their
flow for eons. Errant thought or true suchness—it is simply a matter of
the difference between delusion and enlightenment. If you try to forcibly
annihilate errant thought and seek true suchness without enlightenment,
how can you get to see true suchness? The concluding line says, "If you
can accord with true practice for a moment, you annihilate the defilement of countless wrongs." Then you can be perfectly clear.

2

FUNDAMENTALLY THERE IS NO ORIGINATION OR
  EXTINCTION, YET WE INSIST ON SEEKING DIVISIONS
  MARKING BIRTH AND DEATH.

AS FOR SIN AND MERIT, THESE TOO ARE BASELESS; WHEN
    HAS THE SUBTLE BODY EVER INCREASED OR DECREASED?
I HAVE A ROUND CLEAR MIRROR, WHICH HAS HITHERTO
    ALWAYS BEEN COVERED;
TODAY I POLISH IT SO IT REFLECTS THE UNIVERSE, AND
    MYRIAD IMAGES ARE CLEARLY REVEALED.

The fundamental essence of enlightenment, true suchness, has no origination or extinction; there is no possibility of increasing or decreasing it.
It is because of attachment to objects that there is origination and extinction, birth and death. This is just like a mirror being covered, that is all.
If you can polish away the accumulated dust of past influences, it is round
and bright, without defect. Using this to reflect the universe, myriad
forms are clearly revealed. What producing or destroying them is there?

3

THE ESSENCE OF THE SELF ENTERS THE ESSENCE OF THE
    BUDDHAS; THE ESSENCE OF BUDDHAHOOD IS
    EVERYWHERE THUS.
FROM ON HIGH THE COLD LIGHT SHINES IN THE COLD
    SPRINGS; ONE MOON APPEARS IN A THOUSAND PONDS.
ITS SMALLNESS IS SMALLER THAN A HAIR, ITS GREATNESS
    FILLS THE UNIVERSE;
HIGH AND LOW DO NOT RESTRICT IT, IT MAY BE SQUARE OR
    ROUND; WHAT LONG OR SHORT, DEEP OR SHALLOW CAN
    YOU SAY IT HAS?

The essence of the self, the essence of buddhahood, the essence of
human beings in all nations and lands are all the same, not more in sages,
not less in ordinary beings. It is like the single disc of the bright moon
appearing in a thousand ponds. This essence can be small, can be great,
can be high, can be low, can be square, can be round, can be shallow, can
be deep, can be long, can be short—yet it is not confined to small or
great, square or round, high or low, shallow or deep. It is just that ordinary people use it every day but do not know it.

4

THE PRINCIPLE GOVERNING THE TEACHING
FUNDAMENTALLY HAS NO DOCTRINE; THE EMPTINESS
THAT EMPTIES EMPTINESS ALSO IS NOT EMPTY.
QUIET AND CLAMOR, SPEECH AND SILENCE, ARE ORIGINALLY
THE SAME—WHY BOTHER TO TALK OF A DREAM IN A
DREAM?
THERE IS NO FUNCTION IN THE FUNCTION THAT HAS
FUNCTION; EFFORT IS APPLIED IN THE EFFORTLESS
EFFORT.
IT IS LIKE THE FRUIT NATURALLY REDDENING AS IT RIPENS
—DO NOT ASK HOW TO CULTIVATE THE SEED.

The Buddhas' expositions of doctrine really have no dogma; when a
Buddha speaks of emptiness, it is really not empty. The doctrineless doctrine is called true teaching; nonempty emptiness is called true emptiness. True teaching, true emptiness, quiet or clamor, speech or silence—it
is just a matter of unconsciously following the laws of God; what doctrine
is there to preach, what emptiness is there to expound? To insist on
preaching doctrine and expounding emptiness is like talking of a dream
in a dream—how can you know the essence of true teaching, true emptiness? Tranquil and unperturbed, yet sensitive and effective, sensitive and
effective yet tranquil and unperturbed, this is "no function within function having function, applying effort within effortless effort." That there
is "no function within function having function" means that the teaching is based on emptiness; that one "applies effort within effortless
effort" means that there is teaching within emptiness. The teaching basically empty, emptiness having a teaching, it is neither true nor false, not
existent nor nonexistent. Round and bright, unobscured, after a long
time there is spontaneous release, just as fruit naturally ripens on a tree.
This itself is cultivating the true seed of the essence of enlightenment—
there is no more need to ask how to cultivate the seed.

5

GOOD OR BAD—FORGET THOUGHTS ALL AT ONCE; LET
NEITHER PROSPERITY NOR DECLINE CONCERN THE MIND.

IN DARK AND LIGHT, NOW CONCEALED, NOW REVEALED,
  FLOAT OR SINK AS YOU MAY; ACCORDING TO YOUR LOT,
  EAT WHEN HUNGRY, DRINK WHEN THIRSTY.
SPIRIT CALM, SERENE, EVER TRANQUIL, ONE MAY SIT OR
  RECLINE, SING OR HUM.
THE AUTUMN WATER IN ONE POND IS BLUE AND DEEP;
  WHEN THE WIND BLOWS, DO NOT BE STARTLED, LET IT
  BE AS IT IS.

The overall meaning of this poem is in the lines "Spirit calm, serene, ever tranquil, one may sit or recline, sing or hum." Once the spirit is calm, good and bad, prosperity and decline, dark and light, obscurity and prominence, floating and sinking, do not enter the mind; passing the days according to circumstances, you sit and recline, sing and hum, untrammeled, free, without thought or worry, like the autumn water in a pond, blue and deep, without waves even when there is wind—what fear is there of vexation or upset?

6

NO NEED TO TRY TO ANNIHILATE OBJECTS; ENLIGHTENMENT
  IS AN ARTIFICIAL DEFINITION.
MATTER AND VOIDNESS, LIGHT AND DARK, ARE BASICALLY
  EQUAL; STOP DIVIDING REALITY AND FALSEHOOD INTO
  TWO.
WHEN YOU UNDERSTAND, IT IS CALLED THE PURE LAND
  —THERE IS NO MORE INDIA OR TS'AO CH'I.
WHO SAYS PARADISE IS THE WESTERN HEAVEN? WHEN YOU
  UNDERSTAND, AMITABHA APPEARS IN THE WORLD.

The essence of enlightenment is originally round and bright, clean and naked, bare and untrammeled, not matter, not void, not light, not dark, not real, not false. Those who understand this attain buddhahood on the spot—what's the need to try to extinguish feelings about objects? It is because so many people do not understand, that the Buddhas and bodhisattvas provisionally defined enlightenment, to get people to return to the immediate by way of the gradual, so as to realize buddhahood.

Enlightenment means the true way, in that by returning from error to truth there is a gradual awakening.

7

OTHERS, SELF, BEINGS, LIVES; HOW CAN WE DIVIDE THAT
    AND THIS, HIGH AND LOW?
REALITY SPONTANEOUSLY SHINES THROUGHOUT, WITH NO
    "I" OR "THEY"—ONE NEED NOT SEEK IT THOUGHT
    AFTER THOUGHT.
HAS SEEING WHAT IS RIGHT EVER BEEN SEEING WHAT IS
    RIGHT? HEARING WHAT IS WRONG IS NOT NECESSARILY
    HEARING WHAT IS WRONG.
VARIOUS FUNCTIONS HAVE NEVER CONTROLLED EACH OTHER
    —IN LIFE AND DEATH, WHO CAN HINDER YOU?

Others, self, beings, lives, that, this, high, low, I, they, seeing, hearing, right, wrong—these are all artificial characterizations. If you can penetrate them all with shining awareness and see through them completely, not being concerned with them, then life is as is, death is as is, life is all right, death is all right too; life and death present no obstacle, and you naturally understand life and death.

8

IF YOU CULTIVATE PRACTICES AND CHARITY WHILE
    DWELLING ON APPEARANCES, THE RESULTING REWARDS
    WILL BE LIMITED TO CELESTIAL AND HUMAN SPHERES.
IT IS LIKE SHOOTING AN ARROW UP AT THE CLOUDS; IT WILL
    FALL, SIMPLY BECAUSE THE FORCE COMES TO AN END.
HOW CAN THAT COMPARE TO UNFABRICATED REALITY?
    RETURNING TO THE ORIGINAL, REVERTING TO
    SIMPLICITY, GOING BACK TO PRISTINE PURITY,
OBJECTS FORGOTTEN, FEELINGS ENDED, GOING ALONG
    WITH NATURAL REALITY, THEREBY YOU REALIZE
    ACCEPTANCE OF THE TRUTH OF NONORIGINATION.

Formless form is true form. True form does not come from the fruits of practices or charity performed while dwelling on appearances. It comes from reverting to pristine purity and simplicity, forgetting objects and ending feelings. When you find the true form, every action, every stillness, is natural reality; you spontaneously attain acceptance of the truth of nonorigination. The *Śūraṅgama Sūtra* says, "This person thereupon attains acceptance of the truth of nonorigination." A commentary on the sutra says, "True suchness is called nonorigination. Truth has no contamination; knowledge of truth is called acceptance."

9

ONCE YOU HAVE CAUGHT THE FISH OR THE RABBIT YOU
    NATURALLY FORGET THE NET AND THE TRAP.
THE RAFT TO CROSS THE RIVER, THE LADDER TO THE
    HEIGHTS: ONCE YOU HAVE REACHED THE GOAL, THEY
    ARE ABANDONED.
BEFORE YOU ARE ENLIGHTENED, YOU NEED EXPLANATIONS;
    AFTER ENLIGHTENMENT, VERBALIZATIONS BECOME
    WRONG.
EVEN THOUGH THESE LINES BELONG TO NONCONTRIVANCE,
    THEY TOO ARE TO BE SHED.

A net is a means to catch fish; once you get the fish, you can forget the net. A trap is a means to catch rabbits; when you get the rabbit, you can forget the trap. A raft is a means to cross a river; when you reach the shore, you can leave the raft. A ladder is a means to climb up high; when you reach the height you can leave the ladder. These are similes for words as a means to understand principles; when the principles are understood, one can forget the words. Though the lines about forgetting the net and trap, abandoning the raft and ladder, are telling people to understand true essence and fundamentally are in the realm of nondoing, one cannot immediately wind matters up with nihilistic inaction. By mere nihilistic inaction, how can one reach the state of sublime awareness of true thusness? It is necessary to shed this nondoing before one can deeply attain self-realization.

10

AFTER ENLIGHTENMENT, DO NOT SEEK QUIESCENCE; GUIDE
THE DELUDED ACCORDING TO CONDITIONS.
WHEN VIEWS OF ANNIHILATION AND ETERNITY ARE
PRESENTED, THERE ARE EXPEDIENTS TO GUIDE BACK TO
REALITY.
FIVE EYES, THREE BODIES, FOUR KNOWLEDGES, SIX
PERFECTIONS AND MYRIAD PRACTICES CULTIVATED
EQUALLY,
ONE ORB OF ROUND LIGHT, A FINE JEWEL HELPS OTHERS
AND CAN ALSO SAVE ONESELF.

Buddhism considers realization of essence first, but that does not mean
that after enlightenment there is then empty nothingness. It is necessary
to take this empty essence back to reality; only this is the true essence of
buddhahood. Therefore the text says not to seek quiescence or extinction
after enlightenment, but to guide the deluded for the time according to
conditions. Guiding the deluded is the reason for practicing expedients
and doing good works.

The five eyes are the celestial eye, the eye of wisdom, the objective eye,
the enlightened eye, and the physical eye. The three bodies are the pure
body of reality, the complete body of reward, and the innumerable
created bodies. The four knowledges are the great round mirror knowledge, the knowledge of essential equality, the subtly observing knowledge, and the knowledge of practical accomplishment. The six perfections are generosity, discipline, tolerance, diligence, meditation, and
wisdom. The myriad practices are all expedients and good works. The five
eyes, three bodies, four knowledges, six perfections, and myriad practices
simultaneously cultivated inwardly and outwardly, the basic essence of
true thusness becomes clearer and clearer with refinement, like a brilliant
jewel, penetrating obscurity, bringing the hidden to light. Helping others
as well as oneself, it is always useful—how could it be just emptiness
alone?

11

I SEE PEOPLE THESE DAYS EXPOUNDING ESSENCE WHO JUST
   BOAST OF QUICKNESS IN REPARTEE;
BUT WHEN THEY MEET ACTUAL SITUATIONS THEY ARE ALL
   THE MORE DELUDED—HOW ARE THEY ANY DIFFERENT
   FROM THE IGNORANT?
WHAT IS PREACHED SHOULD BE PUT INTO PRACTICE—ONLY
   THEN IS IT CALLED SPEECH AND ACTION WITHOUT
   DEFECT.
IF YOU CAN USE THE SWORD OF WISDOM TO CUT THE
   JEWEL, THIS IS CALLED THE TRUE KNOWLEDGE OF THE
   ENLIGHTENED.

The important point of this verse is in the last line. The true knowledge
of the enlightened is all-pervasive; this is the sword of wisdom. By that
true knowledge one can get rid of error and return to truth, so it is called
the sword of wisdom. Because that true knowledge is round and bright,
unobscured, ever present, it is called a jewel. To cut the jewel does not
mean to obliterate it but to take it in, not allowing the shining of the
light to operate outside. When speaking in terms of substance it is called
a jewel, when speaking in terms of function it is called the sword of wisdom. The sword of wisdom, the jewel, and true knowledge are all one,
not three things.

This true knowledge is not obtained by talking; it can only be real if it
is cultivated by personal practice. If one cannot personally practice it and
only wants to talk about it, considering a quick wit to be insight, one will
be confused in actual events—what will be accomplished? Therefore
when it says "If you are able to use the sword of wisdom to cut the jewel,
this is called the true knowledge of the enlightened," only when the
words and actions are complete is it really true knowledge. Verbal quickness in repartee is not true knowledge.

12

IF YOU WANT TO UNDERSTAND THE SUBLIME PATH OF
   BIRTHLESSNESS, IT IS ALL A MATTER OF SEEING THE TRUE
   MIND FOR YOURSELF.

THE TRUE BODY HAS NO FORM, AND NO CAUSE EITHER; THE
PURE SPIRITUAL BODY IS JUST THUS.
THIS PATH IS NOT NONBEING AND NOT BEING, NOT IN
BETWEEN, NOT TO BE SOUGHT THERE EITHER.
WHEN BOTH EXTREMES ARE DISMISSED, ABANDON THE
MIDDLE; ONCE YOU SEE IT, THIS IS CALLED SUPREME.

Once you see the true mind, this is the sublime path; there is no need
to seek the sublime path elsewhere. The true mind is unstained, unattached, unperturbed, unmoved, formless and soundless; this is also
called the pure spiritual body. This mind, this body, is not existent, not
nonexistent, yet both existent and nonexistent. It cannot be sought in
being, cannot be sought in nonbeing, and cannot be found in neither-
being-nor-nonbeing. Since none of these three apply to it, try to think
what it is. When you see this, you immediately transcend to birthlessness;
this is called the sublime path of the supreme one vehicle.

The true body and true mind are originally one; in terms of substance
it is called the true body, in terms of function it is called the true mind.
Substance and function as one, body and mind forgotten, physically and
spiritually sublimated, merging with the Tao in reality—isn't this what
birthlessness means?

GLOSSARY

aberrant energy Energy produced or activated by external influences, by inner emotions, or by arbitrary conceptions. It is called aberrant in the sense of being conditioned and obstructing autonomy or preventing realization of the true self.

absolute one The name of a god used to symbolize the unified mind.

Altair and Vega Stars whose meeting symbolizes union of yin and yang.

Amitabha A Buddha representative of compassion, infinite light and life, in the sphere of "Ultimate Bliss" *(q.v.)*.

auxiliary techniques Exercises for producing health and bliss.

bamboo A symbol of emptiness in the sense of emptying the mind of ordinary preoccupations in order to make it receptive to higher knowledge.

bathing A relaxation of intensive effort in spiritual practice, to prevent excess of striving from resulting in counterproductive impulses such as eagerness or unbalanced force. The term is also used to refer to "washing the mind," which is related to the former usage in the sense that concentration is held to also require "cleaning" out mental contaminants that may be retained or even exaggerated in the effort to focus the mind on something else.

birth and death The ongoing process of material and psychic change. A common Buddhist term, it is used to refer to attachments to transient particulars, with the resulting subjection to mental pressures and states caused by a conflict between the craving for stability and the actuality of evanescence. Hence the term is often used synonymously with bondage or suffering.

birthless Objectively, this means "nonorigination," the principle that as all things are interrelated and have no independent existence in themselves, beginnings are a matter of definition and not of inherent reality. Subjectively, birthlessness means the mind is not compulsively aroused and does not fabricate illusions.

black ox A Ch'an Buddhist term for the ignorant, unregenerate mind: the ox turns "white" as the mind is purified and illuminated.

black tiger   A symbol of "true lead," which stands for the mind of Tao or the primal root of consciousness.

Bodhidharma   The reputed founder of Ch'an Buddhism in China.

bodhisattva   A Buddhist term for an awakened person who is consciously dedicated to the total welfare of all living beings.

body of reality   A Buddhist term for pure objectivity or pure awareness.

both countries   Yin and yang, the mundane and the celestial, tranquility and action.

buddha land   The environment of fully awakened consciousness.

celestial and human spheres   In Buddhist terminology, as used here, celestial and human spheres refer to states of bliss and social order, considered as lesser rewards of ethical and religious practices which are not thoroughly purged of selfishness or attachment. It should be noted that "celestial" has quite different connotations in Buddhism and Taoism: in Buddhism, it can be almost derogatory, since it stands for blissful states which are considered a potential hindrance to enlightenment; in Taoism, it is positive, referring to the realm of enlightened consciousness.

celestial essence   The original essence of consciousness, before being affected by mundane influences and confined within habit.

celestial immortality   A state of mental refinement in which emotional and intellectual attachments to objects of the world, including the ego, have been removed, and one is no longer ultimately identified subjectively with the individual body or personality, so that consciousness is "spacelike" and merged with objective reality.

celestial jewel   The highest state of perfection envisioned by Taoist enlightenment.

center   The point of balance, the state of mind before it is affected by feelings; it also stands for will, sincerity, intent, and truthfulness, as the hub of experience. The state of balance of the celestial and the earthly, of detachment and involvement, of firmness and flexibility.

Chang Chien   A famous traveler, used in this treatise as a symbol for yang.

Chang San-feng   A famous Taoist adept of the Ming dynasty, traditionally considered an inventor of the popular exercise system known as T'ai Chi Ch'uan.

cinnabar   Symbol of the energy of consciousness.

cinnabar crucible   The human mind.

closed room   This term refers to the practice of concentration in which the energy of awareness is not allowed to "leak" outside into distraction or emotive effervescence.

conscious essence   The essence of mind or nature of awareness.

conscious knowledge   The range of awareness or data available to consciousness.

counting others' treasures   A Buddhist expression for nonparticipatory study of the externals of a developmental system.

crescent moon furnace The mind of Tao; the image of the crescent is often used to represent the emergence of the "light" of the primal mind from the "shadow" of acquired conditioning.

crucible The "vessel" in which the "elixir" is "cooked." It is variously defined: it can refer to mind (cf. *cinnabar crucible, gold crucible*), or to the qualities of firmness and flexibility, or determination and adaptability.

cultural cooking The practice of "nonstriving" or "nondoing," which involves tranquil preservation of clarified consciousness to prevent it from scattering in distraction; calmly watching over the mind. "Cultural" means gentle, without force.

dark Symbol of unknowing: the human mind is said to be light outside and dark inside, in that its awareness plays on objects and not on inner essence; the mind of Tao is said to be dark outside and light inside, in that it is not fixed on externals but is aware of inner essence. Dark can thus mean unknowing in the sense of ignorance or in the sense of detachment.

death-impulse The force of mortality, impermanence, decay: associated with the dissipation of life energy, and with habituation to transient things.

demons Obstructions on the path. According to Lu Yen in *Wu Chen Pao Fa Chiu Yu Ching*, anything can be the path, including demons, while anything can be a demon, including the path. There are said to be inner demons and outer demons; the way to overcome them is said to be to silence the mind and master thought.

Dipankara An ancient Buddha, symbol of primordial enlightenment.

doing Practice involving conscious effort and striving, such as effort to escape the force of mental habit so as to experience the original mind and gain autonomy; striving to extract the primal energy of consciousness from accretions of experiential history.

dust Sense objects, or the realm of the ordinary senses; often used in a general way to refer to the mundane world and/or the products of mental agitation arising from contact with the world in the absence of inner freedom.

earth The medium of the joining of the conscious human mind and the subconscious mind of Tao; referred to as intent, or will. Also associated with the "center," standing for sincerity, truthfulness, or faith, as a unifying force in the human being. Note that this is different from the *I Ching* sign *earth*, which is italicized in the text of the translation.

earthen pot This term has the same meaning as "earth," but here is represented as a metaphysical container or locus in which various elements of mind are concentrated and unified. In psychosomatic Taoist yoga the "earthen pot" is assigned an actual physical location, in the region of the solar plexus, the center of the trunk, this spot being used as a focus of concentration.

earthly soul Used in the present text to symbolize real knowledge. It is referred to as yang ("soul") within yin ("earth") because real knowledge is primordial (unconditioned) and hence yang, but is ordinarily hidden, hence yin.

east "In the east" means within oneself.

elder water The unified energy of consciousness from which real knowledge is derived.

elixir A general word for the energy, capacity, and function of life and consciousness: various terms such as gold elixir, great elixir, outer elixir, inner elixir, and restored elixir are used in the context of different aspects or stages of the spiritual "alchemy."

embryonic breath An ancient hibernation technique; also refers to a state of composure and profound tranquility, in which the breath is imperceptible and the mind does not give rise to any impulses.

emptiness Metaphysically, emptiness means that phenomena are not objectively just as they subjectively appear to be; practically speaking, it refers to a state of mind which is not prejudiced by subjective assessments, a state of clarity and directness. In Taoism this is referred to as "emptying the human mind."

enlivening Unification of mind, balanced combination of the various elements of mind in such a way that they complement each other and work together harmoniously and constructively.

essence The essence or nature of mind.

extraction This term has several meanings: (1) extraction of hardness of the mind of Tao; (2) extraction of excess conscious knowledge of the human mind; (3) extraction of false yin and yang. It thus is used to mean: (1) removal of vehemence of effort associated with bypassing the human mind and bringing forth the mind of Tao; (2) stilling of excess intellectual activity; (3) removal of undesirable qualities of weakness and aggression, or other analogous extremes of passive and active attitudes and behavior. In sum, extraction means lessening or removal of qualities or energies which inhibit balanced development at any given point in the process of the spiritual alchemy.

false feeling Subjective feelings and emotions conditioned by physical states, thoughts, or external influences.

false fire Volatility, passion, intellectually or emotionally conditioned consciousness.

false nature The acquired temperament and personality formed by historical and environmental factors.

false yin and yang Extreme, isolated, or unbalanced manifestations of passivity and activity. For example, weakness/force; cowardice/aggression; quietism/arbitrary action; vacillation/stubbornness.

fire Consciousness, awareness; also, concentration.

fire and water Conscious knowledge in the human mind (fire) and real knowledge in the mind of Tao (water). These are represented by the corresponding *I Ching* trigrams ☲ and ☵. *Fire* ☲ has one yin in the center, representing the contaminant of mundane conditioning mixed into consciousness. *Water* ☵ has one yang in the center, representing the celestial or primordial hidden inside the mundane. The standard Chinese characters for fire and water are also used to stand for anger and lust, or for spirit and vitality.

firing process A general term for procedure, course of practical work; also spoken of in terms of specific firing processes.

five energies returning to the origin A state of mental and physical collection, used to recover the original energy. It is described as "The body unmoving, the mind unstirring, the nature tranquil, feelings forgotten, the physical elements in harmony." It is also said to be practiced by not using the external senses.

five eyes A Buddhist term for the range of potential perception available to humans: the flesh eye, which is the ordinary organ of sight; the celestial eye, which is the power of clairvoyance; the wisdom eye, which is the power of intuitive insight; the objective eye, which is the power to see things as they are in reality; and the enlightened eye, which is the power to see both absolute and relative truth, encompassing all the other eyes.

floating clouds Thoughts, feelings, objects; the evanescent world.

flower pond Openness of consciousness.

flowing pearl Open awareness.

four forms or *four signs* Metal and wood, water and fire; these stand for sense and essence, vitality and spirit. Hence combining the four forms means unification of the human being, with the mind of Tao and the human mind united, sense and essence joined, and energy and consciousness combined.

four fruits A Buddhist term for stages of development culminating in individual mental freedom. Various psychic powers are associated with attainment of these stages. The usage of the term in this text appears somewhat idiosyncratic.

four knowledges A Buddhist term for complete consciousness: the round mirror knowledge, which means impartial awareness; knowledge of equality, which means insight into the relativity of all things; observational knowledge, which means discernment of particulars; practical knowledge, which is application of understanding in action.

frog in a well The mind enclosed in narrow subjective views.

furnace Variously defined: sometimes referred to as flexible obedience, in the sense of following proper procedure; as receptivity, in the sense of being aware of the qualities of each time so as to be able to adjust the "firing" accordingly; or as constant alert observation. See also *crescent moon furnace.*

furnace of evolution The inner energy of life, kept aglow by conscious attention; also the external world of change, used consciously for self-refinement.

gold crucible   The mind in its original, uncontaminated state.

gold elixir   The primordial energy of life; also referred to as a combination of innate capacity and innate knowledge.

gold immortal   One who has restored the original capacity and energy of life, and refined them so that they are free from contamination by mundane conditioning.

great elixir   The maturation of the spiritual state realized by unification of mind and recovery of potential.

Great One   A god used to symbolize unity.

Great Ultimate   Primordial unity of being.

Great Vehicle   A Buddhist term for the overall endeavor leading to the perfection of both the individual and the community.

hall of brightness   A spot in the brain, used by some Taoists as a focus of attention in certain concentration exercises.

Heart Scripture   The Buddhist *Prajñāpāramitāhrdayasūtra*, the shortest Buddhist scripture, summarizing the emptiness of absolute existence.

heavenly soul   Symbol of conscious knowledge, referred to as yin within yang, in the sense of mundane conditioning being mixed in with primordial consciousness.

Hsing-lin   A Taoist adept, disciple of Chang Po-tuan, author of *Wu Chen P'ien*.

Hsueh-tou   An eminent Ch'an master (980–1052), especially noted for his poetry.

Hui-neng   The sixth patriarch of Ch'an Buddhism (638–713).

hundred foot pole   A Ch'an Buddhist term alluding to a transitional state of inner emptiness, stillness, and detachment.

increasing and decreasing   Increasing conscious access to the mind of Tao, decreasing the inhibiting conditioning of the human mind.

incubation   A phase of practice associated with "nondoing" and "bathing" *(q.v.)*, and the "cultural fire": concentration may at first be tainted with eagerness, anticipation, vehemence, and so on; thus the practice of "bathing" in the sense of purification is applied, removing contamination from intense concentration in the "martial" phase. This is called "incubation" in the sense of carefully nurturing the embryonic state of initial enlightenment to maturity.

Independent Seer   Name of a bodhisattva *(q.v.)* in the Heart Scripture *(q.v.)*.

inner elixir   The originally inherent potential which has been "recovered" after being "lost" to temporal conditioning and is refined after being "returned inside."

jackals   A Buddhist term for exponents of doctrines which hold to something relative as being absolute.

Kaśyapa The name of an outstanding disciple of the founder of Buddhism, said to have received the "special transmission outside the doctrine" from which Ch'an Buddhism is supposed to derive.

Kuan-yin Chinese name of Avalokiteśvara, a Buddhist bodhisattva representing the embodiment of compassion. In the *Saddharmapundarīkasūtra,* Kuanyin is said to have thirty-two forms, or specific adaptations to the needs of those ready to be liberated. Kuan-yin is one name of the Independent Seer *(q.v.),* but two names are used in this text to indicate two specific contexts in which the associations evoked are different.

K'un-lun A Central Asian mountain chain, representing: (1) west-metal-true sense-the mind of Tao; (2) primordial unified energy, the source of all being. In psychosomatic meditation systems of the "lesser vehicle" of Taoism, the K'un-lun also is used as a code word for the head.

lead crucible Lead stands for real knowledge and true sense; thus the lead crucible is the receptacle of this knowledge, the mind of Tao.

leak In Buddhism, this term means psychological clinging or mental contamination; in Taoism, it means drainage of energy.

life-impulse The essence of consciousness.

lion A symbol of a Buddha, particularly associated with the power of transcendent wisdom; the roar of the lion means the refutation of all dogmatism, through the principle that whatever is conditioned and dependent is empty of inherent reality.

living midnight Midnight symbolizes the state when the human mind and its discriminatory consciousness are silent; living means it is the point at which the potential of the mind of Tao is released. Living also means that properly accomplished "darkness"—cessation of the activity of the human mentality—is not oblivion, as open awareness remains as a channel of access to higher experience.

martial refining Concentrated effort to master feelings, get rid of delusions, remove acquired conditioning, and restore the original mind.

Master Lu Lu Yen, also known as Lu Tung-pin, a T'ang–Five Dynasties Taoist adept, traditionally considered an ancestor of the Complete Reality schools. Regarded as a spiritual immortal and a functionary in the celestial hierarchy, Lu is believed to have retained sufficient energy after physical disintegration to be able to project manifestations of himself, and is said to have appeared repeatedly over the centuries. Many writings and sayings are attributed to him.

Master Ts'ui Ts'ui Chih-chen, a Taoist adept said to have lived in the Latter Han dynasty. His *Ju Yao Ching,* a treatise on spiritual alchemy, is esteemed in the Complete Reality tradition.

medicinal substances Essence and life, essence and sense, real knowledge and consciousness, innate capacity and knowledge, vitality, energy, and spirit are all called medicinal substances, ingredients of the "elixir" of spiritual immortality.

mercury   Symbol of the essence of consciousness. Also associated with flexibility and with instability, the mercurial nature of the human mind; hence it must be stabilized by combination with the "lead" of real knowledge of the mind of Tao.

metal   Being firm and strong, metal symbolizes the true sense of real knowledge, which is unequivocal.

metal in water   Symbol of the primal root of consciousness, unified vitality or energy, real knowledge in the mind of Tao, innate natural goodness. It is referred to as yang within yin, represented by the trigram *water* ☵.

metal man   Symbol of the mind of Tao.

mid-autumn   The fifteenth day of the eighth lunar month; the full moon, representing pure yang as full illumination or revelation of the original state of the mind of Tao.

midnight and noon   Midnight, as the starting point of morning, represents the beginning of activation of yang, the real knowledge of the mind of Tao; noon, as the starting point of evening, represents the beginning of yin, the conscious knowledge of the human mind. Midnight is the mind of Tao emerging actively, noon is the human mind receiving it passively; midnight is the beginning of transcendence, noon is the beginning of reintegration with the world.

mind-monkey   The unruly mind, jumping from one object to another.

morning and evening   Active and passive phases of praxis. Active practice is referred to as doing, striving, and martial firing. Passive practice is referred to as nondoing, nonstriving, and cultural cooking. Hence morning and evening means breaking through the accidental or acquired to reach the essential or primal, then stabilizing and preserving this accomplishment.

mysterious female   A representation of the combination of yin and yang, flexible receptivity and unequivocal sense. This term, from the *Tao Te Ching*, is one of those defined in many different ways. It is sometimes referred to as the basic mind, or open consciousness.

mysterious pass   This term, one of the most important in Taoist alchemy, has numerous definitions. Psychosomatic meditation systems associate it with particular points in the body, variously locating it behind the navel and in front of the kidneys, between the genitals and kidneys, in the umbilical region, on the top of the head, or on the forehead. These are considered lower or "sidetrack" systems: in the higher teachings the mysterious pass is referred to as the celestial mind, or the middle, and it is also said to be completely metaphysical and to have no location. It is also said to be where yin and yang divide, where essence and life abide, the lair of spirit and energy, found only in profound abstraction. The opening of the mysterious pass is a critical experience in Complete Reality Taoism: descriptions of it resemble those of "seeing essence" *(q.v.)* in Ch'an Buddhism. In sum, the mysterious pass may be viewed as an orientation point in concentration practice: in auxiliary or elementary methods, it is concrete, while in advanced methods it is abstract.

Naga girl In the Buddhist *Saddharmapundarikasūtra,* a young girl who attained sudden enlightenment; commonly used to represent transcendence of social and temporal distinctions.

natural real fire or *natural fire of reality* Spontaneous awareness without conscious effort; equated with the "cultural fire." It is called natural and real because it represents the consciousness purged of artificiality, the reality of the original mind.

negativity Mundane conditioning, bondage to things of the world.

ninefold restoration Restoration of the original celestial mind, freed from bondage to accumulated habit and acquired personality.

nine heavens Nine is the number of yang: thus nine heavens stands for pure yang, which is the celestial, unconditioned, primal state.

nine-restored gold liquid Purified real knowledge.

nine transmutations Transmutation of conscious energy into the celestial purified state, represented by the number nine, which stands for yang.

nine years Some presentations of Taoist practice speak of "nine years facing a wall," a stage entered into after stabilization of consciousness, devoted to becoming thoroughly immune to the influences of objects and feelings.

nonleaking In Buddhism, this term signifies freedom from mental contamination; in Taoism, it means that energy is not wasted.

nonorigination See *birthless.*

other This term may be used to mean an enlightened teacher, whose perspective is beyond the scope of self-centered subjectivity; it is also used to refer to everything outside oneself, from which one's "investment" of concern-energy needs to be recovered in order to gain autonomy. In sexual yoga it is used to refer to one's partner.

other shore A Buddhist term for consummation, attainment, and transcendence.

outer elixir This term may be used to refer to mineral or vegetable potions, or to the energy-circulation exercise known as the waterwheel. In the present commentary, "outer" is taken to refer to the condition of something vital in oneself being "lost," as it were, by becoming bound up in external objects.

outer furnace This term refers to the use of action in the world as a means of self-refinement.

pearl in the poor one's clothes An allusion to an allegory in the Buddhist *Saddharmapundarikasūtra:* a benefactor sews a pearl into the clothes of a drunken sleeper. Unaware of this, the latter lives a life of poverty and hardship until he meets the benefactor again and has the hidden pearl pointed out to him. Discovering the pearl, he becomes wealthy. The pearl symbolizes the buddha-nature, the potential of enlightenment, said to be hidden beneath the "clothing" of acquired conditioning.

phantasmic body   The physical body, called phantasmic because it lacks permanent reality.

polar energies   Yin and yang.

positive   Yang, as that which is "celestial," unconditioned, primal.

Power of Tao   The *Tao Te Ching*, one of the most widely read classics of Taoism.

punishment and reward   Punishment is "repelling yin," getting rid of mundane conditioning. Repelling yin to the point of balance, being in the world yet not being controlled by things of the world, is symbolized by the autumn equinox, and by punishment and death. Reward is the emergence of the unconditioned primal mind; the spring equinox represents emergence to the point of balance, being free yet remaining in the world voluntarily.

quicksilver   Another term for mercury, symbolizing the conscious knowledge in the human mind.

quietism   The habit of taking quietude or detachment as an end rather than a means; this is diagnosed as a misunderstanding and an illness in both Ch'an Buddhism and Complete Reality Taoism.

reality body   The original unified essence of the human being.

reality eye   A Buddhist term for objective awareness without distorting projections on the part of the observer.

realm of dust   The realm of the senses; the ordinary world.

recognizing a thief as your child   A Ch'an Buddhist expression meaning to mistake the conditioned portion of the mind as the true mind, or to take function for essence.

return   Recovery of the original mind.

River Diagram   An ancient diagram of cosmology based on the five elements.

sane energy   Energy which is not influenced by external objects or by subjective thoughts and feelings.

seeing essence   A Ch'an Buddhist term for direct experience of the original mind without the intervention of conceptualization.

sevenfold reversion   Seven is associated with yang and fire, and fire with consciousness: sevenfold reversion, or seven-reversion, is a term for restoration of consciousness to reality, removal of subjective distortions.

seven-reverted cinnabar   Stabilized consciousness, restored to its primal state.

Shakyamuni   Epithet of the founder of Buddhism.

shutting the coccyx   In sexual yoga, contraction of perineal muscles to stop the flow of semen and prevent ejaculation in the male is felt as pressure in the coccyx, one of the critical points on which attention is focused in the waterwheel exercise.

sidetrack methods   Auxiliary techniques of limited scope, obsession with which diverts the practitioner and inhibits full development of human potential.

signlessness   A Buddhist term meaning that things in reality are not identical to the descriptions projected on them by the mind which conceives of them.

silver   A symbol of real knowledge.

silver within water   Real knowledge concealed by temporal conditioning.

six perfections   Six modes of practice recommended in Buddhism for simultaneously developing oneself and benefiting others.

six psychic powers   Capacities believed in Buddhism to be released in the process of liberation of the mind: clairvoyance, clairaudience, total recall, mental telepathy, psychic travel, and ability to terminate all contamination in the mind.

spirit of discrimination   The conceptualizing mind.

spiritual body   The basic essence of consciousness.

spiritual sprouts   The incipient activation of the living, creative potential of the original mind.

suchness   A Buddhist term used to refer to objective reality and to the purified mind.

Śūraṅgama Sūtra   A Buddhist scripture especially favored by Ch'an Buddhists and Complete Reality Taoists since the Sung dynasty.

swallowing saliva   A common Taoist hygiene practice for vitiating poisons naturally occurring in food.

three bases   Heaven, humanity, and earth: also associated with spirit, energy, and vitality, which are called the upper, middle, and lower bases. These are considered fundamental elements of the macrocosm and microcosm.

three bodies   In Taoist usage, this term refers to the "real original body," corresponding to youth, the "strong body," corresponding to maturity, and the "declining body," corresponding to old age. In Buddhist usage (written differently in Chinese but ordinarily translated the same in English), the term refers to three aspects of the completed human being, corresponding to the physical presence and actions, the psychic presence of knowledge and bliss, and the most subtle presence of essence.

three components   Heaven, earth, and humankind.

three fields   Three "fields of elixir" corresponding to the vitality, energy, and spirit. In psychosomatic exercises, these fields are assigned physical locations in the lower trunk, midtrunk, and head.

three flowers gathered on the peak   In psychosomatic Taoist practice, this refers to the unity of vitality, energy, and spirit in the upper field of elixir. In the present commentary it is used figuratively for a state of realization.

three realms   A Buddhist term for three domains of mundane experience: the realm of desire, in which emotions are involved; the realm of form, purely aesthetic and intellectual, without emotion; and the formless realm, without desire, concept, or any sort of concrete form.

three vermin   Consumptive or degenerative forces represented as vermin or parasites anciently said to be in the three fields of elixir and to eventually cause death; thus they represent dissipation of vitality, energy, and spirit.

202

thusness Suchness *(q.v.)*; being as is, without the imposition of artificial definitions; also called true thusness.

Triple Analogue *San Hsiang Lei,* a Taoist classic of the Latter Han dynasty.

triple world The totality of the three realms *(q.v.)*.

true emptiness A Buddhist term for pure potential, called "empty" because of absence of limitations, inconceivability, ungraspability, and openness.

true lead Symbol of real knowledge and primordial energy.

true seed Real knowledge; same as true lead.

Ts'ao Ch'i The place where Hui-neng, the sixth Ch'an Buddhist patriarch, taught in southern China; hence generally associated with Ch'an.

Tzu-hsien A Taoist adept in the third generation of the southern school of Complete Reality Taoism, disciple of Hsing-lin *(q.v.)*.

Ultimate Bliss A Buddhist paradise, said to be a realm free from the obstructions to enlightenment ordinarily encountered on earth; in Ch'an Buddhism it is said to be within oneself.

unminding A Ch'an Buddhist term for inner freedom and equanimity.

valley spirit A symbol of open awareness.

war Inner struggle against the compulsive force of personality and habit.

water of celestial unity In ancient cosmology the element of water was associated with the sky and the number one; this is used in alchemy as a symbol for the primal unity of being.

waves Mental disturbance.

Western Heaven The "pure land" of Ultimate Bliss *(q.v.)*, nominally said to be in the west, esoterically said to be in oneself.

wild fox A Ch'an term for an aberrated practitioner.

wind External influences.

wind and thunder at midnight Disturbance taking place at the critical juncture where the human mind quiesces and the mind of Tao emerges.

winter solstice The point of quiescence of the habit-ridden human mentality and emergence of the mind of Tao; equivalent to midnight.

wood and metal Symbols of essence and sense.

yellow female True intent, or truthfulness, the medium or "go-between" through whose agency yin and yang are united.

yellow path The "middle way" or "center" *(q.v.)*, standing for balance.

yellow sprouts The emergence of the "living potential," or original energy of life, as it becomes freed from preemptive habit.

Yuan-tu-tzu A Taoist adept in the sixth generation of the northern branch of the Complete Reality school, teacher of the famous expositor Shang-yang-tzu.

READINGS

For an extensive bibliography of works on Taoism and alchemy, see Joseph Needham's *Science and Civilization in China,* 5 vols. (Cambridge University Press).

For studies of Chang Po-tuan and his successors, including a translation of the *Wu Chen P'ien* from the point of view of chemistry, see the works of Tenney Davis in *Proceedings of the American Academy of Arts and Sciences* 73 (1939–40), and *Journal of Chemical Education* 16 (1939).

For observations of contemporary Taoism in Taiwan, see the works of M. R. Saso; for historical and anthropological studies, see the works of H. Maspero and H. Welch.

For recent Chinese bibliographical and historical studies, see Ch'en Kuo-fu's *Tao Tsang Yuan Liu K'ao* (Hsiang Sheng Publishing Co., Taiwan, 1975) and Ch'en Yuan-an's *Nan Sung Ch'u Hopei Hsin Tao-chiao K'ao* (Hsin Wen Feng Publishing Co., Taiwan, 1976).

For information on Taoist meditation in contemporary Taiwan, see Li Lo-ch'iu's *Fang Tao Yu Lu* (Chen Shan Mei Publishing Co., Taiwan, 1965).

The works of Liu I-ming may be found in *Tao Shu Shih Er Chung* (Hsin Wen Feng Publishing Co., Taiwan, 1982).

Other commentaries on the *Wu Chen P'ien* may be found in volume 14 of *Tao Tsang Chi Yao* (Hsin Wen Feng Publishing Co., Taiwan, 1976).

A useful compendium of Complete Reality Taoist lore may be found in *Chung Ho Chi,* which is in volume 17 of *Tao Tsang Chi Yao,* and in volume 2 of *Tao T'ung Ta Ch'eng* (Hsin Wen Feng Publishing Co., Taiwan, 1974).

Information on the life of Chang Po-tuan may be found in *Hsuan Men Pi Tu* (Tzu Yu Publishing Co., Taiwan, 1965), and in *Li Tai Shen Hsien Shih* (Hsin Wen Feng Publishing Co., Taiwan, 1978).

Some information on Taoist alchemical terminology may be found in Tai Yuan-ch'ang's *Hsien Hsueh Tzu Tien* (Chen Shan Mei Publishing Co., Taiwan, 1961); somewhat less specialized is Li Shu-huan's *Tao Chiao Tzu Tien* (T'ien Tao Company, Hong Kong, 1980).

CPSIA information can be obtained at www.ICGtesting.com
Printed in the USA
LVOW122353060313

322947LV00001B/10/A